11/01

A PRAIRIE MOSAIC

AN ATLAS OF CENTRAL NEBRASKA'S
Land, Culture, and Nature

EDITORS
Steven J. Rothenberger
    Professor of Biology
Susanne George-Bloomfield
    Professor of English

EDITORIAL BOARD
Bruce Elder
    Professor of Acounting and Finance
Allan Jenkins
    Associate Professor of Economics
Kenneth Nikels
    Dean of Graduate Studies and Research
Michael Schuyler
    Dean of the College of Natural and Social Sciences

LAYOUT AND DESIGN
Melody Hansen
    Designer, UNK Graduate
Richard Schuessler
    Art Director, Associate Professor of Visual Communications & Design

COVER PAINTING
Ernie Ochsner "Lincoln Creek, Summer Storm"
    Provided by Museum of Nebraska Art

CARTOGRAPHY
Gordon Bennett
    Associate Professor of Geography

Publication supported by the Omaha World-Herald Foundation
Published by the University of Nebraska at Kearney

©2000 University of Nebraska at Kearney
ISBN - 0-7392-0512-9

FOREWARD FROM CHANCELLOR

The University of Nebraska at Kearney is delighted to present A Prairie Mosaic. This multidisciplinary piece of scholarship offers a singular view of the heart of Nebraska and its peoples. Our rich prairie land–yesterday, today, and tomorrow–provides living and working experiences that reflect the American pioneer experience. The industry and perseverance of the stalwart peoples who settled on Nebraska's wind-swept plains continue to inspire and nourish us today.

These pages contain thirty informative articles treating the natural and cultural essences of the prairie experience. From a review of Nebraska's physical and climatic characteristics through a look at the delivery of higher education through new technological advances, these writings give a reliable introduction to the expertise of the faculty at Nebraska's premier scholarly teaching university. The splendid research and fine analysis contained in these pages will hold your interest as you reflect on the history and politics of the only state with a unicameral form of government. You will revel in the commentaries on the art and literature indigenous to the "land where the West begins." Like our students, who benefit daily from the intellectual challenges found in our classrooms, you, too, will appreciate the keen insights of distinguished professors.

Speaking for the University, I wish to acknowledge the creative and research efforts of a stellar faculty. The University also recognizes with gratitude the Omaha World-Herald Foundation and John Gottschalk, president and chief operating officer of the *Omaha World-Herald*, for its generous underwriting of the publication costs of A Prairie Mosaic.

Gladys Styles Johnston
CHANCELLOR
UNIVERSITY OF NEBRASKA AT KEARNEY

MIXED**PRAIRIE**

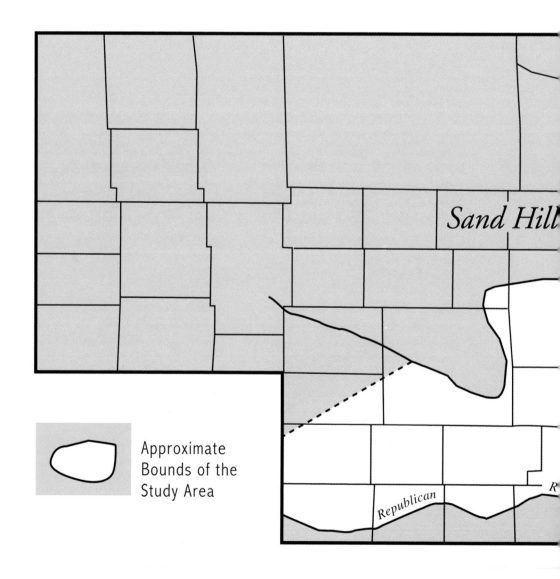

Sand Hill

Approximate
Bounds of the
Study Area

Republican

R

A PRAIRIE MOSAIC

To all of those who love the prairie...

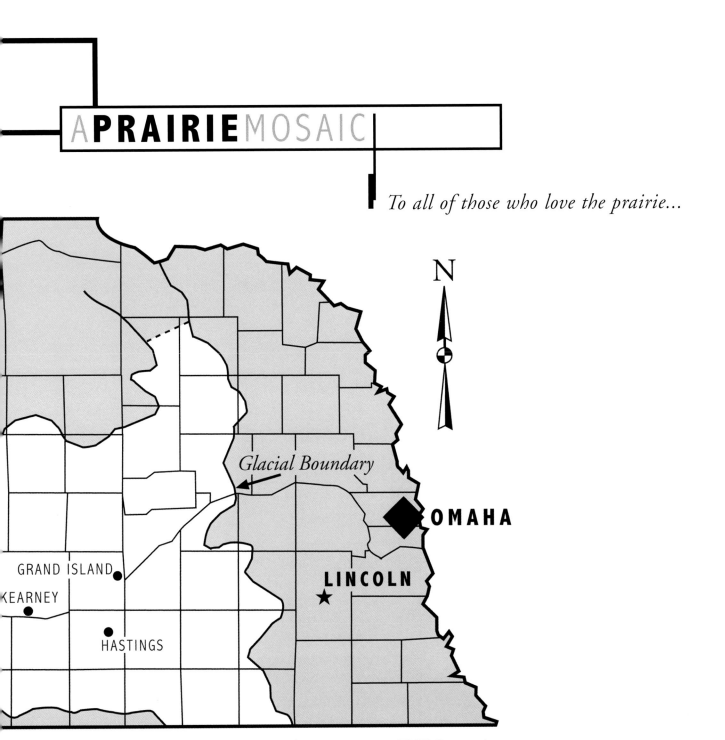

N

Glacial Boundary

OMAHA

LINCOLN

GRAND ISLAND

KEARNEY

HASTINGS

Map by G.E. Bennett, UNK Geography

A PRAIRIE MOSAIC

TABLE OF CONTENTS

HISTORYLAW

ECONOMICS
POLITICSSOCIETY

INTRODUCTION

Steven J. Rothenberger, Professor of Biology

The concept for A Prairie Mosaic originated shortly after the successful publication of The Platte River: An Atlas of the Big Bend Region in 1993. Geographically, prairie is the dominant ecosystem of this region. Therefore, a second, prairie-based book was a logical choice to consider. Initially, there was concern that the original material necessary for this volume would be difficult to find. However, a number of interested and talented potential contributors urged us to move forward with this project. An even stronger force was our love for this land, the central Nebraska prairie, and the fact that the prairie has so many stories to tell. This collection of articles and poems is an attempt to illustrate the complexity of the prairie, along with some of the major biological, historical, cultural, and social forces that play a role in the lives of those who have settled in this region. Although this work scarcely scrapes the surface, we are hopeful that the reader might discover or, at least, better appreciate this region and its successes.

Once deemed "the Great American Desert" by Major Stephen Long and chronicled as unfit for habitation by others, the Nebraska Prairie has risen in its perception, stature, and importance. The Plains traditionally represented nothing more than an area to cross when one was going somewhere else. Change was destined to occur. The Homestead Act of 1862 opened these lands to settlement and to new generations of immigrants, who were determined to make a living on the land. New towns and villages were formed, mainly along well-known trails or within the east-west corridor of the transcontinental railroad.

According to Professor Wayne Fields, a specialist in Midwestern literature, "the Plains have historically scared the heck out of people." Initially, all of the early explorers were accustomed to the hills and forests of the east. "Their idea of good and evil, progress and regress, existence and nothingness were oriented to trees and hills." Modern literature treats this land much more favorably. Writers, such as Willa Cather, Mari Sandoz, and John G. Neihardt, wrote with passion about the prairie and its people, but, at the same time, made no attempt to disguise its harshness. Writer and theologian, Martin Marty, reminds us that Great Plains literature provides a "sense of place," a *locus standi* as author Wright Morris would say. When interviewed, Morris acknowledged that "the prairie conditions what I see, what I look for, and what I find in the world to write about." It is this same Prairie heritage that stimulates and inspires numerous creative works by artists, writers, and naturalists. In some special way, the best of the human spirit and all it can achieve thrives here.

Prairie roots have quietly helped to shape a nation.

Is there a certain hardiness of the spirit, a kind of perseverance and resourcefulness that is a part of living here? Nebraskans point with pride to a long list of nationally known personalities who called Nebraska home. While the prairie was their "sense of place," most achieved success and fame elsewhere. They left behind an ordinary, predictable landscape to search for something else. But the quality of life here often remains their point of reference. Those who remain to call the prairie home face many challenges to maintain the "good life," but they are a resilient, educated citizenry with well-grounded values. Just as the Native Americans adeptly utilized the land, the plants, and the animals, modern prairie cultures must conserve nature and her resources and adapt to changing environmental and economic conditions in order to survive into the future.

In A Prairie Mosaic, we present the Nebraska prairie to our readers. We chose the central Nebraska region because it is the heart of the Great Plains. It lies on the 100th meridian where the semi-arid west begins. Most of central Nebraska is mixed-grass prairie, but to the north and west, it gives way to the Nebraska Sand Hills, the largest single grassland in North America. The tall-grass or "true" prairie encroaches from the east, while the unique sandsage prairies are found in southwestern Nebraska. To the south, the Republican River Valley forms a convenient transitional boundary.

A Prairie Mosaic is organized into four major sections. Chapter One describes Geography, Climate, and Biology; Chapter Two presents History and Law; Art and Culture comprise Chapter Three; and Chapter Four centers on Economics, Politics, and Society. Photographs by Solomon Butcher, interspersed throughout the chapters, highlight the changes that have occured on the prairie over the past one hundred years.

As these works were compiled, it became apparent that it is impossible to capture the complexity of this region in any single volume. However, the thirty-six contributors bring with them a wealth of experience and expertise in teaching, research, writing, or creating works that emanate from the prairie. All of them are or have been associated with the university in some way, making this publication something that is uniquely UNK. Each contributor tells a special story in his or her own way. The creative layout and design of this book was accomplished by UNK graduate Melody Hansen and assisted by Professor Richard Schuessler of the Graphic Arts Department. It is a privilege to combine these contributions into a volume that can be enjoyed far into the future.

"Serene Lake" *Gary Zaruba*

ZARUBA

to my friend the landscape painter
by don welch

Bobbing on a meditative sea,
think one thought per century.

Take your time,
look for the first notice of land.

Eventually, when a tableland
appears above the warm waters,

arm yourself with the seeds
of grasses and wild flowers.

And what passes as wind.

Begin.
Paint south to north.

Love slow going
and the richness of alluvial earth.

Treat every rhizome as worth,
every root, every tuber.

Bolder than cardinal flowers,
paint lady slippers, paint stargrass blooms.

Age like the bluestem,
comfort the ground with heather asters,

let the sky humble you.

And occasionally look up,
listen to the melodies of larkwork.

GEOGRAPHY CLIMATE
BIOLOGY

THE SETTING:

A REVIEW OF THE GEOLOGY AND PHYSIOGRAPHY OF THE NEBRASKA PRAIRIE

M. Stanley Dart, Associate Professor of Geography

The landscape of the Nebraska prairie is not an "easy" one. To the untrained or unappreciative eye, the landscape of the prairie is hardly one to evoke the awe produced by snow-capped peaks or pounding waves upon a rocky shore, where it takes only a smidgen of courage to extend one's mind to the power of such places. However, the prairie landscape is one which asks— in fact, demands—our fullest and most complete attention, our deepest strength, and our clearest eyes. There are those who choose to pass on through—not making the effort to understand and see. But for those who stop off for a while on the prairie, the rewards to the intellect, the body, and the soul are rich, indeed.

Some Geologic History

The Nebraska prairie landscape is the product of the interactions between a variety of geomorphic and geologic processes. Throughout most of the Mesozoic Era, 240-66 mybp (million years before the present), Nebraska lay beneath a shallow trans-continental sea into which various sands, silts, and limy clays were deposited. Among these were the Dakota Group, a collection of sandstone and mudstones deposited along the edges of the shallow seas; the Colorado Group, composed of limy shales; and the Pierre Formation, a shale representing deposition in a near offshore

environment. As a result of more recent deformation of the continental crust, this association of Mesozoic and earlier sediments lie buried beneath tens to hundreds of feet of later wind and water deposited material. They are exposed at the surface only along the eastern edges of the Nebraska prairie and, occasionally, in the lower portions of major river valleys.

By the late Cretaceous Period, in the area now occupied by the Rocky Mountains, the continent began a slow and persistent uplift. This Laramide Orogeny, or mountain building episode, marked the end of the Mesozoic Era and commenced the Cenozoic Era.

As land rose during the Laramide Orogeny, the streams that developed sought paths to the sea by following the general easterly regional slope. In some areas of western Nebraska, the older Cretaceous rocks were completely stripped away by erosion. But, commencing in the mid-Tertiary Period (37 mybp), sands and gravels from the mountains were transported outward from the highlands and spread in a broad apron across the Great Plains. These stream-borne alluvial sediments lie on top of and in sharp contrast to the older Cretaceous materials beneath. Today, this aggregation of alluvial materials is present as the Ogallala Formation.

Though it has been subsequently modified by erosion, the Ogallala Formation once extended outward onto the plains from

Sandhills near Sargent, 1887   Butcher Collection

southern Canada to northern Texas and from the base of the mountains to eastern Nebraska (Fig.1). In Nebraska, the Ogallala Formation has a thickness of over one thousand feet in the central portion of the Sand Hills. However, within the Nebraska prairie region, the Ogallala decreases in thickness from west to east and north to south. Generally, the Ogallala is not present east of a line from Norfolk (in northeastern Nebraska) to Hastings (south-central).

The importance of the Ogallala Formation to the Great Plains and to the Nebraska prairie region can not be over-emphasized. The Ogallala is the principle aquifer from which groundwater is extracted for agricultural, municipal, and industrial use. Along the southern and eastern fringes of the Nebraska prairie, where the Ogallala is thin or absent, groundwater availability is reduced.

Of interest, as well, is the role that volcanic activity has played in the geologic history of the Great Plains. During the mid-Tertiary (37-17 mybp), regular volcanic activity throughout the Rocky Mountains and western mountain systems contributed huge volumes of volcanic ash that were carried to the east and deposited across the Plains. While the 1980 eruption of Mt. St. Helens, Washington, produced a dusting of ash across Nebraska within a few days following the event, the volcanic vigor of the preceding thirty-seven million years was

several levels of magnitude greater. As recently as ten million years ago, a series of volcanic events in southern Idaho produced dense and suffocating clouds of ash which swept fiercely across the northern Plains and were deposited to depths of up to a foot. These events are recorded in the dramatic fossil assemblage at Ash Fall Fossil Beds State Historical Park near Orchard in north-eastern Nebraska.

As the mountains to the west continued to rise, two contrasting processes began to affect the Great Plains. First, the plains began to "dry out." The western mountain mass formed a barrier to the movement of moist air from the Pacific into the continental interior. The reduction in moisture allowed grasslands to expand across the plains. Second, streams draining the western highlands began the slow process of reworking and redistributing the alluvial materials that had been deposited by earlier streams. By the beginning of the Pleistocene Epoch or the "Ice Age" (2 mybp), most of the Nebraska prairie would have looked much like the savanna areas of Africa–a broad plain of low relief crossed by a few larger year-round flowing streams and ephemeral streams which held water only seasonally.

Nebraska and the "Ice Age"

Though the landscape of the Nebraska prairie has evolved through the last sixty-six

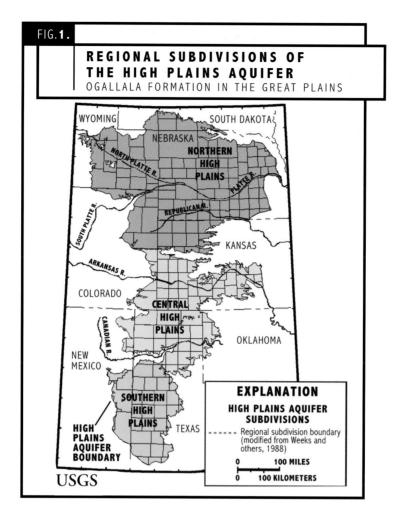

FIG.1.

REGIONAL SUBDIVISIONS OF THE HIGH PLAINS AQUIFER
OGALLALA FORMATION IN THE GREAT PLAINS

WYOMING

SOUTH DAKOTA

NEBRASKA

NORTHERN HIGH PLAINS

NORTH PLATTE R.

PLATTE R.

REPUBLICAN R.

SOUTH PLATTE R.

KANSAS

ARKANSAS R.

COLORADO

CENTRAL HIGH PLAINS

CANADIAN R.

OKLAHOMA

NEW MEXICO

SOUTHERN HIGH PLAINS

TEXAS

HIGH PLAINS AQUIFER BOUNDARY

USGS

EXPLANATION

HIGH PLAINS AQUIFER SUBDIVISIONS

- - - - - Regional subdivision boundary (modified from Weeks and others, 1988)

0 — 100 MILES

0 — 100 KILOMETERS

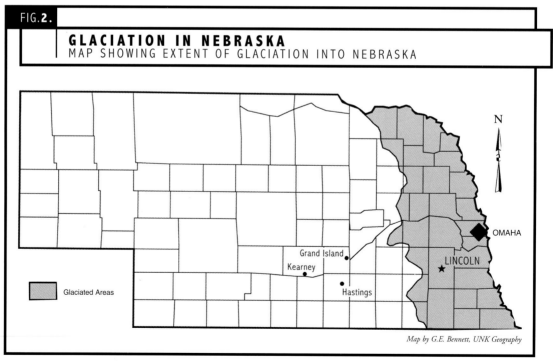

FIG.2.

GLACIATION IN NEBRASKA
MAP SHOWING EXTENT OF GLACIATION INTO NEBRASKA

N

OMAHA

Grand Island

Kearney

LINCOLN

Hastings

Glaciated Areas

Map by G.E. Bennett, UNK Geography

Skeletal remains at Ash Fall Quarry   by Susanne George-Bloomfield

non-glaciated areas caused dramatic alterations to the pre-glacial landscape. Glacial development in the mountains to the west altered drainage systems, caused renewed erosion of the upland areas, and developed a suite of sediments poised to flood outward onto the plains. In association with the reorientation of eastern river systems, vast quantities of glacial meltwater and glacially derived sediments spilled out of the Rocky Mountains into streams discharging across the plains. The Missouri, Platte, Arkansas, and Rio Grande Rivers (or their predecessors) all served to resculpt the land and provide a new increment of alluvial sediment to their valley systems.

The onset of glaciation also altered climates across the plains. It is assumed that the climate of the plains has varied between cooler and drier conditions and warmer and wetter conditions over the last 100,000 years. Particularly important are those times of lower precipitation when vegetative ground cover and, specifically, grasses, were more sparse. Without a consistent vegetative cover, the loose, fine-particle colluvium found along hill-slopes of the uplands and alluvium of the river valleys became mobile. Prevailing westerly and northerly winds began a slow but sure winnowing process in which the finer silts, clays, and volcanic ash were separated from the coarser sands. From the valley floors of those streams carrying glacial meltwater, very fine particles, referred to as glacial "flour," were blown out of the valleys and deposited along adjacent uplands.

Loess–Painted by the Wind

While sands were being shaped into dunes across the north-central part of Nebraska, giving rise to the Sand Hills, finer (0.01-0.05 mm diameter) particles, called loess, blanketed the adjacent areas to the south and east. It is evident that the principal periods of loess deposition were not contemporary with the development of the Sand Hills. Most of the principal loess formations in Nebraska are older than

million years or so, the advent of the Pleistocene epoch brought the most profound changes to the land. Over a two million year span, glacial ice spread periodically across the northeastern quadrant of North America. In Nebraska, the maximum western extent of glacial ice reached only extreme eastern Nebraska along a line from just east of Norfolk to southeast of Fairbury (Fig. 2).

Prior to glaciation, eastward flowing streams following the regional west-to-east slope reworked the vast surface of Tertiary alluvial materials. During at least the Kansan glacial stage (≈1,000,000 ybp), the eastern portions of these streams were blocked by the mass of glacial ice in eastern Nebraska. The Missouri River itself flowed northeastward and entered into the Atlantic Ocean along the North American coast near present Hudson Bay, Canada. But glacial ice blocked this route to the sea, and the Missouri, and other streams like it, were redirected to the south along the glacial edges. At one or more times, the combined streams flowing from the western mountains and the eastern streams supported from glacial meltwater adopted paths that moved southward along the glacial margin, exiting the state through the drainage of the present Blue River and, possibly, other river valley systems in southeastern Nebraska.

Even though the western eighty percent of Nebraska was not covered by ice, the effects of continental and alpine glaciation on climate and stream flow regimes in

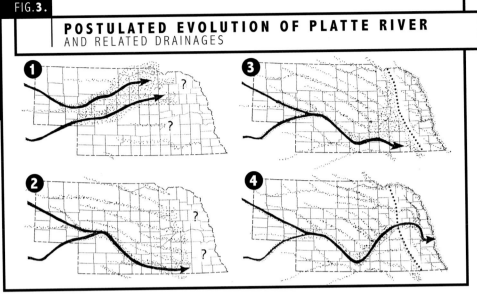

FIG. **3.**

POSTULATED EVOLUTION OF PLATTE RIVER
AND RELATED DRAINAGES

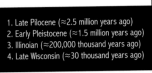

1. Late Pilocene (≈2.5 million years ago)
2. Early Pleistocene (≈1.5 million years ago)
3. Illinoian (≈200,000 thousand years ago)
4. Late Wisconsin (≈30 thousand years ago)

Sketch maps showing postulated drainage patterns when there was glacial ice in eastern Nebraska. Solid lines show main ancestral drainage of Platte River. Heavy dotted line represents terminal moraines of one or more pre-Illinoian glacial maxima, undifferentiated. Stippled pattern indicates probable areas of long-term fluvial deposition before and after the suggested dates. Queried where eastward extent of fluvial deposition unknown.

Maps by Conservation and Survey Division, University of Nebraska

10,000 years while the Sand Hills appear to have been shaped only within the last 5,000 to 8,000 years. The likely sources of loess include the silts and clays (derived principally from sediments deposited by glacial meltwater) blown from river valleys and extracted by the process of deflation from the loose alluvial materials laying across the exposed Ogallala formation.

Loess deposits are the typical surface materials of the uplands of the Nebraska prairie. Loess accumulations along the eastern and southern margins of the Sand Hills exceed 90 feet in thickness with a maximum of 143 feet in southeastern Lincoln County. Loess thickness decreases with distance to the east and south of the Sand Hills, ranging from twenty to fifty feet in upland areas paralleling the Platte and Elkhorn Rivers, for example, and decreasing to only a few feet in the upland areas of the eastern portion of the state, such as in Jefferson and Saline counties.

While loess is the predominant surface material of the Nebraska prairie, it must be noted as well that eolian (wind) sand deposition occurred in some areas separate from the Sand Hills. During a period of reduced stream flow in the North Platte River, perhaps 10,000-12,000 ybp, migrating sand dunes blocked the flow of the river along a stretch in northwestern Keith County backing the waters of the river approximately forty miles upstream and creating ancient Lake Diffendal. Along other portions of the central Platte and lower

Loup Rivers, alluvial sands were blown out of the river beds and deposited as linear dune fields along the south sides of their flood plains.

The Physiography of the Nebraska Prairie

The Nebraska prairie can be broadly subdivided into three principal physiographic regions: 1) the Dissected Loess Plains; 2) the Loess Plain/Rainwater Basin; and 3) Alluvial Valleys.

By the end of the glacial period, approximately 9,500 ybp, the landscape of the Nebraska prairie probably resembled a broad, gently rolling plain, mantled by loess, stretching from the edges of the Sand Hills to the south and east. The remnants of this plain can still be seen. They are most obvious in the southeastern portion of the Nebraska prairie stretching from Phelps County on the west and bounded by the Little Blue, Big Blue, and Platte rivers on the south, east, and north. This area is known as the Loess Plain or Rainwater Basin.

Bisecting the plain from west to east was the Platte River. Over the previous 200,000 years, the river system had shifted its course back and forth across the east central part of Nebraska in response to flow and deposition variations which occurred within the basin and in the glaciated portions to the east (Fig.3).

The regional slope of the Nebraska prairie is from the northwest to the southeast. A casual perusal of a map showing the drainage system of the area shows that most streams follow this regional gradient. Examples include the South, Middle, and North Loup rivers lying north of the Platte River and the Big and Little Blue rivers to the south (Fig. 4). The Platte stands in contrast to these in that it follows a west to east path until it enters the glaciated region in the eastern part of the state. The drainage systems to the north and south of the Platte River have developed subsequent to the deposition of loess on the uplands. It is also notable that, within the Nebraska prairie section, the Platte's principal tributary streams enter the main river from the north while no major (and few minor) tributaries enter from the south.

The Dissected Loess Plain

On either side of the Platte River Valley, an upland area, called the Dissected Loess Plain, consists of hilly land with moderate to steep slopes. On the north side of the Platte Valley, this physiographic area extends along a southwest to northeast line from central Dawson County to Madison County and includes all or parts of Custer, Buffalo, Sherman, Valley, Greeley, Howard, Nance, Boone, Antelope, Pierce, and Holt counties. South of the Platte Valley, the Dissected Loess Plain encompasses the Republican

River Basin across southern Nebraska from Hitchcock to Nuckolls County.

The surface material of the Dissected Loess Plain is principally loess. Streams, extending their headwaters to the north and west, have progressively cut into the original loess plain. In some of the upland areas, remnants of the original plain (locally called "tables") remain, particularly in those areas farthest from rivers and streams (for example, Valley, Greeley, and central Custer counties).

Local topographic relief is smallest/lowest in areas near to the Platte River Valley but increases dramatically to the northwest. For instance, near Ord (Valley County), the elevation of the North Loup River is at 2,000 feet above sea level while two miles to the southwest, elevations reach 2,310 feet. The landscape of the Dissected Loess Plain is typically quite hilly. Most of the land is in slope with local relief of 50 to 150 feet quite common. Flat land, where it exists, is on the uneroded uplands between drainages or in the valley floors (Fig. 5).

Throughout the dissected plains section of the Nebraska prairie, where hillsides have been over-steepened by natural (erosion) or human (excavation/cultivation) processes, sharply vertical slopes result and frequently persist. Loess has a very high angle of repose, the maximum slope or angle at which a material will remain stable. In pure, undisturbed

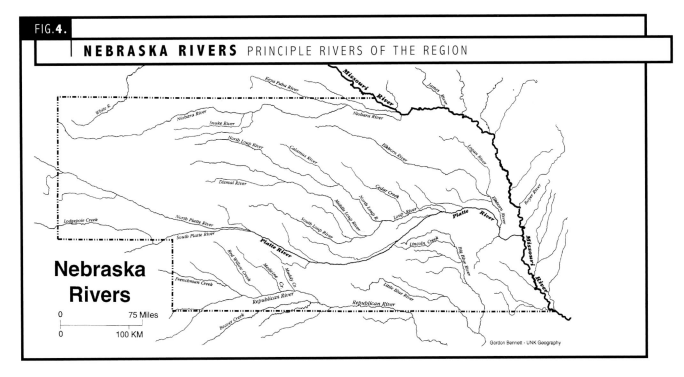

FIG.4.

NEBRASKA RIVERS PRINCIPLE RIVERS OF THE REGION

Nebraska Rivers

0   75 Miles

0   100 KM

Gordon Bennett - UNK Geography

FIG.**5.** An uneroded table   by Stan Dart

deposits, exposed loess can form slope angles greater than 75°. However, if these steep exposed slopes are attacked by running water or over-saturation, they quickly become unstable. Slow to rapid mass movements (creep, block sliding, etc.) cause slope alteration (Fig. 6). Water, running from an upland, across and down a steep exposed slope to a lower area, can erode headward in dramatic fashion. For example, in Custer County, attempts have been made to drain water from wetlands on upland "table" areas. Drainage ways were directed to the edge of the uplands, unfortunately resulting in deeply incised "canyons," which have rapidly progressed headward into previously undissected areas on higher tables (Fig. 7).

Many hillslopes in the dissected loess plain develop semi-horizontal, narrow, elongated step-like "terraces"–often referred to as "catsteps"–which appear to criss-cross hillsides. It might be assumed that these catsteps are simply trails worn into the hillside by the regular passage of livestock. They are, more properly, the result of slow slippage of loess block units along deteriorating hillslopes. Weathering of exposed loess induces vertical or near vertical planes along which slippage may occur. The planes become lines of weakness on the slope, and loess blocks, under the influence of water and gravity, are able to slowly move down slope. The presence or absence of catsteps is dependent upon the angle of the slope (more pronounced on high angle slopes)

and vegetative cover (more cover, fewer catsteps). Grazing animals take advantage of catsteps in their movements and frequently enhance the magnitude of slippage in heavily grazed areas.

The gradients of streams crossing the Dissected Loess Plain provide insight into stream processes. Most stream gradients in the section, that is, the change in vertical elevation over a horizontal distance, tend to be in the range of six to seven feet/mile with the higher gradients in the upstream portions of basins and the lowest gradients in the lower portions of basins. For example, the Missouri River, as it abuts Nebraska, has a gradient of one foot/mile. The gradient of the Platte River, from North Platte to Columbus, ranges from 6.7 feet/mile (west) to 6.2 feet/mile (east). At its juncture with the Loup River at Columbus, the Platte's gradient drops substantially to less than five feet/mile, reflecting the increased sediment load and discharge of the combined streams, and is only four feet/mile at its juncture with the Missouri.

In comparison, the South, Middle, and North Loup rivers, Cedar River, and Beaver Creek have gradients ranging from four feet/mile in their lower portions to more than seven feet/mile in their upper portions. Frenchman Creek (Chase County) and Red Willow Creek (Hayes County) each have gradients in excess of nine feet/ mile in their upper reaches. The gradients of ephemeral/ seasonal tributary streams to these rivers may

FIG.**6.** An exposed loess slope in Powell Canyon, Custer County, 1901   Butcher Collection

FIG.**7.** Mason City "ditch" erosion   by Stan Dart

*Eight miles south of Odessa
in the Great Plains Rainwater Basin
we discover Funk Lagoon,
a sprawling network of wetlands.*

*In late February, on a slate-gray day
we drive down the gravel roads
and see the snow geese in the fields
storing up energy
for the long flight north.*

*Their wings are tipped black,
but otherwise their bodies are all white—
one color the spirit may take
in its ascent.*

*And when a colony of them lifts off
from the stubble of last year's corn,
circling and whirling above the shallows
of rainwater and snow melt,
the air ripples with the beating
of their wings.*

U.S. Fish and Wildlife Service

FIG.**8.** Aerial photo of a portion of the rainwater basin topography

exceed one hundred feet/mile. The potential for headward erosion by tributaries into the dissected plain in the upper portions of these stream systems is considerable. Headward erosion will continue on all portions of this area, and, progressively, the proportion of undissected uplands to sloping terrain will decrease.

It is interesting to speculate how the face of Nebraska will appear in another ten thousand years. In Frontier and Lincoln counties as well as Hamilton County, tributaries of the Republican River (Medicine Creek and Muddy Creek) and of the Big Blue River (Lincoln Creek and others) extend to within a few thousand yards of the Platte River. Should headward erosion along these streams continue as it has for the last few thousand years, it is reasonable to assume that one or more of these streams might intersect the Platte, causing the river's course to change again as it continually seeks the shortest route to the sea.

The Loess Plain–Rainwater Basin

The Loess Plains region of south central Nebraska is frequently referred to as the Rainwater Basin. The region encompasses some 4,200 square miles within the 17 counties lying south of the Platte River from Phelps County (west) to Butler County (northeast) to Jefferson County (southeast). This area lies almost exclusively within the basins of the Little Blue and Big Blue rivers, which originate within the region and exit to the southeast. As the name implies, loess is the principal sub-surface material and serves as the parent material for upland soils. The topography of the Loess Plains is characterized by a flat to gently rolling surface with numerous closed depressions.

The Loess Plain is truly a product of the wind. It can be compared to the Dissected Loess Plain in that the surface material is the same wind-deposited loess derived from alluvial valleys and the Sand Hills to the north. Here, the loess has been only minimally dissected by stream erosion, and the overall drainage system is quite irregular and undeveloped. Over broad areas, the undulating surface consists of shallow basins of interior drainage. Lacking any outlets, basins may collect local snowmelt and rain water from areas of a few acres to several square miles. In places, basins have been breached and drained as headwaters of nearby streams have advanced into the poorly drained areas where outlets have formed across low divides between basins (Fig. 8).

The origins of the basins are clearly a result of wind erosion and the process of deflation. During arid periods when surface vegetation is less dense, fine soil particles are scoured out, causing the surface to be deflated. Soil particles are deposited on leeward/downwind edges of depressions, creating a low barrier.

The basins are characteristically shallow with flat bottoms and gently sloping sides. They range in area from less than an acre to more than forty acres. Few lie much lower than five feet below the surrounding land. Similar structures in the High Plains of northern Texas are called "playas," a Spanish term referring to basins which collect water seasonally. Taken as a group, basins tend to reflect elongated circular shapes that are oriented along a northwest to southeast line paralleling the principal wind direction during the periods of formation. Low crescent shaped ridges are present along the southern edges of larger basins. If one were to view a basin in cross-section, the southern end would be more gently sloping than the northern end– a reflection of the grading effect of wind-formed waves along the down-wind end.

Radiocarbon dating analysis indicates that basin formation has occurred episodically during arid/semi-arid periods from 20,000 to 25,000 ybp to 5,000-7,000 ybp and again 3,000-4,000 ybp. During each of the periods, existing basins were enlarged and new basins were formed.

It is suggested as well that biological processes have acted in concert with the wind to enhance and perpetuate the basin-forming processes. Basins collect rainfall and snow melt, holding water for varying lengths of time. Some larger basins contain water year around while smaller basins may hold water only into the late spring and summer. In the past, the water and associated vegetation served as focal points for animals, particularly buffalo, who would feed, drink, and wallow in the shallow water. As basins seasonally dried out, the broken and powdered soil in and around the basins would be freely available to the winds of winter. From season to season, a compounding cycle emerges: more water, more animals attracted; more animals attracted, more disturbance of the soil; more disturbance of the soil, more deflation, creating larger basins which, then, hold more water.

The bottoms of most basins are composed of very fine clay particles which have settled in the still, standing waters. A clay layer, which may range in thickness from only a few inches to as much as six feet, forms an effective, impervious barrier to the vertical movement of water. That is, surface water which collects in a basin is unable to permeate into the sub-soil. Likewise, groundwater from below is normally unable to move upward into a basin.

The soils in wetland basins are regular, definable, and reflect the hydrologic and vegetative character of basin environments. In basins permanently occupied by water, the Massie silt loam soil type predominates in the lowest, wettest parts of depressions. Water is generally present during the summer months, and, when undisturbed by drainage or cultivation, Massie soils support a plant community of cattails and bullrushes. In slightly shallower and fringing areas that are seasonally flooded, the Scott soil type– a silt/clay loam–supports a plant community dominated by smartweed. As the depth of water and the frequency of inundation decrease, the Fillmore and Butler soil types (also silt/clay loams) prevail with the Butler soils inundated only during the highest water events and only for short periods of time. All of these soils are poorly suited to cropping. However, they have very high value as habitat for wetlands wildlife.

It is estimated that prior to settlement, the Loess Plains contained more than 4,000 major wetland basins covering nearly 100,000 acres along with many hundreds of smaller basins. By the late 1800s and early 1900s, the flat ground and fertile soils attracted farming activities. Initially, basins were not cultivated. It was easy to plow around them, and the tight, clayey soils were both non-productive and difficult to cultivate. In the Post World War II era, mechanical innovations allowed larger tracts of land to be cultivated and "inconvenient" portions, like the basins, to be drained and tilled. The construction of rural road systems and associated ditches further encouraged the drainage of basins since, in many cases, the shortest distance for a drainage line would be a half-mile to the closest road ditch.

With the advent of large scale center-pivot irrigation technology in the 1970s, many

BLOWOUT

Sunset, among the sandhills,
those ancient glaciers of grass.
Standing on blacktop,
looking out beyond a fence line,

we watch the fungus of a blowout
look back. What began
as a small prairie flaw
is a gape, a yawn,

bringing a hillside down
and swallowing the sun.
Don't we too try to hide
from the wind?

Don't we arm ourselves
against something invisible,
blind, meaning no harm,
and most of the time on the other side

of our imperfections,
until that day it gets in,
and finding a fault,
a crack or a crevice,

blindly begins?
(from Plain Sense)

DON**WELCH**

FIG.**9.** Photograph of a river terrace

by Steven Rothenberger

portions of the Loess Plain which previously supported hay cropping or pasturing came under cultivation and irrigation. Many basins have been drained and tilled while other basins have experienced increased siltation from run-off on adjacent cultivated ground. According to Nebraska Game and Parks Commission data, on average, seventy-three percent of all acreage in the Rainwater Basins is cultivated and fifty-nine percent of all cropped acreage is under irrigation. In Phelps County, for example, ninety-three percent of all cropped land is irrigated while only twenty-one percent is irrigated in Nuckolls County.

Alluvial Valleys and River Systems

The streams and valley systems of the Nebraska prairie are reflections of the land they drain and the variety of climatic and geomorphic conditions which have influenced the physiography of the region over the past several tens of thousands of years. Every stream has what is called a base level, which is the level or depth to which it can erode. The ultimate base level of the earth is, of course, sea level. As a practical matter, the lowest elevation that any Nebraska stream could erode its channel (under current conditions) is the elevation at which that stream joins with any other stream. In the case of the Platte River, for instance, this is the elevation at which the Platte enters the Missouri River at Plattsmouth.

During the successive glacial advances and retreats of the Pleistocene, world-wide sea levels fluctuated by as much as three hundred feet. As seas levels declined, river systems world-wide graded (or eroded) their basins in response. During inter-glacial periods, as sea levels rose, stream systems alluviated (deposited material) in response. Similarly, streams continually adjust their channels and regimens in response to the volume of water (discharge) and/or the sediment (load). Over the long term, a stream will reach an equilibrium where the gradient of the stream is sufficient to carry both the volume of water and the sediment load produced in the river basin.

The principal river systems of Nebraska have all responded in one way or another to the variable hydraulic conditions associated with both the glacial period–when ice covered the eastern one-fifth of the state–and the various inter-glacial periods. The records of alternating periods of erosion and deposition are preserved within the alluvial materials associated with river flood plains and adjacent riparian and valley slope associations. While it is unusual for any one stream system to contain a complete record of all cycles, comparisons of evidence from several river systems allow for clearer understanding of the evolution of river systems.

Terraces are physical features composed of alluvial materials deposited when a river flowed on a floodplain that stood at a higher

FIG.**10.** Photograph of a portion of the North Loup River near Ord   by Steven Rothenberger

elevation. If a stream's capability to erode is increased (by lowering its base level, increasing its discharge, decreasing its sediment load, or a combination of any/all of these), the stream will cut downward through the alluvium of the flood plain. Quite frequently, along the edges of old floodplains, portions of original alluvial sediments will remain as alluvial terraces paralleling the valley. Subsequent erosion may destroy entire terraces, but, in many cases, terrace remnants and fragments can be found along most river systems in the Nebraska prairie section (Fig. 9). Archeological evidence suggests that terraces were frequently sites of aboriginal habitation and use.

Conversely, many of Nebraska's rivers flow across flood plains composed of thick deposits of river-deposited alluvial material. Deposition within a river system can happen when one or any combination of the following occurs: increased base level, decreased discharge, and increased sediment load. In portions of the Platte River Valley, alluvial fills are in excess of one hundred feet deep and lie directly on the eroded surface of the underlying Ogallala formation. This is a clear indication that, at one time, the Platte River (and its predecessors) had cut downward sufficiently to reach this depth– most likely during a period of glacial maximum when base levels were lower– and has subsequently refilled the valley with alluvial silts, sands, and gravels as base levels rose again during inter-glacial

periods. T.M. Stout has identified six cycles of valley erosion and fill in Nebraska from the glacial period to present. In many river valleys, terraces or portions of terraces formed during this period are still evident.

The rivers of the Dissected Loess Plain lying north of the Platte River include the Loup River system (South, Middle, and North), the Elkhorn River, and their associated tributaries (Fig. 10). Each of the principal segments of these rivers originates in the Sand Hills, with the Loup system, including the Calamus and Dismal Rivers, penetrating farthest to the west.

The Sand Hills origins of these streams significantly influences their flow characteristics. Within the Sand Hills, the sandy surface material is extremely permeable, allowing rainfall and snowmelt to infiltrate rather than run off. As a result, there are very few surface flowing streams or well developed drainage networks in the Sand Hills. However, the infiltrated water becomes part of the extensive ground water system of the Sand Hills, and, where the land surface intersects the groundwater table, some type of water feature appears. In some cases, the water table appears as a lake, wetland, or spring. If the water table intersects a stream valley, ground water seeps into the stream system and, as surface water, drains from the area. Since groundwater is released slowly but very consistently into a stream, that portion of the stream's flow that can be attributed to groundwater seepage

FIG.**11.** A channelized stream segment.

(base flow) is very regular and constant. Since there are few surface tributaries available to contribute run off from short term events (storms, rapid snow melt, etc.), streams do not show rapid increases or decreases in discharge in response to these events. For example, the Loup River system is extremely unlikely to flood or experience significant seasonal variations in discharge for these reasons.

This contrasts with stream systems which drain the Dissected Loess Plain south of the Platte River and the Rainwater Basin/Loess Plains of south central Nebraska. The Republican, Little Blue and Big Blue rivers, and tributaries, originate on or are mostly contained within areas where the soil parent material (loess) is much less permeable than the sands of the Sand Hills. Water derived from surplus rainfall and snowmelt flows downslope and enters into tributary streams which collectively enter into the main stems. During storms, when precipitation rates may exceed infiltration rates, considerable quantities of overland flow will reach stream segments in short periods of time and may cause flash flooding. Often, equally rapid declines in flow occur as the mass of water moves through the system. Similarly, rapid snow melt and rainfall on saturated or frozen soil can produce the same results.

One factor which moderates stream flow in the upper/western portions of the Loess Plain is the generally flat topography, lack of extensive stream development, and the presence of deflation basins. Basins act to

hold rainwater and snowmelt. Surface water that moves as overland flow will have greater potential to infiltrate into the soil as it moves towards low areas.

Within the Dissected Loess Plain, bluffs rise sharply away from the lowlands, often in a series of steps along terraces. Hillslopes are frequently blanketed with colluvial materials resulting from mass movements, such as creep, slumping, and block sliding. In places of recent movement or rapid erosion, the underlying unweathered loess may be exposed in vertical faces.

Characteristically, the valley floors and floodplains of streams in the Nebraska prairie are wide and flat. Floodplain sediments are primarily composed of varying fractions of silts and sands. The principal streams meander across the contemporary floodplain and, in areas where sand is present as part of the debris load, braiding occurs within the channel. Within meander belts, active undercutting and point bar deposition causes progressive sideways gradation of the floodplain, often producing meander cutoffs which form occasional small lakes or wetland areas.

In some areas, stream segments have been artificially channelized or straightened for a variety of reasons. Often, channelization permits bottomland to be more extensively and efficiently cultivated. Channelized streams provide more direct and rapid removal of excess water in times of flood. Some streams are channelized and rerouted because their natural courses lie in the way of some type of land development (Fig. 11).

However, channelization significantly disrupts the regimen of streams which have, over the long course of time, developed an equilibrium which allows for the efficient passage of water and sediment through the system. The effects of channelization are several. By straightening a meandering channel, the gradient of a stream is increased, which immediately increases the velocity of water flowing in the stream. Increasing velocity then increases the energy in the stream available for carrying sediment, allowing water to commence erosion of the bed and sides of the channel. The channelized portion of the stream degrades.

A downstream segment of a channelized stream that is not altered and allowed to remain in its equilibrium state will be impacted by upstream modification. Water from the modified segment entering the unmodified section will carry a greater sediment load, but the velocity will be reduced as it enters the unmodified segment. Consequently, the new sediment load will be redeposited in the natural segment, and the level of the stream bed will be raised. As a result, the downstream segment will be more susceptible to flooding because the volume of space previously occupied by water is now filled with sediment.

The stream segment above the modified channel will also respond to the change. With increased velocity and increased erosive power, erosion of the upstream channel will increase, causing that segment to be progressively lowered. Tributary streams will commence downcutting as well, and a new cycle of erosive energy is generated.

Channelization is not the only way stream equilibria are negatively altered. Any modification which causes change in the velocity of water or sediment load can stimulate adjustments to the flow regime. Most notably, removal of vegetative cover increases both run-off and sediment loads. Soil compaction and processes which create impermeable surfaces, such as paving, decrease infiltration and increase run-off. All of these alter slope angles and affect the time interval between water moving as over-land flow and its entrance into a stream. Loess, when exposed in slopes, is highly erodible. Within the Dissected Loess Plain particularly, land use practices which

encourage increased run-off are significant contributors to the alteration of streams and their adjacent riparian areas.

The Nebraska prairie is the product of a combination of geologic, geomorphic, and climatic processes which have interacted over millions of years. The lands and streams of the Nebraska prairie are productive and sustaining as a result of this unique combination of processes. Just as there have been slow and progressive natural changes in the land through that time, human activities on the land have and will continue to have significant impact. By recognizing the complex interplay of natural processes and human utilization, the character of the landscape of the Nebraska prairie can be preserved and sustained.

Selected**References**

Baltensberger, B.H. 1985. Nebraska: A geography. Boulder, CO: Westview Press.

Bentall, R. 1991. Facts and figures about Nebraska rivers. Water Survey Paper No. 73. Conservation and Survey Division. Institute of Agriculture and Natural Resources, University of Nebraska-Lincoln.

Bleed, A. and C. Flowerday, eds. 1990. An atlas of the Sand Hills. Resource Atlas No. 5a. Conservation and Survey Division. Institute of Agriculture and Natural Resources, University of Nebraska-Lincoln.

Nebraska Game and Parks Commission. Characterizations of wetland and upland habitats. Rainwater basins best management practices manual.

Diffendal, Jr., R.F. 1991. Plate tectonics, space, geologic time, and the Great Plains: A primer for non-geologists. Great Plains Quarterly, 11:83-102.

Diffendal, Jr., R.F. and F.A. Smith. 1996. Geology beneath the primary management systems evaluation area (MSEA) site southwest of Shelton, Buffalo County, Nebraska. Geological Survey Report of Investigations No. 11. Conservation and Survey Division. Institute of Agriculture and Natural Resources, University of Nebraska-Lincoln.

Elder, J.A., V.H. Dreeszen, and E.C. Weakly. 1973. Topographic regions map of Nebraska. GRM-4 Conservation and Survey Division. Institute of Agriculture and Natural Resources, University of Nebraska-Lincoln.

Feng, Z., W.C. Johnson, and R.F. Diffendal, Jr. 1994. Environments of aeolian deposition in South-Central Nebraska during the last glacial maximum. Physical Geography, 15:249-261.

Keech, C.F. and R. Bentall, 1982. Dunes on the plains: The sand hills region of Nebraska. Resource Report No. 4. Conservation and Survey Division. Institute of Agriculture and Natural Resources, University of Nebraska-Lincoln.

Schultz, C. B. and J.C. Frye. 1968. Loess and related eolian deposits of the world: Volume 12. Proceedings VIIth Congress. International Association for Quaternary Research. Lincoln, NE: University of Nebraska Press.

Stout, T.M., et al. 1971. Guidebook to the late pliocene and early pleistocene of Nebraska. Lincoln, NE: University of Nebraska Conservation and Survey Division.

Swinehart, J. B., J. Goecke, and T. C.Winter. 1988. Field guide to geology and hydrology of the Nebraska Sand Hills. Geological Society of America Field Trip Guidebook. Gregory S. Holden (Ed.).

Swinehart, J.B., et al. 1994. Quaternary geologic map of the Platte River 4 X 6 quadrangle. Map I-1420 (NK-14). United States: United States Geological Survey.

Weaver, J.E. and W.E. Bruner. 1948. Prairies and pastures of the dissected loess plains of Central Nebraska. Ecological Monographs. 18:507-549

WEATHER AND CLIMATE

ARBITER OF LIFE ON THE PRAIRIE

Marvin Glasser, Chairman of the Department of Physics and Physical Sciences

Hanging on the wall of many of the one room school houses that dotted the prairie until mid 20th century was a painting of a bison standing in a desolate wintry expanse. The bison was depicted facing into the wind and the horizontally driven snow of a raging blizzard. The shaggy denizen of the plains appeared oblivious to the hazards of a weather event that would cause other residents of the prairie, including humans, to perish if not sheltered. Protected by its thick mane and using its sharp hooves to dig through the crusty snow, it thrived on the other dominant life form characterizing the prairie, native grasses. The bison, more than anything else, epitomizes the role of adaptation to the harsh weather in this unique region and is also a symbol of the impact that humans can have when they intervene with nature. Although the bison thrived and adapted to the weather of the plains of North America for tens of thousands of years and in numbers that stretched the imagination, they were nearly swept into extinction in a few short decades by the wave of adventurers and settlers that came to the plains. Even the vast expanse of prairie that was the bison's habitat has been tamed and fragmented into ever diminishing patches by its human inhabitants. In the long run, however, weather and climate have been the architect of the plains and they will, acting in conjunction with human activity, remain the final arbiter of what the plains will become in the future.

In order to understand the nature of the prairie province, it is important to examine the role of weather and climate in the formation of the plains and in the shaping of its residents. Weather, by definition, is the combined descriptions of temperature, wind, rainfall, and other conditions of the atmosphere at a given time and place. Climate, on the other hand, is the cumulative effect or average of weather over extended periods of time along with the record of extremes that can be derived from it. The purpose of this discussion is to provide insight into the processes of climate and weather unique to the prairie. By way of illustration, some of the normal aspects of weather and climate are considered along with a few of the more spectacular features which distinguish the prairie of North America from any other region on Earth.

I. CLIMATE CLASSIFICATION
Climate and Vegetation

When the first settlers moved from the American colonies toward the west, they were undoubtedly struck by the dramatic changes that occurred in the vegetation as the almost continuous canopy of eastern forests gave way to seemingly endless expanses of treeless grasslands. It is natural to wonder what causes such dramatic differences in the ecology of various

Kearney house wrecked by cyclone, June 4, 1908   Butcher Collection

regions. When Koeppen was contemplating climatic classification in the late 1800s, botanists were in the final stages of drawing up the first worldwide maps of natural vegetation. He was impressed, as the settlers must have been, that the earth's vegetation was organized into uniquely different zones separated by narrow boundaries of rapid transition. His classification, published in 1900, was based on the recognition that vegetation growing naturally without the interference of humans could be considered as an overall climatic indicator because it integrates all weather elements together over extended time periods. The final result of vegetative growth in a region represents the totality of the climate of the region.

Determining the Boundaries

The usefulness of devising a classification scheme for climate, in order to provide an overall appreciation of its effect on a region, should be apparent. If the early settlers could have known what we now know about the climate of the prairie, they could have been saved from some very costly mistakes. As Koeppen refined the classification, he narrowed the climatic characterizations down to a few major zones. He then determined the particular monthly temperature averages or temperature-precipitation combinations that related to each region, in order to identify the rapid transition zones between ecological

groupings of plants. He determined, for instance, that if the temperatures for the coldest month of the year averaged below 64°F, most tropical plants would cease to grow. This temperature criteria became the poleward limit of tropical climates.

Why Temperate Climates Are Not Really Temperate

In Koeppen's climatic classification, the eastern portion of the Nebraska prairie is designated as temperate, which is characterized by four to seven months with temperatures averaging above 50°F. Just to the south, in Kansas, the climate is considered to be subtropical with at least one month averaging above 65°F and having eight or more months averaging above 50°F. Average monthly temperatures of above 50°F have been recognized as a significant threshold of growth for many domestic crops. Corn, for example, ceases productivity when the temperature falls below this limit.

Temperate climates are further subdivided into continental and oceanic climates. This point recognizes a factor not lost on the residents of the prairie as they struggle to adapt to the dramatic temperature changes that can have them exposed to warm, humid tropical air masses from the Gulf of Mexico at one moment only to be abruptly engulfed by cold, dry Polar air masses from Canada. From the point of view of the day to day

Nothing cuts distance like a fence.
The dust, strung taut as wire,
hums sterile songs. The posts
of moments, dried and gnarled, dig in.

Grief tamps them down, walks on,
sliding its hand along the barbs.
In the sluffed dirt the prints of our boots
hang on, signatures of strain

and thin-lipped laughter. Lips crack
and break. There are soul-cleats
on our tongues, salt-cells
in the wounds of sepia weather.

from The Georgia Review

weather, "temperate" would appear to be a misnomer, since great extremes occur in these climatic zones, especially in the interiors of large continents. However, from the point of view of averages, the climate is temperate. The extreme variations of temperate continental climates are only found in the Northern Hemisphere, since the continents in the Southern Hemisphere have no land masses to produce polar air, and oceans separate the continents from the extreme cold air of the Antarctica.

Rainfall Isn't Everything–Evapotranspiration

The western half of the Nebraska prairie, according to Koeppen's climatic classification, is semi-arid due to its location in the rain shadow to the east of the Rocky Mountains. Determining the boundary between humid and dry regions has been the major bugaboo in practically every attempt to classify climate, since no one line of equal precipitation can serve to delineate it. The reason for this is that moisture availability for plant growth depends not only on precipitation but also on other moisture losses from the plant and the soil. It remained for Thornthwaite in 1944 to shed the greatest light on the problem of the distinction between humid and dry climates. He coined the word "evapotranspiration" to describe the moisture loss from vegetated soils, and he eventually realized that it was potential evapotranspiration (the amount of moisture that would be lost if there was unlimited water) that should be balanced against rainfall. The potential to evaporate water is, of course, largely dependent upon temperature and wind. As any farmer knows, the greatest need for water comes during the hottest part of the growing season. On the other hand, a region which is generally cold, like the arctic tundra, receives less water than most deserts and still maintains wet marshy conditions.

Timing–Important as the Amount of Rainfall

Another source of concern for those attempting to grow crops in the marginal conditions of the prairie is the timing of the precipitation. Koeppen was also aware that it isn't just the amount of annual precipitation which is important, but rather it is the timing of the precipitation in relation to the growing season that is even more significant. He developed formulas for three types of precipitation regimens: one in which the precipitation is spread uniformly throughout the year; one where it is concentrated in the winter months; and one with the precipitation concentrated in the growing season.

The Nebraska prairie is of the latter type, having a well-defined peak of precipitation in the growing season during April and May. These months have a total precipitation of more than five times the precipitation in January, the driest month. In the Koeppen scheme for climate classification, the boundary between the semi-arid western portion of the prairie and the temperate continental, eastern grasslands coincides

(NASA Photo STS001 10 010)

FIG.**1.** Panorama of the Prairie and the Platte River

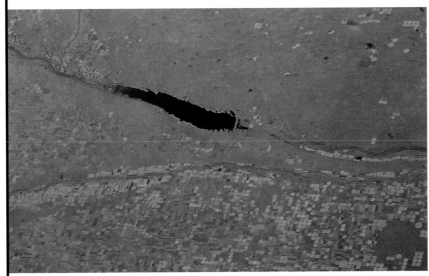

(NASA Photo STSO73 704 037)

FIG.**2.** Evidence of Human Activity on the Prairie

Panorama of the Prairie and the Platte River

This astronaut photo shows the general setting of the prairie region of Nebraska. The photograph is a panorama from northern Kansas at the bottom to South Dakota at the top. Taken by astronauts in April 1981, the view includes the western half of the Nebraska prairie and some of eastern Colorado and Wyoming. The dark circle at the top left of the photo is the Black Hills. The Pine Ridge area and the Niobrara River valley are visible as dark strips just south of the Black Hills. The arc of the Great Bend region of the Platte River starts on the left of the photo at about Lexington and stretches westward across the center of the photo before dividing into the North and South Platte Rivers. Lake McConaughy is the prominent reservoir on the North Platte River. In the lower part of the photo, the Republican River drainage basin can be seen with its reservoirs. The dark region near the upper right margin of the photo is the artificially planted Nebraska National Forest.

Evidence of Human Activity on the Prairie

This photo was taken by astronauts from a shuttle flight at the end of October in 1995 using a 250 mm lens. The stippled regions south of the Platte River are an indication of agricultural activities. In this close- up photo, there is no mistaking the impact of human activity where the shapes of the individual fields are evident. The dam at Lake McConaughy and the circular fields of the center pivots can easily be identified. There are fourteen years between the above photo (STS00110 0010) and this photo. This 1995 photo clearly shows that there are center pivots being introduced into the Sand Hills north of the Platte River. This view of extensive agriculture in a semi-arid area with insufficient natural rainfall raises the intriguing question of sustainability, considering the wide range of climatic variation, which is characteristic of the region. Further complicating the fate of irrigated agriculture in a semi-arid climate is the issue of human-induced climate change that many scientists expect in the future.

If one could have taken a photo from this vantage point prior to the arrival of the settlers, one might have been lucky enough to see one of the great bison herds that were reported by early explorers. Immigrants passing through described herds large enough to hold up the progress of wagon trains for hours or even days. With estimates of bison throughout the plains regions ranging in the tens of millions, one could be sure that there would have been many bison in such a snapshot of the past.

FIG.**3.**

DAILY TEMPERATURE VARIATIONS
NORTH PLATTE, NEBRASKA IN JANUARY 1995

Temperature Variability
The daily maximum and minimum temperatures for North Platte, Nebraska, for January 1995 show the variability characteristic of the winter season for the prairie provinces. Not only do day to night temperatures vary by as much as 40˚F, as on January 31, but the temperatures from day to day are more likely to be extreme rather than average. For example, the average maximum temperature for January for the past 30 years is 34˚F, but 21 days of the month are either much colder or much warmer than the norm.

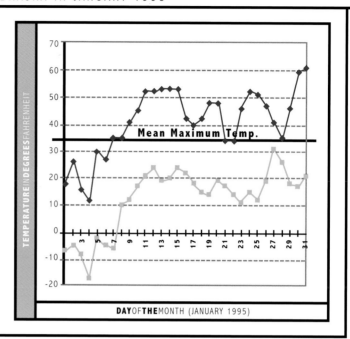

with the twenty inch climatic isoline for annual precipitation, which also is near the 100th meridian. The southern boundary of the prairie region grades into the subtropical continental climate which lies to the south in Kansas near 37° north latitude. In reality, the climate of the plains region can fluctuate on the time-scale of years between the three climatic types: semi-arid, temperate continental, and subtropical continental. The implications of this for the practice of agriculture on the prairie is considerable, particularly in connection with the cycles of drought which plague residents of the prairie.

The Astronaut Perspective

Originally, the region west of the 100th meridian was vegetated primarily by bunch grass and was adapted for grazing. As can be seen in the astronaut photos (Fig. 1), much of the grassland has been plowed under for agriculture. As with all subhumid-semiarid regions of the world, grassland soils are excellent. Their fertility encouraged farmers to plant crops in climatically hazardous regions, which experience precipitation amounts that are below normal more years than they are above normal. Humans have interceded with technology in the constant

struggle to support agricultural crops in a climate that produced grasslands (Fig. 2).

NASA photos taken of Saudi Arabia show that even the desert can be made to bloom as long as water is applied. It should be noted, however, that it is reported to cost between fourteen to thirty dollars per bushel to grow wheat in Saudi Arabia, using center pivot irrigation. The water comes from deep and ancient aquifers. Once the water is pumped out, it will not be replaced for millennia.

Irrigation from the great Ogallala aquifer, which underlies part of the Nebraska prairie region, can forestall some of the effects of drought. But in the long view and in the court of nature, it will be climate which has the final say as to the future for life on the prairie.

II. WEATHER VARIABILITY
Everyone Talks About It

The subject of weather is a constant source of conversation and a frequent brunt of complaint in many cultures. But, for the inhabitants of the prairie, these discussions recognize the underlying reality that weather not only changes rapidly but undergoes swings of great extremes. It is not without merit to say that there is no such thing as "normal" when referring to weather on the prairie. For example, the highest temperature for days in January for North Platte over the last thirty years indicates that the average high for January is about 34°F. A graph of the actual daily maximum and minimum temperatures for North Platte in 1995 illustrates that for most of the days of the month, the temperatures are either much colder or much warmer than average (Fig. 3).

Living on a Battlefield

Why are the day to day weather contrasts so exaggerated in the prairie provinces of Nebraska and on the Great Plains of North America? The rapid and extreme weather changes that occur here can be attributed to two major factors. One is the geographic setting and the other relates to the way the weather machine works, i.e. characteristics of the global circulation. In the most fundamental sense, global circulation is the result of temperature differences at the earth's surface. These temperature differences are, in turn, created by unequal solar heating. For example, the Polar regions receive little direct solar energy and reflect most of what they receive back into space, leaving the surface and the atmosphere cold.

In the tropics, on the other hand, the sun is high overhead throughout the year. Much of the sun's energy goes into evaporating water, leaving the equatorial regions with humid and hot climates. On the average, the tropics have an excess in energy and the Polar regions have a deficit. Weather and circulation is a direct response to the redistribution of this excess energy from the tropics toward the polar regions. Living in the midlatitudes between these two regions exposes residents to continual fluctuations of weather, as air from the tropic and polar regions pass through, mingle, and exchange energy. The consequence is a weather war zone in which weather rapidly changes and sometimes becomes violent.

The Great Rocky Mountain Barrier

The second factor involved in producing extreme weather on the plains is related to the particular geographic circumstances of the prairie. The north-south barrier of the Rocky Mountains has the effect of reducing the westerly flow typical of the midlatitudes and allowing the contrasting air masses from the polar and tropic regions to move more freely north and south. About half of the energy exchange between the tropics and the polar region is due to the exchange of these air masses. The midlatitudes are, in a very real sense, a battleground between these thousand-mile-wide pools of air moving to carry excess energy from the tropics to higher latitudes. The spinning earth deflects the air masses so that, in the Northern Hemisphere midlatitudes, the surface winds have a component from the west. In most parts of the world, this westerly flow tends to deflect air masses to the east, reducing the southward penetration of cold air. Only on the prairie of North America does a great north-south mountain barrier allow the deep incursions of air mass into enemy territory.

Oceans: The Great Moderator

Another geographic factor which is important in producing weather extremes is the central continental location of the prairie. Bodies of water both absorb and release heat more slowly, since they store more heat than land. The atmosphere over or near oceans undergoes much less change in temperature, both from day to night and from season to season, than locations isolated in the interior of continents. The most dramatic testimonials to this set of circumstances are the more than normal share of blizzards, thunderstorms, tornadoes, hail, floods, and droughts impacting the ecology of the prairie and affecting the lives of the residents.

III. WEATHER EXTREMES
Winter on the Prairie–Blizzards

Winter has its own brand of life-threatening weather. Though not as violent as the tornado, a blizzard can hold large areas of the plains in its icy grip. To live through a winter on the plains is to realize the truth of the perspective that normal conditions are a fiction of averaging extreme weather together. It is not unusual for daily high temperatures to soar into the 60°F range on a sunny, snow-free day in January, the coldest month of the season. This can

ASHES

*The sky
that
gave breath
to her ancestors
now
chokes
her children.
All will
return
to dust
unless
we stop
closing
the sky.*
CHARLES**PEEK**

FIG.**4.**

MEAN ANNUAL SNOWFALL AND SNOW COVER
UNITED STATES, 1961-1990

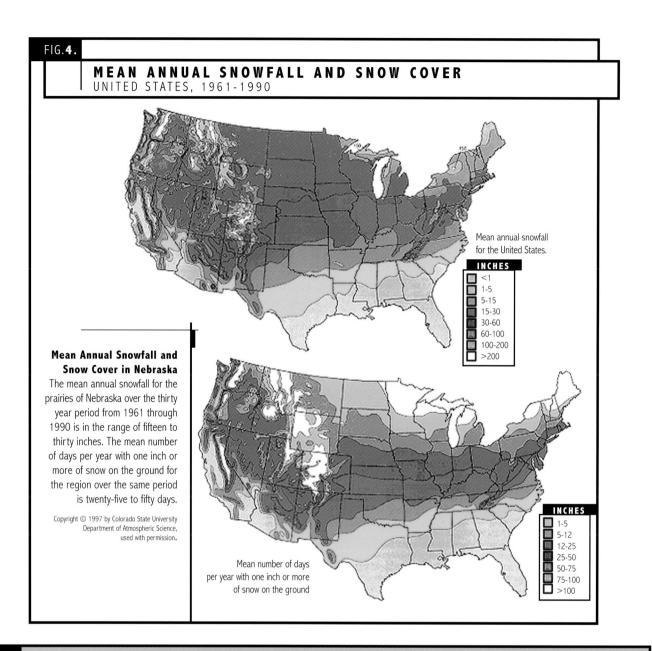

Mean annual snowfall
for the United States.

INCHES
☐	<1
☐	1-5
☐	5-15
☐	15-30
☐	30-60
☐	60-100
☐	100-200
☐	>200

Mean Annual Snowfall and Snow Cover in Nebraska

The mean annual snowfall for the prairies of Nebraska over the thirty year period from 1961 through 1990 is in the range of fifteen to thirty inches. The mean number of days per year with one inch or more of snow on the ground for the region over the same period is twenty-five to fifty days.

Copyright © 1997 by Colorado State University Department of Atmospheric Science, used with permission.

Mean number of days
per year with one inch or more
of snow on the ground

INCHES
☐	1-5
☐	5-12
☐	12-25
☐	25-50
☐	50-75
☐	75-100
☐	>100

DATA RECORDS OF SNOW ON THE PLAINS—A HISTORY OF EXTREMES

Snow storms can occur in any of eight months of the year in the Nebraska prairie region. The following data is from the climate information for Grand Island, Nebraska.

On average, 31 inches of snow falls during the winter season on the central plains.

The greatest snowfall for a season was 85 inches, which occurred in 1914-15. This was followed by a close second in the 1983-84 season with 70 inches.

The least snow to fall in a season since records have been kept was three inches in 1907-08.

A late snow of four inches and a hard freeze on May 28, 1945, ruined the regions gardens and crops.

A three-day ice and snowstorm on November 25-28 in 1983 brought everything to a halt in the central plains and ushered in the coldest December on record with seven days in a row of temperatures that never rose above zero degrees Fahrenheit.

Halloween in 1991 was shut down by Nature's trick of one to two feet of snow.

The earliest snowfall of over one inch occurred on September 20, 1995, when three inches of snow fell.

In the fall of 1997, a storm with an intensity that was estimated to occur only once every 200 years swept out of the Rocky Mountains on the last week end in October. It left behind up to 50 inches of snow in the mountains and utterly paralyzed cities along the front range. Snowfalls of one foot were widespread across the plains region, and some areas received over two feet. Much of the snowfall occurred in thunderstorm events, with lightning, thunder, and rates of accumulation of 3-4 inches per hour. Because the snow came before a frost had prepared the vegetation, trees still had most of their leaves. Power outages from falling limbs were the worst on record, reminding residents that prairie snowstorms can overwhelm everything in their path and that even our most vital technologies can fail in the onslaught.

Platte River Winter Scene

Winters on the prairie are often harsh, but they also can have a softer side. Here the Platte River catches the first inhabitants on a sandbar, the cockleburr, silhouetted in the low winter sun.

photo by Marvin Glasser

For residents of the plains around Grand Island and Kearney, the blizzard of January 16, 1996, can serve as a reminder of the descriptions of blizzards that their parents and grandparents can so vividly recall. While many other blizzards have occurred which had more snow, were more intense, or were more widespread, the suddenness and timing of the event makes it a memorable experience for anyone caught in its grip. We can give dispassionate descriptions of such storms as being the consequence of energy exchange on a grand scale between the tropics and polar regions and to the quirk of geography, in which the Rocky Mountains block the westerly winds, allowing the dramatic conflict of air masses. This, however, does not seem adequate to describe an event that so dramatically and abruptly confronts us with the powerlessness of our own efforts or that of our technologies to withstand the force of nature on a rampage.

The arrival of the cold front in the region in the midafternoon hours caught the maximum number of people either on the roads, at their places of business, or in activities away from home, such as shopping or at school. The rapid transition from unusually warm days, which tends to lull one into a state of complacency, began with rain which quickly froze on everything. Even though residents are generally accustomed to adjusting to poor road conditions in winter, the sudden icing was followed by blinding snow, so that it was impossible for even experienced drivers, confronted with intermittent zero visibility and no traction, to avoid accidents or to end up having an abrupt off-road encounter, i.e. hitting the ditch.

By one count, 140 cars were in the ditches off Highway 30 along the 40 miles between Grand Island and Kearney, and many of these became buried in the ensuing drifting. Everywhere in the region, drivers abandoned cars as they became stuck, even in the roadways as they became fearful of driving blind. The motto for the day became "if you are safe, stay where you are." The majority of the population, as a result, became stranded wherever they were, wisely avoiding exposing themselves to the dangers of the storm. University classrooms, schools, stores, shopping malls, and churches, wherever there was shelter, became the overnight resting places for hundreds of citizens and travelers.

For many, memories of the experiences associated with the storm will remain for a lifetime and become the grist of tales passed on to their children and grandchildren. Stories about people and the effect of the storm on their lives filled regional papers. In one case, motorists coming into Kearney from the north drove off the main highway onto graveled country roads to avoid the glasslike surfaces of the paving and roads already blocked with stranded cars. These roads, too, became impassable. As darkness fell, a cadre of a car and two delivery trucks pulled into a farm yard near the roadway, beckoned only by the faintly visible yard light. Finding no one at home and fearing frostbite, a side door to the garage was jarred open. This allowed the freezing travelers to enter the house through an unlocked door. As the evening progressed, several more stranded men struggled to the same house until there were twelve travelers grateful to be sheltered from the storm. With shelter, heat, and a working phone they made calls to allay the fears of friends and family and felt lucky to be safe.

Because all landmarks disappear in the whiteout of a blizzard, the stranded travelers were not sure how far they were from Kearney. Someone had noted the farm owners' name on unopened mail on the dining room table in attempting to gain a clue as to their location. At one point, the phone rang and the call was answered. It was the owner of the farm, on vacation in a distant state, who had mistakenly dialed his own phone while trying to reach a hired hand. The owner, confused at first, asked who he was speaking to and was surprised to hear that the person answering the phone gave their location as being his house. Realizing that there were strangers in his house resulted in some understandably tense moments until the situation was explained.

True to the character of those who live on the plains, the owner extended a warm welcome and offers of food and other essentials to the uninvited strangers, who spent the night playing pool in the recreation room. When snow plows cleared the roads, the grateful refugees left behind more than enough money to cover the cost of food and utilities. It is surprising, especially in light of the life-threatening wind chills of -40˚F, that although there were some frost bite victims, no one lost his or her life as a direct result of the storm.

be followed by the passage of an Arctic cold front which, in a matter of an hour or less, reduces the temperature dramatically and may also usher in a blizzard. A snow storm is given the status of a blizzard if visibility is reduced to less than 450 feet, and winds gust to 35 mph or greater. On the prairie, blizzards can become even more severe, having winds greater than 45 mph that reduces visibility to zero and are accompanied by bitter cold temperatures. The combination of wind and cold can produce life-threatening wind chill conditions, which have the cooling equivalent of -40°F to -80°F. Frostbite can occur in less than a minute when skin is exposed to these conditions.

The Frailty of Technology in the Face of Nature

If blizzards are preceded by warm weather and precipitation starting as rain that changes to ice and then to blinding snow, the stage is set for one of the most disruptive events of the winter season on the plains. Ice initially coats the roadways and may break down power and phone lines. The net effect is to bring to a snarled and tangled end all normal travel and communications. Weather like this serves to alert everyone living in the region, or the unwary traveler caught in its grip, that the forces of nature can totally take control of one's life for a few hours or even a few days. These storms, classified as midlatitude wave cyclones, can have sizes and intensities that rival and even exceed that of most hurricanes.

Experiencing such a storm causes one to ponder the hardships suffered by early settlers and the many travelers on the great trails that passed through the region. Many were without adequate clothing or supplies and were accustomed to the more sheltered conditions of the eastern forests. Residents who dug into the prairie and used the sod for thick walled houses, called soddies, found adequate protection, but those traveling through or caught in the open were at great risk in these violent and unannounced storms.

Snow and Agriculture

The effect of blizzards on agriculture is primarily related to the impact on cattle and other livestock. The storm itself may pose a direct threat to the livestock or indirectly thwart efforts to feed and care for them. Strong winds break snowflakes into small crystals, which may pack to the extent that drifts become hard enough to walk on. Cattle tend to face downwind in such storms and may move for miles with the wind, crossing fences and becoming difficult to find. It is not uncommon for cattle to end up in towns where there is more shelter.

Bison, which are much better adapted to the weather of their native prairie, tend to face into the wind. The thick coat of shaggy hair that covers their head and front quarters serves them well as protection from the coldest windchills. A herd of snow-encrusted bison in a storm tends to evoke sympathy for their condition. The layer of snow, however, serves to further insulate the bison from heat loss and to shield them from the wind-chill effect, so their condition may not be as stressful as appearances would indicate. In addition to the effects on livestock, the occurrence of snow, especially snow which comes without wind, is important for its protection, or insulation, of winter wheat crops and for supplying water to soil profiles.

Annual Snowfall and Days of Snow Cover

The distribution of snowfall for the plains can be determined from the Mean Annual Snowfall graphic produced by the Colorado Climate Center (Fig. 4). Five to fifteen inches of snow fell, on average, in the southern portion of Nebraska for the period 1961 through 1990, while fifteen to thirty inches are average for northern Nebraska. The Mean Number of Days per Year with one inch or more of snow on the ground is twenty-five to fifty days in Nebraska for the same period. Anyone who has lived in the region and is old enough to recollect the weather over this period will likely have the impression that the frequency and amount of snowfall has decreased in recent times. That impression is accurate. Determining whether the recent milder and more snow-free winters for the region are the result of some natural cycle or have a connection with atmospheric changes induced by human activities is an interesting but difficult issue.

Mammatus clouds   Photographer Marvin Glasser

Tornado Sky
Mammatus clouds, as seen in this photo, form on the underside of the anvil cloud portion of a thunderstorm. The anvil part of the thunderstorm, or cumulonimbus cloud, is sheared off the top of the thunderstorm by jet speed winds at the top of the weather layer. This photo shows the appearance of clouds from a thunderstorm approaching Kearney in a late afternoon summer storm. The feature is the result of severe turbulence, and it derives its name "tornado sky" because of its frequent association with intense storms that produce tornadoes. When the descending blobs of cloud are arranged in rows, as in this photo, it is sometimes called a "corncob sky" by natives of the prairie. The coloration of the clouds is due to the rays from the setting sun.

Were the winters experienced in the early 1900s more severe than those today, or is this a trick of memory like the length of the fish that got away? The weather records over most of North America indicate a decrease in recent decades in the number of days in the year with snow cover. Snow cover going into spring has decreased by an average of seven days statewide in Nebraska. The decrease has been greater in the east than in the west. It should be noted that fewer days with snow cover by itself can cause the weather to be warmer because snow reflects up to ninety percent of the sunlight. Without snow the ground warms and, in turn, heats the atmosphere. This may have been caused by a shift in the winter storm track to the west.

Even though there has been an overall decrease in the number of snow days for the winter season, snows are coming earlier in the fall. There is also evidence of a decrease in the total amount of snowfall in recent decades. The decreases in snowfall and persistence of snow cover could be the result of a temporary warming trend, or they may be the first signal of something much more significant. Many climatologists consider these changes to be an early sign of global warming and that the warming may be the result of increased greenhouse effect, resulting from excess carbon dioxide produced by human activities.

Spring and Severe Storms–Thunderstorms: Explosions in Slow Motion

The prairie province in Nebraska has a high incidence of severe thunderstorms. The most intense of these spawn tornadoes, with the greatest frequency in Nebraska being in the spring. These prominent weather events also result from the grand scheme of energy exchange between the tropics and the polar regions. Thirty percent of the excess energy transported from the tropics, on a global average, is in the form of latent heat in water vapor. This energy is released as heat when vapor converts back to its solid and liquid phases in clouds and storms. The more water vapor available, the more potential there is for severe thunderstorms and, consequently, the higher risk of tornadoes. An ordinary thunderstorm releases as much energy as a medium-yield nuclear weapon. Fortunately, the energy release from converting water vapor into cloud droplets and ice crystals is spread over hours, rather than being released in an instant. The resulting energy of the storm is still violent enough to produce the most devastating atmospheric phenomena, tornadoes.

Tornado Alley

The high incidence of thunderstorms in the region to the east of the Rocky Mountains is related to the unique fact

A shelf cloud signaling the approach of a thunderstorm

STORMS A SERPENT IN THE SKY

In the process of recounting the role of weather in shaping the prairie, it would be remiss to not include some insight into the sheer wonder of the display put on by weather. The attention of visitors to the region is often attracted to the day and nighttime panorama of the sky. This is particularly true for those who come from cities where their vision of the sky is obscured by city lights, tall buildings, or pollution. Even early settlers, used to the security of the eastern forests, were struck by the great vistas of grasslands with unobstructed views from horizon to horizon. Some express surprise at being able to see weather coming. Natives, more familiar with the signs in the sky, find clues to approaching weather systems or even signals that indicate an immediate need to seek safety. In this photo, the shelf cloud, somewhat unusual in that it has two layers, is created by a gust front and signals the approach of a thunderstorm accompanied by strong winds. In dry years, these winds pick up dirt and create menacing, dark walls of dust, indicating the loss of precious topsoil. In earlier times, the stinging tongue of this serpent (lightning) could have ignited dry grasses, causing walls of fires to race across the prairie.

that it is the only region in the world where polar continental air masses have such easy access to warm, humid air masses from the tropics all year long. Plentiful water vapor for energy, rapidly moving cold fronts, and adequate surface heating for lifting and starting the energy release through condensation are important factors in the production of frontal thunderstorms. These conditions are maximized in Tornado Alley, which starts in the panhandle of Texas and extends north through the centers of Oklahoma and Kansas into Nebraska.

Another ingredient that is necessary for forming thunderstorms intense enough to produce tornadoes is the presence of a Polar Front Jet Stream above the thunderstorm region. These fast moving rivers of air at the top of the weather layer aid in exporting air out of the thunderstorms so that inflow can continue underneath the base of the cumulonimbus cloud. This helps replenish the water vapor that supplies energy to the storm. In air mass thunderstorms, which are isolated from frontal lifting, surface heating is important in initiating uplift. The most violent thunderstorms occur when a tongue of warm dry air out of the southwest overrides a humid air mass from the gulf. The stable dry layer suppresses lifting until a rapidly moving cold front can cause convection to break though explosively, producing the rapid growth needed for a severe thunderstorm.

IV. DROUGHT AND SETTLEMENT ON THE PRAIRIE

The Great American Desert

Although hundreds of thousands of emigrants had passed through the prairie region on the great trails by the mid 1800s, only about 2,700 settlers actually lived there. Most of these residents lived near military installations and trading posts. Congress had designated the region as Indian Territory and forbidden settlement between 1821 and 1854, when Nebraska became a territory. An additional impediment for settlers coming with the hope of farming was the stigma of the "Great American Desert" written across existing maps of the Platte Valley region. This epitaph for the prairie was the consequence

of an expedition westward along the Platte River led by Major Stephen Long in 1820.

Almost Wholly Unfit for Civilization

No one would be more surprised than Long to see the region today, after his botanist and geologist had characterized its "hopeless and unreclaimable sterility" that should "forever remain the unmolested haunt of the native hunter, the bison and jackal." Long, in his final report, concluded, "In regard to this extensive section of the country I do not hesitate in giving the opinion, that it is almost wholly unfit for civilization and of course uninhabitable by a people depending upon agriculture." It has long intrigued climatologists how a grassland with substantial vegetation could have been incorrectly identified as "desert."

In Long's defense, it appears from a study of tree ring width that at the time of Long's expedition, the region was undergoing extreme drought, possibly worse, in relative terms, than the great drought of the 1930s. Long may have, indeed, seen a "Great Desert" with dormant, overgrazed grasses and blowing dust. What Major Long and the expedition geologist and botanist could not have known was that two great gifts had been bestowed on the region by eons of geological and climatological processes: deep fertile grassland soils and a world class aquifer.

Rain Will Follow the Plow

Drought has had an important effect on the pattern of settlement and agriculture on the plains, and it is likely to continue to be one of the more profound concerns for residents in the future. A severe drought in 1860 caused many to abandon their farms. Settlements remained sparse on the prairie until the Homestead Act, which became effective on January 1, 1863, allowed the head of a family, for a filing fee of ten dollars, to claim 160 acres of land for free if they lived on it for five years. Three years later, the Union Pacific began laying track in the Big Bend area of the Platte River, on the way to completing the first intercontinental railroad in 1869. This markedly improved the hauling of freight and passengers to the region. These factors, coupled with a nearly

NASA photo. STS049 92 071

SANDSTORM VIEWED FROM SPACE

If astronauts had been circling the Earth on "Black Sunday," they might have viewed something like the scene above. This astronaut photo catches a giant sand storm in the Sahara Desert. The wall of sand is several thousand feet high and extends in a great arc for more than a hundred miles. Similar storms crossed the Dust Bowl. Laden with sand and precious top soil, these events scoured the land left unprotected where the settlers turned over the sod.

Most dust storms in the 1930s were smaller, being only a few tens of miles across, and were associated with the gust fronts of thunderstorms. The irony of thunderstorms without rain was not lost on the settlers who already felt that nature was conspiring against them. Drought and dust work hand in hand to produce this effect.

Although rain may fall from a thunderstorm cloud, if the air is very dry the raindrops evaporate before reaching the ground. As a result of evaporation, cool air columns are formed, and these descend to the surface, spreading out ahead of the storm to produce the gust front or, in this case, dust front. Dust in the atmosphere, in turn, tends to stabilize clouds, reducing their ability to produce rain. In one sense, the settlers may have been correct, because droughts are a conspiracy of factors in which the conditions producing them act to perpetuate them. When this process does not reverse itself, it is called desertification. Desertification is a process of global concern. While natural cycles in rainfall are contributing factors to this process, in most cases, the initiating event is the actions of human activities, including overgrazing and the use of poor agricultural practices

Dust Storm as it reaches Franklin, Nebraska, 1935

Colorado Dust Storm 2, Baca County, 1935   by J. H. Ward

STORMS   **"BLACK SUNDAY"**

A Day of Infamy in the Dust Bowl

 On April 14, 1935, a great dust storm rolled out of Colorado and across Oklahoma. Where the brunt of the storm was felt, residents recollected that the day was very still. Birds fled ahead of it across the sky. Some took photographs and some prayed. To all, it was like a curtain falling on a vast stage turning the day to darker than night.

The plow, one cause for the Dust Bowl   by Arthur Rothstein

unbroken period of twenty years of favorable weather between mid 1860 and mid 1880, enticed more settlers.

As more land became occupied in the eastern regions of the prairie, the overflow of settlers moved on to less favorable regions of the western prairie. Drought, grasshoppers, and a national depression intervened briefly to slow the region's development in the years between 1874 and 1877. Land speculators, anxious to dispel the stigma of the Great American Desert, assured prospective settlers that there was enough rainfall to support agriculture, and even offered the claim that "rain will follow the plow." While their arguments were spurious, the years of above normal rainfall encouraged many new settlers.

Prolonged Drought : The 1930s

Unfortunately, drought returned to the Great Plains in the late 1880s and continued into the 1890s. The combination of crop failures and the economic depression of the Panic of 1893 reduced the population of some western Nebraska regions by as much as fifty percent. Even those used to the variability of the prairie climate could not have been prepared for the unprecedented and prolonged drought of the 1930s. The litany of human and economic suffering is remarkable in its variety and extent, but the

image, which haunts survivors of the decade-long drought and those who look back for its lesson, is that conjured up by the Dust Bowl.

The Dust Bowl

The Dust Bowl was, in reality, a ninety seven million-acre piece of the High Plains extending from Texas into Nebraska. Many have theorized about the causes of the Dust Bowl, beyond the obvious association with drought and wind. Was this disaster mostly an unusual climatic change, or was it an ecological disaster caused by a misunderstanding of the limits of human intervention on the plains? Clearly, elements of both came together to produce the disaster. In the above photo, the vision of the plow, abandoned and being buried by the forces they set in motion, should serve as a symbol to modern-day residents of the prairie. If humans are to continue to thrive in the prairie province, they will need to understand the existing natural constraints of climate and resources that govern and sustain its environment.

A more difficult question for the residents of the plains is, will it come again? It is evident, from the survey of historical climate conditions, that extended drought periods have been common in the past and will likely occur again. What is not as clear is if the

Sod busting   by Fred Hulstrand

Another use for sod   by W.H. Starkjohann

SOD   SOD BUSTING & ANOTHER USE FOR SOD

Four teams of four horses each break virgin sod on the Hulstrand farm in North Dakota. This hand colored photo, taken around 1900-1906, shows fertile soil, produced over centuries by prairie grasses in consort with climate, being exposed to a climate with more than enough variability in precipitation and wind to make its future uncertain.

On the treeless prairie, timber was not available to provide shelter from the harsh weather of the plains. Making use of what was at hand, settlers built homes from slabs of sod. The buildings used some wood for doors and windows and, in this case, to support the sod roof, but the floors were typically left as dirt. To afford further protection, some soddies were dug into the ground. This hand colored photo was taken around 1902 or 1903 of a school house, complete with a privy, located on the prairie in Keya Paha County, Nebraska.

The Aftermath   Photographer Arthur Rothstein

THE AFTERMATH

The fertile topsoil, without its protective cover of prairie grasses and exposed to the elements of weather, lies in piles around a farmer's barn near Liberal, Kansas. The photograph was taken in March of 1936 in the midst of a drought which turned a large portion of the high plains into the Dust Bowl.

lessons that have been learned from that disaster along with the technology and agricultural practices that have been developed will be enough to cope with drought and to avoid major disruption of lives, economy, and food production.

A further complication is the wild card of human-induced, global climate change. Unfortunately, most models of the effects of additional greenhouse warming indicate that even wider swings in climatic conditions are likely in temperature and precipitation. This would not bode well for a region with a proven record of high climatic variability.

Conclusion

The great lesson to be learned from examining the weather and climate of the prairies is that while blizzards and tornadoes are intense, awe-inspiring, and even life-threatening events, it is the variability of weather and climate that humans have the most to fear. It is also clear that the reasons for the type of weather and climate unique to the prairie are known and can be explained in terms of models that take into account the way energy is exchanged between earth, oceans, and atmospheric systems. Unfortunately, what is not known is the precise timing of natural climatic swings, such as drought cycles.

It is known that human induced activities, such as burning fossil fuels and destroying forests, will have an effect on the climate of the earth by doubling the greenhouse gas, carbon dioxide, some time in the next century. It is more difficult to predict the specific timing and intensity of the resulting climatic change that will result for a given region. Will some future drought cycle, or, worse yet, some long term unfavorable climatic change, overwhelm the technology that supports agriculture on the grasslands of the prairie? Or will improved technology and favorable climatic changes further transform the prairie to agriculture? Climatic change and the actions of humans will undoubtedly determine whether the bison and grasslands

Just because
no one sees

the pods
of the milkweed

slowly open
on the prairie

on a cold October night
doesn't mean

we should ignore
their white silken treasure

readying itself
for flight

on a sunny afternoon
when the cottonwoods

are turning gold.
Who can say

if the prairie dogs
sun-bathing

on the hillside
have come to see

the air show,
but when a trio

of pods burst open
and the white silken parachutes

float over the prairie
meadow

even the sharp green tips
of the yucca

crane
in anticipation.

will once again become the dominant feature of the plains, whether agriculture will flourish, or whether the Great American Desert will become, in fact, a desert.

Selected References

Doesken, N. J. and A. Judson. 1998. The SNOW booklet: "A guide to the science, climatology, and measurement of snow in the United States." 2d ed. Ft. Collins: Colorado State University.

Holmgren, P. S., M. W. Schuyler, and R. Davis. 1993. The Big Bend country of the Platte River: A history of human settlement. In The Platte River: An atlas of the Big Bend region. Eds. A. Jenkins and S. George. 58-74. Kearney: University of Nebraska at Kearney.

Lydolph, P. E. 1985. The climate of the earth. Totowa: Rowman & Allanheld.

Palecki, Michael. 1996. Nebraska's climate past and future. Nebraskaland. 74 (1): 106-101.

Schneider, Stephen H. 1996. Encyclopedia of climate and weather. 2 Vols. New York: Oxford University Press.

THE PRAIRIE BELOW GROUND

Harold G. Nagel and Marvin C. Williams, Professors of Biology

Early visitors to the grasslands of Nebraska probably had very little thought about the plant parts found below ground or their importance to the prairie. John Weaver, one of the pioneer prairie ecologists at the University of Nebraska, whose specialty was prairie plant roots, must have felt that no one but him thought roots were important. However, time has demonstrated that his assumption was incorrect. In fact, it seems today as if everyone is interested in prairie roots and soil ecology—but there are still only a few persons willing to work with soil ecology. Range management personnel have recently joined the soil ecology bandwagon, and they have concluded that soil condition is even more important to the health and productivity of rangeland than is the plant community growing on the rangeland.

Development of the Soil Community

In a forest, most of the biological activity is above ground and is relatively easy to observe. Biologists have known for years that the prairie is different from the other major biomes, such as the deciduous forest made up of trees which lose their leaves each year. The prairie has a disproportionate amount of activity below ground, making it more difficult to study. Compared with the root penetration of a tall tree, for example, prairies have a relatively deep penetration

and expansive growth of roots (Fig. 1). In fact, prairie plants are usually credited with having at least half to as much as two-thirds of their total plant growth present as roots. This differs from crop plants, which have only about forty to fifty percent of total biomass as root weight compared to above-ground biomass. This indicates that one would find about two to three tons per acre of roots in mixed-prairie. Because prairie plant roots have a lifespan of about three years, the mixed-prairie needs to produce almost a ton of new roots per year, or as much as the biomass of grasses aboveground.

Since most prairie plants are perennial, the carbohydrates manufactured by the leaves during the growing season are stored in the roots over the winter. The plant will then have adequate energy and nutrients to start growth the next spring. This is an important fact about prairies. If a prairie is overgrazed and not enough sugars are stored in the roots of a plant, that plant is placed at a competitive disadvantage and may die out over a few years. If this happens frequently, most or all of the desirable or native prairie plants may be eliminated, the case on many central Nebraska pastures and rangeland today.

Another reason that prairie plants may have evolved deep root systems was to stratify or spread out the root system, which greatly reduces competition between individual plants. Some prairie forbs have root systems that penetrate the soil to a depth of ten to twenty feet. Here, these forbs (broad-leaved, non- grassy plants, usually with showy flowers) take up water and nutrients and do not compete with the grasses which generally do not penetrate to this depth.

Plants have evolved other diverse life-style mechanisms which reduces competition. For example, prairie plants with a C3 photo-synthetic pathway, having a maximum photosynthesis between 20°C and 30°C (68-86°F), are mainly active in spring and fall or are found in shaded locations. On the other hand, the C4 plants, having maximum photosynthetic activity at about 30 to 40°C (87-104°F), are more active during summer in full sunlight.

If one takes a section of prairie sod to about thirty centimeters (about twelve inches) in depth, and looks at the roots under a large magnifying glass or a dissecting microscope, one will likely find that there is a root hair in every visible portion of the soil. In fact, textbooks state that there is a root hair every 0.02 millimeters.

The great biomass of roots and amazing abundance of root hairs is thought to be an adaptation to sparse soil moisture in the mixed-prairie. Although plants require extra energy to produce these extensive root hairs and extra root system depth, it apparently pays off in the evolutionary game called survival. A study of the relationship between soil strata and primary productivity on the Willa Cather Memorial Prairie located near Red Cloud, Nebraska, has been recently completed. It was found that, in spite of the extremely numerous roots in the topsoil, the "A" horizon, no statistical correlation existed with that layer and productivity. However, the "B" horizon, or subsoil, was highly correlated with primary productivity. In fact, about sixty percent of the variation in productivity was accounted for by the amount of water in the "B" horizon.

When the North American continent was invaded by Europeans, the land that they settled closely resembled that of Europe. Because of their plentiful rainfall, both the eastern United States and Europe were vegetated by deciduous forests. During the thousands of years of development of the most recent forest soil, a large proportion of the nutrients were leached out by the abundant rainfall. Meanwhile, in the prairie soils, the vast root system and more sparse precipitation allowed most, if not all, of the nutrients originally present to remain in the soil.

As pioneer farmers cleared the trees, they expected that ten to fifteen years later they would have to move on to new land, as the old wouldn't yield much anymore due to low soil fertility. Fertilizer practices weren't

FIG. 1.

RELATIONSHIP OF ROOTS IN MIXED-PRAIRIE
DEPTH IN FEET

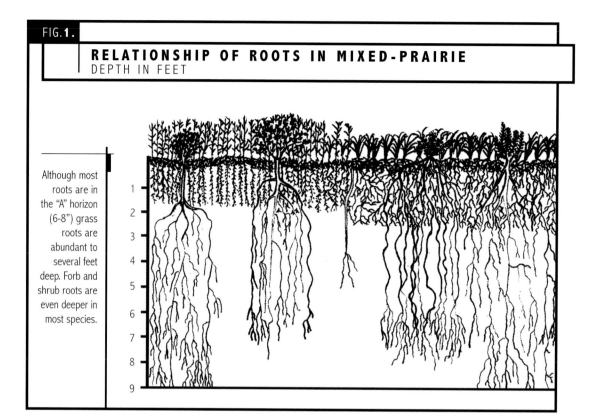

Although most roots are in the "A" horizon (6-8") grass roots are abundant to several feet deep. Forb and shrub roots are even deeper in most species.

prevalent at this point in history. When the settlers moved into the "Great Desert" of the central prairies, they didn't know what to expect, as there were no comparable prairies in Europe. A prairie soil surely couldn't yield much, they assumed, since it wouldn't even grow trees! They did find the sod very tough to break, even with special sod-breaking plows.

The pioneer farmers tilled the prairie soil for ten years, and it still yielded well if it rained. They farmed it twenty-five years, fifty years, and now, over one hundred years later, the land is still producing. Even with irrigation, most prairie soils require only the addition of nitrogen to produce great yields. We owe our prairie heritage a great deal for the fertile soil it left for us.

However, the prairie plants can't take full credit for the rich soil. The land also inherited very rich, nutrient-diverse parent material out of the Rocky Mountains. The parent minerals, including the feldspars (loaded with calcium, potassium, magnesium, etc.) the apatites (phosphorus), and the micas (potassium, etc.), were abundant in Nebraska's parent soil material. In addition, the prairie soil was still young and had not yet had time for serious weathering and

erosion losses. The moderate climate has also helped to preserve the nutrients.

PRAIRIE SOILS: IMPORTANT ORGANISMS
Vascular Plants

When one observes the prairie, it is probably not surprising that vascular plants, especially grasses, provide most of the weight of living organisms. An upland hay meadow will produce one to two tons of dry hay in a year of above average rainfall and a ton per acre in a year of average rainfall. Since this live organic matter (biomass) is at least matched and often exceeded by roots in the soil, vascular plants contribute at least two tons per acre in a given year. Since prairie vascular plants may produce as much as four tons per acre under some conditions, they are, undoubtedly, the most important organisms in the prairie.

"The Fungus Among Us"

When it comes to weight of organisms in the soil, the fungi would most commonly be in second place. Most people know fungi only when a mushroom's fruiting body emerges from the soil during its reproductive phase. In reality, members of this group are in the soil constantly in

FIG.2.

RELATIVE SIZES OF SOIL ORGANISMS
SIZE COMPARISONS

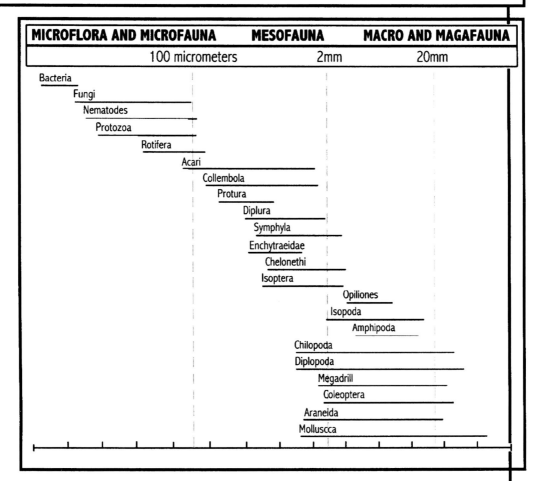

MICROFLORA AND MICROFAUNA	MESOFAUNA	MACRO AND MAGAFAUNA
100 micrometers	2mm	20mm

Bacteria
Fungi
Nematodes
Protozoa
Rotifera
Acari
Collembola
Protura
Diplura
Symphyla
Enchytraeidae
Chelonethi
Isoptera
Opiliones
Isopoda
Amphipoda
Chilopoda
Diplopoda
Megadrill
Coleoptera
Araneida
Molluscca

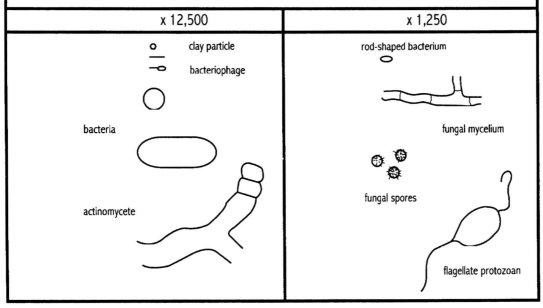

x 12,500	x 1,250
clay particle	rod-shaped bacterium
bacteriophage	
bacteria	fungal mycelium
actinomycete	fungal spores
	flagellate protozoan

FIG.**3.**

DOMINANT ANIMALS IN MIXED-PRAIRIE SOILS
ORIBATID MITE AND SPRINGTAILS

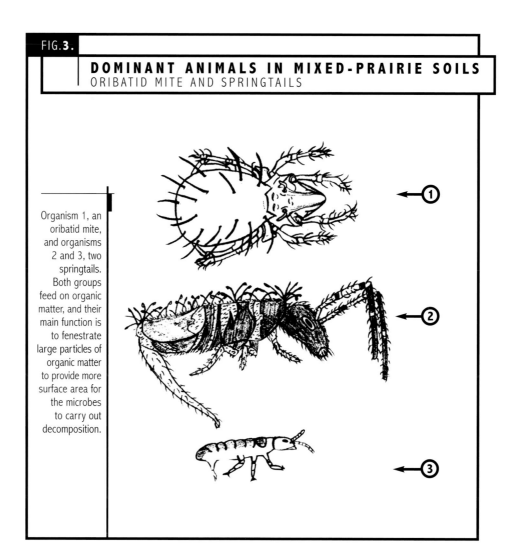

Organism 1, an oribatid mite, and organisms 2 and 3, two springtails. Both groups feed on organic matter, and their main function is to fenestrate large particles of organic matter to provide more surface area for the microbes to carry out decomposition.

the vegetative or non-reproductive form, referred to as the hyphal stage. The most important functions of fungi in the soil are to decompose organic matter, that is, the dead organisms, and to function as mycorrhizae, a fungus-root interaction in which fungi live with the roots of vascular plants and may assist the plant roots in the uptake of nutrients, primarily phosphorus, and water.

To the casual observer, one of the more noticeable aspects of fungi in soils are the species that produce "fairy rings." A fairy ring starts in one spot, with a species of fairy ring fungus decomposing the organic matter in a spot. This spot then turns brown or yellow due to the toxic effects of the decomposition by-products or, perhaps, because the fungal activity water-proofs the soil surface. The fungus grows outward into fresh sod, and the added fertilizer left behind after decomposition causes the grass to grow dark green just outside the ring. The fungus advances, and the ring expands in diameter each year. Rings have been observed up to one hundred foot or larger in diameter in Nebraska, and other rings have been dated to be eight hundred years old.

Actinomycetes and Bacteria

Actinomycetes are bacteria-like organisms that live in the soil and produce its characteristic smell. Most species of actinomycetes are decomposers, which break down dead organisms; however, they are not as abundant as either bacteria or fungi. Some of them are also active in manufacturing antibiotics, and some fix nitrogen into forms that can be used by plants.

Bacteria are highly diverse organisms, especially when viewed from a functional standpoint. They are involved in nitrogen fixation, nitrogen conversion (e.g., nitrite to nitrate), and with several other chemical cycles in the soil. Mostly, however, they are important as decomposers of organic matter. Many species of bacteria, invertebrate animals, and fungi are necessary to break down the complex biochemicals which nature and man add to soils. The breakdown of some biochemicals requires just the proper sequence of bacterial species. It is no wonder that it sometimes requires twenty years or more to decompose half of any particular sample placed in the soil, known as the half life, and humus may have a half life of as much as several hundred years.

Microbes living in the soil are usually underworked when considered on a capacity basis. Most of the decomposers are just barely "idling" and are in a dormant stage, or they may be inactive in a spore stage. This makes it difficult to estimate the total number of microbes in the soil. In one study in Canada, the normal microbial flora was able to decompose as much as one hundred tons per acre of feedlot waste in one season. Normally, in a mixed-prairie, they would receive only about one and one half to two tons to decompose during a year. Bacteria are especially capable of prodigious feats. In compost operations, they take huge amounts of feedlot manure or human sewage and stabilize it by partially decomposing it in just three to four weeks. They do this at a high enough temperature that it kills almost all the pathogenic microbes and weed seeds, so the compost can be safely used as fertilizer on fields and gardens.

Algae

Most people probably associate algae with aquatic systems and not with prairie. There are generally not many algae in prairie soils, but even a few pounds per acre can potentially have a noticeable effect on plant life. This is especially true if the alga is a blue green alga, now called cyanobacteria. Some blue green algae, like some bacteria, are able to fix nitrogen in the soil by taking gaseous nitrogen out of the atmosphere and converting it to a form usable by prairie plants. This process is especially important during succession of prairies, the process which occurs after abandonment of cultivation.

ANIMALS
Microfauna

The smallest animals in the soil, including animals such as protozoa, nematodes, tardigrades, and rotifers (see Fig. 2 for size comparison) are referred to as microfauna. A microscope is required to study these organisms due to their small size. Very little work has been completed to help in understanding their function in mixed grass prairie. Nematodes are especially diverse in their habits, being found in various roles such as plant parasites, predators of microbes, predators on small animals, parasites of animals, plant feeders, and decomposers. The other small animals are mostly predators on microbes.

Mesofauna

Mesofauna includes the middle-sized animals in the soil. They generally require a dissecting microscope at 30X power or higher to see them very clearly. The most abundant animals in mixed-prairie soils, including the mites and springtails (Fig. 3.), are found in this group. Our most extensive work on soil invertebrate populations in central Nebraska have been completed in the river valleys, where earthworms are the most important organism. However, these valley areas are tallgrass prairie, while the surrounding prairies are mixed-grass prairie.

Extensive sampling has been conducted on Juhl's Pearl Harbor Survivors Prairie near Riverdale and at the Willa Cather Prairie near Red Cloud. Study on these two mixed grass prairies over a several year period has given researchers a good understanding of the populations located at these two areas. It is evident that cultivation reduces the number of soil invertebrates considerably, with some groups declining more rapidly than others. Small insects, known as springtails (Fig. 3), appear to be especially sensitive to cultivation, and their numbers become reduced soon after prairie is converted to cultivated crops. On Cather Prairie, mites prevailed over springtails, which were almost rare; at Juhl Prairie, they were about co-equal. One unusual mesofaunal finding on Cather Prairie was the abundance of several rare to uncommon groups, such as Japygidae, Campodeids, and Proturans.

The western harvester ant is in a genus of desert ants. Four or five of these harvester ant species have migrated out onto the prairie-covered plains, occupying only the short and mixed-grass plains, but not living in the tallgrass prairie. This ant builds a large mound, which may weigh as much a ton, dry weight. This ton of soil is brought in from excavation below and during foraging expeditions at the surface of adjacent land. As many as thirty thousand worker ants keep this mound intact against the forces of nature, including wind, precipitation, gravity, and all sorts of animals.

The mound (refer to page 66) is critical to the colony's survival, for it stores the harvested seeds throughout the winter and into the summer. . . Spring season is the hardest on the ant colony. This species harvests virtually one hundred percent of the seeds in the fifty to sixty foot radius within which they forage. Therefore, in spring, except for the stored seeds which they then eat until a new crop of seeds is produced by plants outside the nest, the cupboard really is bare.

The queen constantly lays eggs from early March to September or October, with the first brood becoming reproductive to start new colonies. The rest of the broods produce worker ants, which are essential to replace the dying worker ants. The workers rarely live more than one year in nature.

If the colony cannot replace all the dying workers, the colony will soon die out. This brings us to the second critical reason for the mound, as an incubation chamber for the young ants, known collectively as the brood, which includes eggs, larvae, and pupae. If the brood is kept at optimum temperature and humidity throughout the day, approximately 32°C and one hundred percent, the development time may be halved from the development time at ambient air temperatures. The worker ants achieve this by placing the brood in galleries or chambers just beneath the surface of the mound in early morning, then moving them downward as it gets too hot or dry. By moving them throughout the day, the "nursemaid" workers can greatly speed development into productive, adult worker ants.

To facilitate the maturation process, the ant has evolved very interesting behaviors and capabilities. First, they maintain the cleared area. This area is primarily used to allow sunlight to strike the mound in early morning and late at night, thus greatly increasing the day length when compared to a mound built among the prairie grasses. Next, they build the mound itself. The ant has a "master plan" built in to its brain as to how the mound should look. It always has the long slope to the southeast to provide more area for sunlight to warm the underlying chambers. The slope of the various sides is fairly constant, in spite of varying topographic situations where the mound is built and different materials available from which to build it. Thus, the ant must be able to determine slope and vertical orientation. Somehow, the ant manages to waterproof the surface of the mound, while it is placing the stones, sticks, and soil aggregates on the mound, probably with a secretion from the salivary glands.

The mound, thus, has coarse materials on the surface (gravel) which dissipates the kinetic energy of rain or wind before it reaches the mound proper. Rainfall then runs harmlessly down the slope of the mound without entering it and causing the seeds to mold and rot. This mound covering is vital to the colony. If the mound surface is broken or scraped by man or cow, the workers who normally are bringing in food items will almost all quit foraging for food and one hundred percent of them will be found carrying gravel or sticks until the mound has been repaired, sometimes for as long as several days.

A mound built in the grasses receives almost no direct solar radiation. A colony with no mound but which clears out vegetation around the colony would receive three heat units, while the mound surrounded by the clearing would receive about five heat units. The worker ants respond almost immediately to the increased warmth. This can be demonstrated in the laboratory by placing worker ants and brood around a heat source regulated by a rheostat. As the amount of heat emitted increases, the workers will move the brood further from the heat source; as the temperature decreases, they will move a perfect circle of brood closer to the heat, at the ideal temperature.

The vertical mixing of soil by the western harvester ant is phenomenal. Based upon density in western Kansas, and a average life expectancy of the colony of fourteen years, every square inch of the short and mixed grass prairie would have been occupied at least once during the last fifteen thousand years. This species alone, then, would have "plowed" the entire prairie soil at least once during its development.

After the freezing rain,
the grass so brittle
our boots broke it into shards,

we set out in search of ourselves,
walking on angles of ache,
little bevels of cold.

Japygidae are especially fascinating due to their large posterior pincers, and they eat springtails and mites.

The most important function of mesofauna in the prairie is in causing fenestration of organic matter. This means that they eat holes in leaves, which has the effect of greatly increasing the surface area for the microbes to assist in the decomposition of leaves. Mesofauna are, therefore, very important in the proper functioning of soils as they regulate, to a large extent, the rate of decomposition. Although some of the mesofauna are predators or plant feeders, most of them are involved in some way with decomposition of organic matter. Exclusion studies have shown that if all mesofauna are removed from a soil, the decomposition rate will decline by forty to fifty percent. This may happen annually if chemicals which kill these animals are used in the farming practice.

Macrofauna

Macrofauna includes the more familiar invertebrate animals, such as earthworms, centipedes, millipedes, and most insects. Although not as abundant as the two former groups, the mesofauna and microfauna, the macrofauna usually contribute more weight per unit area. They also function differently, in that they are large enough to eat the organic matter whole, instead of just boring through it. Earthworms are not common in uplands in Nebraska unless the area is irrigated, as the mixed-prairie climate is generally too dry to support much of a population. Little known to most people, exotic earthworms, imported from Europe, have almost excluded the native earthworms. Almost no one recognizes a native species since they are quite small. The large angle-worms, pot worms, fishing worms, and nightcrawlers are all exotic. Only on good quality prairies are there native worms

remaining. On cultivated land, the earthworms are almost all European species. Regardless of their origin, the earthworms do help greatly in forming soil structure.

Soil Structure

Soil structure has to do with how the primary particles of sand, silt, and clay are stuck together. Individual particles of clay, the smallest, cannot be seen even with a common light microscope. Silt particles are also hard to see on a microscope until the larger size limits are viewed. Only sand can be seen with the naked eye, and there only the larger particles.

Most of our mixed-grass soils in Nebraska are composed of wind-transported parent material known as loess. When this loess blew into central Nebraska and settled, it was probably hard packed with very little pore space to hold air. This is a condition known as massive structure. Roots could not penetrate this type of soil, because there was no oxygen for the roots to carry on respiration. A few earthworms in this soil worked wonders, however. The earthworm ate its way through the soil, dropping the leftovers (casts) at the surface of the burrow. When the burrow remained open to the top, water and air moved rapidly into the burrow, thus aiding soil aeration and, therefore, plant growth. Many of these casts remained for long periods, forming at least the early structure in these primitive soils.

Custer County,
Nebraska,

the wind
an old hand
in the windmill's fans,
an ancient motion,

and down deep
a sleeve as dark
as prehistory
is working its way
into a well of memory,

water's anthology
of an inland sea;

and all is coming up
and back,

water's silver sermon
and its age-old text.

And in the windmill's water
there is a prologue
to a song—

Take, drink, *it says,*
and you will know
what the red root knows:

Water is the antecedent
of all blood.

Organic Matter Dynamics in Mixed-Prairie Soils

A number of people are concerned with what is usually referred to as global warming. Many attribute the primary cause of this potential problem to the burning of fossil fuels and the release of carbon dioxide into the atmosphere that has effectively been trapped in coal or oil for thousands of years. Few realize that breaking, or cultivating, prairie soils can contribute greatly to the same process.

How does this work? The prairie accumulated organic matter, referred to as humus, over the ten thousand to fifteen thousand years that recent Nebraska soils have been forming. This time period followed the last glacial activity, which altered the climate so much that "normal" soil development activities either stopped or speeded up greatly. This accumulated humus is much the same chemically as coal or other fossil fuel deposits that contain hydrogen, carbon, and oxygen. The humus accumulated for several reasons. First, the winters were long and cold, causing the growing season to be too short for decomposition of all the plant production from the previous year. Second, not enough oxygen was able to penetrate the soil at critical times for rapid decomposition. Third, inadequate water was present when other conditions were right for decomposition. Last, microbial populations may have been inadequate to decompose the organic matter present.

When soil was cultivated, it suddenly had massive air pockets, which stimulated the decomposition process due to increased metabolic activity of soil organisms. The black surface also warmed up more rapidly in spring and stayed warmer during fall, thus reducing the impact of items one and two above. This was apparently enough to greatly reduce the organic matter content of the soil. After about thirty to fifty years of cultivation, the amount of organic matter plateaued out at about one third to one fifth of the original amount in the prairie soil. This loss of two to five percent organic matter by weight from the soil was in the form of carbon dioxide, which is thought to be a main culprit in the global warming problem.

The addition of organic matter during the development process modifies the soil dramatically. The loess soil had little ability for holding chemicals from being leached out by rainfall percolating through it. The soil had little holding power on the nutrients that were released by weathering the minerals or mineralizing the organic matter in soils. Most soil nutrients have a positive charge and can be carried out of the soil by water, unless there are some negatively charged sites to which they can attach. Almost all of the negative charge in a soil comes from the clays and organic matter. The cation exchange capacity, CEC, as this charge is known, varies with clay mineral type. Smectites, such as montmorillonite, which is common in Nebraska soils, have a high CEC while kaolinites have little cation exchange capacity. With twenty percent clay in the original loess, the original parent material may have had a CEC of ten centimoles/kilogram (cmol/kg), not a very productive soil. With the addition of five percent organic matter, however, this had the effect of adding fifteen cmol/kg of CEC, for a respectable total of twenty-five cmol/kg. Thus, the soil, as modified by the development process, became more productive.

The organic matter serves many other positive functions, such as increasing aggregate stability and releasing nitrogen, phosphorus, and sulfur when decomposed. It also holds the positively charged chemical ions in the soil and keeps them from being leached into the groundwater as rainwater percolates through the soil.

Functions of Belowground Organisms

A summary of the functions of the soil community would include:
1. uptaking nutrients and water
2. converting one chemical form to another
3. buffering the pH(acidity-alkalinity)
4. releasing of nutrients by decomposing the soil organic matter
5. maintaining the porosity of the soil which allows water and air to enter and exit freely
6. fixing nutrients from one location (atmosphere) to another (soil)
7. reducing the leaching of water and nutrients out of the soil (and into the ground water)
8. transforming materials, primary minerals like feldspar, into another (e.g. clay)
9. maintaining energy and nutrient flow throughout the system
10. keeping the soil mixed vertically

The vertical mixing of soil is one that is carried out primarily by large invertebrates and by vertebrate animals such as thirteen lined ground squirrels, badgers, prairie dogs, skunks, and coyotes. Earthworms and ants are two conspicuous invertebrates involved in mixing the prairie soil.

Selected**References**

Carson, R. 1962. Realms of the soil. Chapter 5 in Silent Spring. Boston: Houghton Mifflin Company.

Costello, D.F. 1969. The prairie world. New York: Crowell Co.

Farrar, J. 1997. Loess hills. Nebraskaland 75 (7): 14-25. (Sept./Oct. 1997)

PLANTS OF THE PRAIRIE

THE TRANSITION BETWEEN EAST AND WEST

Steven J. Rothenberger, Professor of Biology

Nebraska's central prairies are a biological ideal. They lie at the convergence of tall grasses from the east, sandhills to the north, southern or Kansas mixed-prairie to the south, and sandsage prairie to the southwest. Eastern species of plants and animals overlap and mix onto the range of their western counterparts. This region represents a unique biological and cultural transition zone. To some, it is a mosaic or patchwork of distinct communities, but to others a melting pot where plants, animals, and people integrate into a way of life. The Nebraska prairie is often portrayed as a large puzzle with clear cut boundaries, when, in reality, species actually intermix or blend together along these boundaries (Fig. 1). The region is also divided on an east-west basis by numerous streams and rivers, trails, railroads, and even modern highways. The Great Platte River Road was and still is a distinct feature that ties all of these parts together. This was the pathway throught the prairie, the convenient corridor for those who dared to cross it. Here where the Great Plains begin, thousands of people once moved westward with their own hopes, dreams, and desires for new beginnings.

As the westward migration of the nineteenth century progressed along the Oregon and Overland (Mormon) Trails, travelers passed through a number of biological as well as geographical zones. Early journals reflected their observations in route, such as vegetation differences, unusual kinds of animals, geographical landmarks (i.e. Chimney Rock), forts, trading posts, and way stations. Subtle biological changes that occurred gradually along the way were not as obvious. Certain species of birds and mammals with eastern affinities disappeared while "western" plants and animals were encountered more and more frequently. The effects of fire, limited precipitation, and grazing produced an environment that was hostile to most woody plants, so it became dominated by perennial grasses and forbs. This lack of woody vegetation on the prairie must have been very disturbing to the immigrant from the eastern United States or from Europe. The endless horizon, unbroken by tree or mountain, was both beautiful and frightening. However unsettling it may have seemed to the pioneers, this vegetation defines the prairie.

Much of central Nebraska's hill country is mantled by loess which is composed of fine wind-blown mineral and silt particles deposited since the first glacial advances of the Pleistocene Epoch (two million years before the present). The rich prairie topsoils rest above these loess deposits. In the river valleys, alluvial silts and sands provide another type of substrate for prairie development. These lowland meadows are often subirrigated and are populated by species

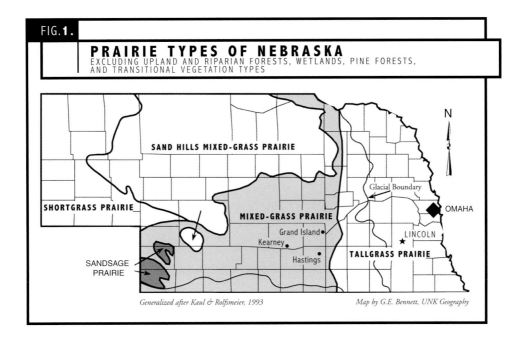

of tall grasses and sedges that are absent from the flora on drier upland sites. Habitat most definitely defines species composition of the prairie.

The prairie in central Nebraska contains species with affinities to five prairie types. These are tallgrass or "true" prairie, mixed-grass prairie, shortgrass prairie, the Nebraska Sand Hills, and sandsage prairie. It is significant that they vary on a topographic basis as well as a geographical basis. For example, the species composition of upland tallgrass prairie sites is much different than that of the lowlands (Table 1). In the valleys, additional runoff and groundwater moisture percolating upward through the soil favors a number of grasses and forbs that would not survive on the drier upland sites. Each of these prairie types consists of a number of communities or plant associations.

Tallgrass Prairie

The tallgrass or "true" prairie once occupied the deeper soils of Illinois, Iowa, and Missouri and formed a large swath from the eastern Dakotas and western Minnesota through eastern Nebraska, Kansas, and Oklahoma to northeast Texas (Fig. 1). This original, unbroken grassland was geographically immense, covering 400,000 square miles. Today, it has largely been replaced by cultivation and roughly

corresponds with what we call the "Corn Belt." Tallgrass prairie generally extends westward into central Nebraska only to about the Grand Island/Hastings area where it gradually gives way to mixed-grasses. However, lowland tallgrass prairies and meadows follow the Platte and Loup rivers farther west into the central Nebraska study area.

The Loup River was once called *Its Kari Kitsu* or "plenty potatoes river" by the Skidi Pawnee who occupied these lands for nearly three hundred years. Botanically, it is a river valley of plenty as it winds through the Loess Hills and Sand Hills of central Nebraska. The Loup's lowlands and wet meadows are storehouses of species diversity, containing more than six hundred documented plant species. Along with the more common tallgrass plants, these low-land meadows are rich in sedges, rushes, mixed-grasses, and forbs belonging to the aster and legume families. Several plants that are especially rare here are small white lady's slipper orchid, northern green orchid, swamp lousewort, wild rice, and white waterlily.

The most prominent tall grasses are big bluestem, switchgrass, and Indian grass. Porcupine grass, green needle grass, tall drop seed, and side-oats grama are also quite common. Forb species vary as to region, but common examples include

TABLE 1

DOMINANT SPECIES OF GRASSES, FORBS, AND SHRUBS BY PRAIRIE TYPE

TALLGRASS PRAIRIE

GRASSES

LOWLAND	UPLAND
big bluestem (*Andropogon gerardii*)	little bluestem (*Andropogon scoparius*)
Indian grass (*Sorghastrum nutans*)	side oats grama (*Bouteloua curtipendula*)
Kentucky bluegrass (*Poa pratensis*)	rough dropseed (*Sporobolus asper*)
prairie cordgrass (*Spartina pectinata*)	prairie dropseed (*Sporobolus heterolepis*)
switchgrass (*Panicum virgatum*)	Junegrass (*Koeleria macrantha*)

FORBS/SHRUBS

asters (*Aster spp.*)	leadplant (*Amorpha canescens*)
sunflower (*Helianthes maximilliani*)	stiff sunflower (*Helianthus rigida*)
Missouri goldenrod (*Solidago missouriensis*)	many-flowered aster (*Aster ericoides*)
snowberry (*Symphoricarpos occidentalis*)	prairie catsfoot (*Antennaria neglecta*)
roundhead lespedeza (*Lespedeza capitata*)	scurf pea (*Psoralea spp.*)

MIXED-GRASS PRAIRIE / SHORTGRASS PRAIRIE

GRASSES

MIXED-GRASS	SHORTGRASS
little bluestem (*Andropogon scoparius*)	western wheatgrass (*Pascopyrum smithii*)
big bluestem (*Andropogon gerardii*)	blue grama (*Bouteloua gracilis*)
Kentucky bluegrass (*Poa pratensis*)	buffalo grass (*Buchloe dactyloides*)
side-oats grama (*Bouteloua curtipendula*)	Junegrass (*Koeleria macrantha*)
blue grama (*Bouteloua gracilis*)	needle-and-thread (*Stipa comata*)

FORBS/SHRUBS

prairie catsfoot (*Antennaria neglecta*)	milk vetches (*Astragalus spp.*)
milk vetches (*Astragalus spp.*)	scurf pea (*Psoralea tenuiflora*)
hoary vervain (*Verbena stricta*)	Russian thistle (*Salsola kali*)
prairie clovers (*Dalea spp.*)	annual sunflower (*Helianthus annuus*)
rigid goldenrod (*Solidago rigida*)	blazing stars (*Liatris spp.*)

SAND HILLS PRAIRIE / SANDSAGE PRAIRIE

GRASSES

SAND HILLS	SANDSAGE
prairie sandreed (*Calamovilfa longifolia*)	prairie sandreed (*Calamovilfa longifolia*)
blue grama (*Bouteloua gracilis*)	sand bluestem (*Andropogon hallii*)
needle-and-thread (*Stipa comata*)	sand dropseed (*Sporobolus cryptandrus*)
sand bluestem (*Andropogon hallii*)	little bluestem (*Andropogon scoparius*)
little bluestem (*Andropogon scoparius*)	blue grama (*Bouteloua gracilis*)
western wheatgrass (*Pascopyrum smithii*)	sand lovegrass (*Eragrostis trichodes*)
sand dropseed (*Sporobolus cryptandrus*)	needle-and-thread (*Stipa comata*)

FORBS/SHRUBS

annual eriogonum (*Eriogonum annuum*)	sand sagebrush (*Artemisia filifolia*)
scurf pea (*Psoralea spp.*)	broom snakeweed (*Gutierrezia sarothrae*)
sand sagebrush (*Artemisia filifolia*)	leadplant (*Amorpha canescens*)
leadplant (*Amorpha canescens*)	sand milkweed (*Asclepias arenaria*)
small soapweed (*Yucca glauca*)	silky prairie clover (*Dalea villosa*)

FIG.**2.** Canada goldenrod is common to lowland sites.

photo by Steven Rothenberger

FIG.**3.** Unusual flower clusters are a feature of rattlesnake master.

photo by Steven Rothenberger

FIG.**4.** Dotted gayfeather is tall and showy during late summer.

photo by Steven Rothenberger

numerous legumes (members of the pea family), sunflowers, goldenrods, and asters (Figs. 2, 3, and 4).

Riparian or riverbottom forest is another plant community type that is associated with rivers and streams that dissect both mixed-grass and tallgrass prairies. Historically, the invasion of grassland by woody plants was restricted by fire, drought, and sometimes grazing. The floodplains associated with the Loup, Platte, and Republican rivers provide some measure of protection for trees, shrubs, and vines. However, trees that were susceptable to fire on the uplands also had to contend with spring flooding on the lowlands. The increase of woody vegetation in these river valleys may be directly attributed to settlement, where flood control and the erradication of fire have been achieved. Here is a transition zone of another kind, the ecotone between prairie and forest.

Occasional savannas once were scattered across the eastern Nebraska prairie. These clusters of trees with understories of grass usually were found on lowlands where moisture conditions were more favorable

and fire was infrequent. Unfortunately, little of this original vegetation remains today. The rich topsoils that once nurtured prairie grasses now grow corn and soybeans.

Mixed-grass Prairie

Mixed-grass prairie is located farther westward where precipitation becomes even more limiting. Tallgrass species are interspersed with more drought-tolerant mid-grass species, depending on the soil type and location. Prominent mid-grass species are western wheatgrass, little bluestem, blue grama, and several species of needle-grass. Some biologists tend to divide the mixed-grass prairie into "southern" and "northern" sections or types. The southern or Kansas mixed-grass prairie is found on calcareous (limestone-based) soils from the Republican River uplands in Nebraska extending south into Kansas (Fig. 1). Some species differences help to separate this region from the typical loess hills mixed-prairie to the north. For example, plants such as Fendler's aster, Fremont's primrose, cardinal-flower, narrowleaf bluet, stenosiphon,

FIG.**5.** Mixed-grass prairie is typical of southern Webster County.   by Steven Rothenberger

and stickleaf mentzelia are at the northern edge of their range in the Republican River uplands. A number of sedges, orchids, and members of the lily family are at the southern edge of their range in the Loup River Valley of central Nebraska. Two of the more colorful prairie forbs are butterfly milkweed and black-eyed susan (Figs. 6 and 7).

The northern or Central Nebraska Mixed-grass prairie is bordered on the north by the Sand Hills and on the east by the transition zone between the tallgrass and mixed-grass prairies (Fig. 1). Much of this mixed-prairie is still intact and is utilized for range cattle production. Productivity of these rangelands is highest during years of above average precipitation and helps to support a significant cattle industry. Major crops on cultivated land are corn, alfalfa, wheat, and soybeans. Big bluestem, a dominant species in the tallgrass prairie, is also prominent here and is especially favored by livestock. Recent studies at 290 sites in the central Nebraska Loess Hills indicated that big bluestem is much more prominent than previously reported. It is more nutritious and palatable to livestock than any other graminoid. Grazing intensity by cattle is definitely a factor in the relative abundance of this species. The density of big bluestem has apparently increased during years of above average precipitation which have occurred since the great drought of the 1930s.

Shortgrass Prairie

Shortgrass prairie occupies the high plains just to the east of the Rocky Mountains and extends into the Nebraska Panhandle. John Weaver, the founding father of grassland ecology, suggested that shortgrass prairie was actually a disclimax, a disturbed region, as a result of grazing and did not merit being labeled as a distinct prairie type. However, a number of prairie ecologists disagree and note a number of species differences to make their point. Some prominent grasses in this region are blue grama, little bluestem, threadleaf sedge, hairy grama and buffalo grass. Sand sagebrush, yucca, western wheatgrass, and prickly-pear cactus are also common on hillsides with choke-cherry, fragrant sumac, western poison ivy, western red current, and woodbine growing in the valleys.

Sand Hills Prairie

The Nebraska Sand Hills is a distinct region of tall and mixed-grass species located primarily north of the Platte River in central and west-central Nebraska. This largest of all North American grasslands covers some 19,300 square miles or nearly twenty-five percent of Nebraska's total land area. The unique feature of this region is grass-covered dunes of sand, the result of millions of years of deposition by water and wind (alluvial and eolian activities). Although a number of alluvial sand formations have been deposited since Oligocene times (nearly 38 million years before present), the present dunes are the result of wind-blown sand formed into large ridges and hills which occurred as recently as eight thousand and five thousand years ago. The sand dunes are, in fact, stabilized by the growth of perennial grasses, such as little bluestem, Indian grass, blue and hairy grama, Indian ricegrass, sand bluestem, Junegrass, needle-and-thread, prairie sandreed, and switchgrass. Without these grasses, these dunes would be subject to Nebraska's prevailing winds and would move just like the dunes in major deserts of the world.

The Sand Hills are exceptionally rich in ground water, even though precipitation is low. The permeable soils and geological deposits minimize runoff and enhance the recharge of underground aquifers. In geological terms, a large accumulation of sands, sandstones, sandy silt, and gravels occur on a layer of impermeable bedrock. These saturated sediments are part of the immense High Plains Aquifer. When groundwater is close to the surface, numerous lakes, marshes, subirrigated meadows, and spring-fed streams occur. These waters feed the Niobrara, the Loup, and the Elkhorn Rivers. The Loup River system is of special importance because of its contribution to the variety of plants and animals found in central Nebraska.

Trees and shrubs are typically more abundant near permanent streams and lakes. Prominent trees in these areas include cottonwood, green ash, boxelder, hackberry, cedar, and American plum. Common native shrubs are Arkansas rose, western poison ivy, chokecherry, snowberry, and sand cherry. The Niobrara and Snake River areas are a source of ponderosa pine and red cedar. Even paper birch from the north intermingles with these species along the western and central reach of the Niobrara. The lower Niobrara valley hosts some typical eastern deciduous trees, such as bur oak, black walnut, and green ash. Most of the Sand Hills remains unforested, but during the past fifty to seventy five years, woody plants have invaded several prairie slopes and uplands, areas that were thought to be

inhospitable to these species. Most of these invasions have likely occurred on disturbed sites near farmsteads and tree rows or on land previously plowed and later abandoned. Another contributing factor is the control of widespread prairie fires resulting from settlement of the area. Nonetheless, botanist Charles Bessey proved that trees can grow in the Sand Hills when his initiative led to the planting and establishment of the Nebraska National Forest near Halsey in 1903.

Another common, woody Sand Hills plant is yucca, also known as soapweed or Spanish bayonet. A diverse group of forbs are distributed within this region, including purple and silky prairie clover, blazing stars, numerous penstemon species, Texas croton, prairie coneflower, scurf pea, sand milkweed, western wallflower, bush morning glory, and western ragweed. Where vegetation is displaced, areas of erosion called "blowouts" occasionally occur. Sand muhly, blowout grass, and prairie sandreed are especially important as they help to stabilize the drifting

FIG.**6.** Butterfly milkweed is uncommon, but prefers well-drained hillsides and calcareous slopes.
photo by Steven Rothenberger

FIG.**7.** Black-eyed susan is common to moist sites in meadows and lowlands.   by Steven Rothenberger

particles. The total flora is only around 750 species, which is quite low for an area so large. The proportion of weedy invaders to native species is also low, which is a reflection of some of the difficulties these plants have becoming established in a sandy environment.

The Sand Hills region may not be as botanically diverse as other grasslands, but differences in soils, topography, evapotranspiration, ground water availability, and water chemistry exist over the region. University of Nebraska-Lincoln Botanist Dr. Robert Kaul, concurring with early studies by R.J. Pool, recognizes seven plant community types in the Nebraska Sand Hills. Significant remnants of the Sand Hills can be found south of the Platte River in Lincoln, Phelps, Kearney, and Hall Counties. One may also find Sand Hills along the South Loup River in northeastern Buffalo County and south of the Middle Loup River in Hall, Howard, and Merrick counties.

Sandsage Prairie

The unique sandsage prairie is relatively common to parts of eastern Colorado and southwestern Kansas, but it is a rare grassland type for Nebraska. It is limited to Perkins, Chase, and Dundy Counties in the extreme southwestern edge of the study area (Fig. 1). Since 1950, a large amount of these grassland acres has been converted to irrigated cropland. Areas that were once open range-

land are dotted with center pivot operations. The declining water table has decimated natural wetlands. The upper reaches of most small streams and creeks in this region are now seasonally dry for much of the year.

Sand sagebrush is the major dominant along with an array of prairie grasses that thrive in sandy soils. These are sand dropseed, sand lovegrass, needle-and-thread, blowout grass, Indian ricegrass, and sand muhly. Some of the more conspicuous forbs are sand milkweed, mentzelia, plains sunflower, blazing star, prickly poppy, snake-cotton, prairie spiderwort, and silky prairie clover. As in the more northern Sand Hills, yucca, broom snakeweed, and leadplant also dot the landscape.

Unfortunately, management has included aerial spraying with herbicides, such as 2, 4-D, to control sandsage in favor of more nutritious grasses. The net result has not necessarily been better pasture. Spraying has also reduced or eliminated more desirable forbs, such as the nitrogen-fixing legumes scurf pea, prairie turnip, and vetch.

Prairie Crossroads

The prairie of central Nebraska definitely represents a cross-roads, an area where cultures, trails, highways, and landforms meet. Far from the monotony often represented in popular literature, the five prairie types that converge are as different as the Germans,

DROPSEED AND SAGE | by DON**WELCH**

Swedes, Danes, Czechs, and Hispanics who
have settled here. While these prairies differ
significantly in appearance and species composition, the transition from one to the next
is nearly invisible to the causual observer.
Biologically, many mysteries and discoveries
remain. Plant and animal distributions in
parts of this area are poorly understood at
best. To the biologist, the area represents
both a challenge and an opportunity. Perhaps
this atlas will help to fill some of these gaps
in our present-day perception of The Prairie.

Selected**References**

Bleed, A. and C. Flowerday, eds. 1989. An atlas of the sand
hills. Conservation and Survey Division, IANR. University of
Nebraska–Lincoln.

Farrar, J. 1993. Sandsage prairie: The cinderella sandhills.
Nebraskaland 71(7):30-41.

Farrar, J. 1997. Loess hills. Nebraskaland 75(7):14-25.

Great Plains Flora Association. 1991. Flora of the Great Plains,
2nd ed. Lawrence: University Press of Kansas.

Hulett, G.K.,C.D. Sloan, and G.W. Tomanek. 1968. The vegetation of remnant grasslands in the loessial region of northwestern
Kansas and southwestern Nebraska. Southwestern Naturalist
13:377-391.

Kaul, R.B. and S.B. Rolfsmeier. 1993. Native vegetation of
Nebraska. Map1:1,000,000, with text. Conservation and
Survey Division, University of Nebraska–Lincoln.

Locklear, J.H. 1997. Shaggy grass country. Nebraskaland 75(5):8-15.

Madson, J. 1982. Where the sky began : Land of the tallgrass
prairie. San Francisco: Sierra Club Books.

Nagel, H.A. and V. Plambeck, eds. 1998. The loess hills prairies of
central Nebraska. Platte Valley Review 26(2).

Reichman, O.J. 1987. Konza Prairie: a tallgrass natural history.
Lawrence: University Press of Kansas.

Rothenberger, S.J. 1994. Floristic analysis of the C. Bertrand and
Marian Othmer Schultz Prairie, a mixed-grass prairie in south-central Nebraska. Transactions of the Nebraska Academy of Sciences
21:21-30.

Steinauer, G. 1998. The Loups: Lifeblood of Central Nebraska.
Nebraskaland 76(5):24-33.

Weaver, J.E. and W.E. Bruner. 1954. Nature and place of transition from true prairie to mixed prairie. Ecology 35(2):117-126.

Weaver, J.E. and F.W. Albertson. 1956. Grasslands of the Great
Plains. Lincoln: Johnsen Publishing Company.

*It is, but isn't pastoral, two women
walking the prairie among the big bluestem
and dropseed grasses, among the bronze
and russets of fall, the sky a light blue,*

*a delicate ache, a subtle exclamation
of color, and the women walking together
remembering what? The rose gentians
of spring? The light combed by the grasses?*

*Their daughters now grown? Perhaps
the lissomeness of their daughters,
their laughter, and their small brown arms
which once waved through these fields?*

*Wild shooting stars of daughters, butterflies
among the milkweed, now far away
in the florescence of basements, shopping
for bargains, flawed seconds, markdowns.*

*In the fall light the women walking together
look down. All around them is autumn,
the dropseed burning with orange,
the white sage ringing them with crowns.*

LANDSCAPE PATTERNS OF THE PRAIRIE

Charles J. Bicak, Professor of Biology

Remarkable diversity characterizes the mixed-grass prairie of the loess hills in central Nebraska. This region extends south and east of the Sand Hills to the Kansas border. Its eastern border begins near Aurora in Hamilton County, extends west to the Colorado border, and south to the Kansas-Nebraska line. The diversity of the prairie is accentuated by both natural and anthropogenic relief. This article outlines landscape features that give the mixed-grass prairie its distinctive look.

The Landscape Concept

The landscape concept integrates scale and diversity in an attempt to understand the prevailing abiotic and biotic makeup of a region. The concept further provides some insight into the functioning of the system: the movement of animals, the transport of seeds of plants, the shifting of soil and nutrients in wind, and water erosion. Hence, an ecological view from the landscape perspective affords an opportunity to shift simply from description of the prairie to prediction regarding changes in spatial heterogeneity and temporal interactions.

Traditionally, ecological studies have operated with the assumption that ecosystems are homogenous. This assumption, however, led to some erroneous assessments of structure and function of ecosystems. Since prairie ecosystems are heterogenous,

it is reasonable to conclude that the fluxes of resources such as water and nutrients are variable as well.

Features of the Prairie Landscape

The mixed-grass prairie is intersected by both anthropogenic corridors, passageways constructed by humans, and natural corridors, which include rivers, streams, ridges, swales, and distinct vegetational borders, such as the ecotone or transition between woodland and grassland.

The geographic boundaries of the mixed-grass prairie in Nebraska are, in fact, defining corridors. The glacial boundary in the east, extending from the South Dakota border in the north to the Kansas border in the south, approximates the eastern corridor. The Sand Hills to the north and west are descriptively characterized by sand soils, and a line of soil demarcation, an edaphic corridor, is apparent. The mixed-grass prairie is approximately bounded by the Republican River in the south. Finally, the western-most point of this triangular region, near the Colorado border, is a consequence of the combined effect of decreasing precipitation, increasing elevation, and a shift toward coarser soils.

The Platte River traverses the heart of the mixed-grass prairie. Trees are a notable feature of the riparian corridor of the Platte. This corridor affords accomodation of a variety of birds and mammals that are less prominent or even absent in the prairie: including white-tailed deer and neo-tropical migratory birds, such as the orchard oriole, the American goldfinch, and the house wren. To the south, the rainwater basin is a dominant feature of the prairie region with some wetland patches exceeding several hundred acres in size. The defining feature to the north of the Platte River Valley is the matrix of upland prairies established by the Loup River system (South, Middle, and North) and the associated tributaries in the watershed. The river/tributary corridors are typically less wooded than the Platte River, yet they are probably equally important in regulating structure and function within the landscape.

Anthropogenic sources of variation in the mixed-grass prairie are many and, probably, rival natural sources in the regulation of plant and animal diversity and density. The most prominent and influential corridor is the east-west expanse of Interstate 80, a four lane highway approximately 100-120 yards wide. Paralleling the Platte River, it passes through some prime wetland areas. Interstate 80 functions as a barrier for the movement of certain animals and plants, especially vegetation with a limited range of distribution of seeds. If patches delineated by roads are large enough for sustainability of populations of organisms, the interstate, and to a lesser extent other roads, may

function somewhat like protective boundaries. The pattern of roads in the prairie varies widely with the township or one mile section lines in the eastern half of the prairie and the less frequent "ranch roads" that follow rivers and drainages in the west.

Windbreaks and fences are also influential corridors in terms of wildlife habitat and plant composition. Patches include row crops, largely corn, and to a lesser extent, soybeans, wheat, sorghum, and milo. Also, farmsteads themselves are a distinguishable and influencing element in the landscape.

There are some interesting examples of a combined natural and human influence on landscape variation. For example, north-facing slopes along drainages are typically cooler and wetter than south-facing slopes. The result may be a rather dramatic difference in plant and animal composition separated by only several yards. The natural effect of the topography may be either enhanced or dampened by human activity, such as cattle grazing, haying, burning, and other management practices.

Overall, the mixed-grass prairie landscape is unique in that it is a composite of row crop production and native prairie. To the east, the land is largely cultivated. To the west, the semiarid conditions only permit management of range for livestock production.

In spring there is one river
where nothing rises to the surface
until the evening hail storm
spreads over the ember field.
This is night and the lilac wild.
You will stand as the water moves
the top soil and blackened seed
and hear with the tasseled wind
a ghost town on a prairie road.
You will find a rising river
search for her over the Great Plains
with its fences and trees uprooted
in spring over the ember field.
This is night and the lilac wild.

Levels of Resolution

Perceptions of the mixed-grass prairie depend on one's level of resolution. The view may be as encompassing as several thousand acres as observed from an airplane, jeep, or horseback. Conversely, the view may be delineated by a patch of only a few square yards in area. Four levels of resolution are described below: landscape (thousands of acres), watershed (hundreds of acres), field (typically less than one hundred acres), and patch (several square yards).

The Landscape

A landscape is a mosaic of patches. The patch mosaic elicits a recognizable and repeatable pattern over thousands of acres. That pattern in landscape in the mixed-grass prairie is marked by expanses of irrigated corn, largely in the river valleys and, to a lesser extent, in upland areas. The upland areas alternatively are marked by native grasses that include representative tallgrass species, such as big bluestem (*Andropogon gerardii*), switchgrass (*Panicum virgatum*),

and Indian grass (*Sorghastrum nutans*). Also mid- and shortgrass species are well represented. These include western wheatgrass (*Pascopyrum smithii*), sideoats grama (*Bouteloua curtipendula*), blue grama (*Bouteloua gracilis*), and buffalo grass (*Buchloe dactyloides*).

The agroecosystems and natural prairie ecosystems are intersected by long corridors that largely extend east and west across the landscape: the rivers, the major highways, and the wooded areas that parallel them. Elevation ranges over several hundred feet, from less than two thousand feet near Red Cloud to three thousand feet near Broken Bow.

To understand this concept of prairie corridors, stand on a hill above any of the communities from Wood River in the east to Gothenburg in the west and view the panorama of prairie and farmstead to the north and corn fields, railroads, river valley, and interstate traffic to the south. From a high vantage point, the remarkable pattern of patches, corridors, and general variation is readily recognizable.

The Watershed

While the landscape encompasses thousands of acres and represents the large, readily recognizable element we may call the grassland, the forest, the desert, or other familiar feature, the watershed may be of a resolution of several hundred acres. A watershed within the mixed-grass prairie may encompass several hundred acres of the loess hills that drain an area, moving water and accompanying materials like nutrients, seeds of plants, and contaminants from one watershed to another within the landscape. While watersheds may appear to be closed systems, they are, in fact, quite open, with substantial transfer of matter and energy in the form of nurients and water from one ecosystem to another.

Funk Lagoon, Rainwater Basin Wildlife Management Area

A "stretch" of the Platte River might also be viewed as a watershed or sub-unit of the landscape. Often, the demarcation of a riparian watershed is both discretionary and anthropocentric. For example, the series of canals that are siphoned from and back to the Platte River between Gothenburg and Grand Island may be considered to represent a series of watersheds.

The Rainwater Basin region is unique in the prairie of central Nebraska as it represents the largest remaining remnant of wetland and watershed catchment along the Platte River system. The Rainwater Basin encompasses two regions. One region is directly south of an east-west line from Kearney to Lexington and includes substantial parts of Kearney, Phelps, and Gosper counties. The other, larger region, is found in parts of eight counties southeast of a line from Columbus to Grand Island. A substantial portion of this basin is within the tallgrass prairie while the western portion is dominated more by mixed-grass prairie vegetation. While much of the area is now in agricultural production, the region is still utilized extensively by migratory waterfowl. The combination of waterfowl, semi-aquatic/aquatic vegetation, and, of course, high water table are the most recognizable and defining features of these composite watersheds in the landscape.

The Field

The field, or stand, encompassses anywhere from one or two acres to perhaps fifty acres. At this level of resolution, the observer notes dominant vegetation forms, for example, the corn field, the pasture dominated by perennial native cool and warm season grasses, or the farmstead with associated corrals and outbuildings.

The influence of humans is most evident at this level of resolution. The observer's eye is drawn to the straight rows in the corn field, the cattle grazing in the pasture, the design and related function of the farmstead.

The Patch

The finest level of resolution is the patch, ranging from less than a square yard to perhaps an acre. At this level, microhabitats are delineated. A few square yards may be remarkably variable. A native shrub, lead-plant (*Amorpha canescens*) or western snowberry (*Symphoricarpus occidentalis*), for example, may cause shading and nutrient and water depletion within its dripline. Another portion of the patch may be dominated by a bunchgrass like little bluestem (*Andropogon scoparius*), while still another area may have a harvester anthill and the frenzied activity of the ants for some distance from the hill. The converse of the anthill is the badger burrow.

Prairie and farmstead emphasizing human influence on a stand   by Hal Nagel

Anthill showing variation at the patch level   by Hal Nagel

Both of these animal features influence plant diversity and density. The landscape at the patch level may be quite diverse, reflecting the same amount of variation as the overall landscape, if only at a finer scale.

The Value in a Landscape Approach

The landscape approach to conceptualizing a region, such as the mixed-grass prairie of central Nebraska, is built upon an ecological hierarchy of organization. Patches make up fields that make up watersheds that define the landscape. Working "up" through this hierarchy is an exercise in understanding how the components of the prairie system work. For example, rates of contamination of groundwater can most accurately be calculated by examining patches and fields. Shifts in plant species composition with heavy grazing, often from more to less preferred species, are also best understood with investigation at these finer levels of organization. Alternatively, working "down" through the hierarchy is an exercise in perception of how the components of the system fit together. The overall pattern of structure and function is revealed at the watershed and landscape levels. Explanation is derived from study of the finer levels of organization while context is provided by the coarser levels.

Since the landscape is a temporal as well as spatial template, it would seem reasonable to base our descriptions of it and prescription for its change on all four levels. Such an approach integrates our view of the prairies that typify Nebraska's landscape. The overlap among the levels and the relationships that link them can be viewed in a model form, with time, space, and the connections among the levels estimated (Fig. 1).

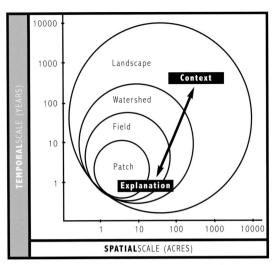

FIG. **1.** A conceptual model of the relationship between spatial and temporal scales in nature and the connection to explanation and context of structure and function in nature.

Rothenberger, S. J., and C. J. Bicak. 1993. Plants. In The Platte River: An Atlas of the big bend region, 18-28. Kearney: University of Nebraska at Kearney.

Urban, D. L., R. V. O'Neill, and H. H. Shugart. 1987. Landscape ecology. BioScience 37(2): 119-27.

Weaver, J. E., and W. E. Bruner. 1948. Prairies and pastures of the dissected loess plains of central Nebraska. Ecological Monographs. 18:507-49.

Weins, J. A. 1992. What is landscape ecology, really? Landscape Ecology 7(3): 149-50.

Selected**References**

Forman, R. T. T., and M. Godron. 1986. Landscape ecology. New York: John Wiley & Sons.

Hopkins, H. H. 1951. Ecology of the native vegetation of the loess hills in central Nebraska. Ecological Monographs 21(2): 125-47.

Lavorel, S., R., H. Gardner, and R. V. O'Neill. 1993. Analysis of patterns in hierarchically structured landscapes OIKOS 67(3): 521-28.

O'Neill, R. V., D. L. DeAngelis, J. B. Waide, and T. F. H. Allen. 1986. A herarchical concept of ecosystems. Princeton: Princeton University Press.

PRAIRIE FAUNA:

A Look at Terrestrial Vertebrates

Gary R. Lingle, University of Nebraska Cooperative Extension Educator

Lying in the heart of the continent and of the Central Flyway, Nebraska's central prairies are renowned as a biological crossroads where east meets west and north meets south. Southern species, such as Great Plains skink, scissor-tailed flycatcher, opossum, and hispid cotton rat are at the northern edge of their range. Likewise, northern species, including Harris' sparrow, northern shrike, and masked shrew, are at the southern edge of their range. Eastern species include gray treefrog, Blanding's turtle, blue jay, northern cardinal, American woodcock, woodchuck, eastern woodrat, and white-footed mouse. Examples of western species near their eastern limit are prairie rattlesnake, black-billed magpie, lazuli bunting, Ord's kangaroo rat, and mule deer. This biological diversity renders the region a perfect place for a naturalist or nature enthusiast of any kind.

The central prairies are drained by three major watersheds: the Republican River to the south, the Platte River in the center, and the Loup River system to the north. These drainages are the most prominent topographic features and generally flow from west to east, creating corridors for species expanding their ranges and stepping stones for migrants moving north and south. Woodland species, in particular, have found the wooded riparian zones along the rivers as excellent habitat for range expansion.

The 100th meridian bisects the region. This imaginary line is often used as a marker to separate humid from arid climate, an important demarcation for agricultural purposes. Lands west of this line typically require irrigation to reliably produce crops. The central prairie lies within some of the most intensely irrigated lands in the world. Hence, much of the native grass cover has been plowed and converted to row crops. Agricultural development within the last 150 years has fragmented the endless vistas of prairie into fields of corn, milo, and wheat with patches of prairie scattered within. For example, over seventy-five percent of the native grasslands along the Platte River Valley have been converted to meet human needs. This has had a tremendous impact, both negative and positive, on wildlife populations. Elimination of the bison and fire suppression have impacted the ecology of the region as well. Fortunately, enough remnant prairie remains to provide vital habitat for many of those species requiring grasslands for their survival.

Terrestrial vertebrates are animals that live essentially on land and have backbones. Major taxonomic classes or groups of terrestrial vertebrates are amphibians, reptiles, birds, and mammals. A brief overview of each of these groups and highlights of a few of the species inhabiting the region follows.

Sandhill Cranes   by Gary Lingle

Birds

The bird life of Nebraska's central prairies is as diverse as the region itself. Over 430 species of birds have been documented in Nebraska, and 3/4 of these species are found here. Not only is there rich diversity, but concentrations of some species are astounding. The most publicized species is the sandhill crane. Over half a million cranes stage along the Platte each March in densities unlike that found anywhere else in the world. This spectacle has fueled an eco-tourism industry that pumps about thirty million dollars into the local economy annually.

Nine to twelve million ducks and geese stage here each spring as well, adding to the region's attractiveness to tourists. The water-fowl are primarily found in the Rainwater Basin, a seven-county region lying south of the Platte River. Geologically, the Rainwater Basin contains a series of shallow, imperme-able depressions formed by the wind and lined with clay, which generally hold surface water from late winter through mid summer. Over a million ducks and geese have been counted at a single basin in recent years. The Rainwater Basin is also an important stop-over area for migrating shorebirds during wet years.

Migration in this area is essentially a year round process. Although January is probably the slowest month of the year in terms of migration, with only thirty percent of the species present at best, can provide surprises. Sandhill cranes and waterfowl appear during warm winters in January, although they typically arrive in mass numbers beginning in mid February and continuing through early March. March is famous for its peak numbers of cranes, waterfowl, and bald eagles.

April ushers in the first wave of shorebirds and bids farewell to the cranes and waterfowl as they depart to their Arctic nesting grounds. The emerging leaves and insects stimulated by May's warming temperatures lures the greatest diversity of migrating species of the year. With a bountiful food supply, the insectivorous songbirds find haven. Warblers, flycatchers, vireos, and thrushes abound, sporting stunning plumage which rivals any species on earth in terms of color. It is possible to tally over 120 species on a good day in early May, while the month itself accounts for eighty percent of the species known from the region.

Nesting species predominate in the summer, although by July arctic nesting shorebirds begin to arrive on their south-ward trek. Peregrine falcons can occasionally be seen stooping mixed flocks of sand-pipers. In August, more southerly species appear as post-nesting dispersal brings in a variety of waders, including snowy egrets, little blue herons, great egrets, and cattle

American Bittern   by Gary Lingle

egrets. Mississippi kites show up in fair numbers some years as well.

Typical fall migration kicks off in September with warblers and sparrows challenging identification by the most experienced birders. Harris' sparrow, LeConte's sparrow, and Sprague's pipit are among the migrants. October and November brings in huge flocks of waterfowl along with winter residents such as bald eagles, rough-legged hawks, northern harriers, and northern shrikes. During mid-winter, raptors are the most conspicuous species, although tree sparrows, dark-eyed juncos, and a variety of finches are the most numerous.

Less conspicuous than the huge congregations of cranes and waterfowl, yet no less important, are the millions of songbirds and other migrants occurring here. Of particular interest is a group of birds known as neotropical migrants, a species that nests in North America but winters south of the border in Latin America. Of the 328 species recorded in Nebraska's central prairie region, fifty-three percent (176 species) are neotropical migrants. Of the 150 species known to nest in the area, forty-five percent (fifty-four species) are neotropical migrants. Conservationists are particularly concerned about neotropical migrants because this group in general has experienced alarming population declines, largely due to habitat loss both on the nesting grounds and wintering areas.

On a continental basis, grassland species have experienced the greatest population declines. Habitat loss, pesticides, and predation, especially by house cats, have contributed to this decline. In one study, it was estimated that the nation's one hundred million cats kill hundreds of millions of songbirds annually, and grassland species are particularly vulnerable. Typical grassland nesters include upland sandpiper, sedge wren, dickcissel, grasshopper sparrow, Henslow's sparrow, bobolink, and western meadowlark. Fortunately, Nebraska's central prairies host thriving populations of these species, reinforcing the importance of protecting habitats vital to many of these birds we take for granted. For example, during a sixteen year breeding bird population study along Platte River wet meadows, four of six species exhibited either stable or increasing populations while, nationally, they all exhibited population declines. The two species that declined in this local study, upland sandpiper and western meadowlark, were responding to changes in management practices which resulted in increased vegetation stature, a condition not preferred by them. The most abundant nesting species found in this region was western meadowlark, followed by common grackle and grasshopper sparrow.

Many of the woodland and shrubland species declining in the east and in the west are finding suitable nesting habitat along the wooded rivers in the central prairies. Red-headed woodpecker, black-billed cuckoo, wood thrush, eastern wood pewee, and field sparrow are fairly common. Bell's vireo and willow flycatcher are two species that are threatened in the Southwest but appear to be doing well here. Orchard oriole, brown thrasher, and loggerhead shrike are other examples of species in decline throughout much of their range, but are stable or, perhaps, increasing in this area. Again, woodland expansion is due, in part, to fire suppression and changes in river hydrology brought about by the construction of reservoirs and water diversion structures. While this has been a bane to some species, such as sandhill cranes and shorebirds, it has been a boom for many others.

Each prairie type found in the region hosts a characteristic nesting population of birds. In the Sand Hills, characteristic species include

Least Tern   by Gary Lingle

Upland Sandpiper   by Gary Lingle

Vesper Sparrow   by Gary Lingle

Bald Eagles   by Gary Lingle

greater prairie chicken, sharp-tailed grouse, long-billed curlew, common nighthawk, horned lark, grasshopper sparrow, and western meadowlark. The mixed-grass prairie hosts red-tailed hawk, Swainson's hawk, killdeer, upland sandpiper, burrowing owl, grasshopper sparrow, and western meadowlark. In the tallgrass prairie, one finds upland sandpiper, sedge wren, dickcissel, grasshopper sparrow, Henslow's sparrow, bobolink, and eastern meadowlark. The shortgrass prairie hosts Swainson's hawk, long-billed curlew, burrowing owl, loggerhead shrike, lark sparrow, lark bunting, and western meadowlark, while the sandsage prairie supports mourning dove, common nighthawk, lark sparrow, Cassin's sparrow, grasshopper sparrow, and western meadowlark.

Six federally listed endangered species occur here, three as transients and three as nesting species. Those found during migration include whooping crane, peregrine falcon, and eskimo curlew (probably now extinct), while nesting species are bald eagle, piping plover, and least tern. Bald eagles are a common winter resident along open portions of the major rivers and established themselves as a nesting species in Nebraska in 1991. Today there are over thirty known eagle nests scattered throughout the state. Least terns and piping plovers nest on the barren sandbars and adjacent sandpits of the Platte and Loup river systems. Habitat loss due to reduced flows and concomitant woodland expansion has resulted in a decline of these birds. Whooping cranes number less than

two hundred in the flock that migrates through Nebraska enroute to their nesting grounds in northern Alberta and their wintering grounds along the Gulf Coast of Texas. The peak of their migration in this area is early April and late October. They utilize wetland and riparian areas, especially in the Rainwater Basin and along the central Platte River.

Birds undoubtedly contribute more economically to the region than any other group of wildlife. Birding, bird feeding, photography, and hunting are the major pursuits. In addition to the millions of eco-tourism dollars generated by crane-watchers, hunters also contribute to the local economy. Waterfowl are perhaps the most sought after game species, followed closely by upland game species such as greater prairie-chickens, sharp-tailed grouse, northern bobwhite, and ring-necked pheasant. Wild turkey and mourning doves challenge hunters as well. Bird feeding activity is growing in popularity as people of all ages in both rural and urban areas discover the joy and satisfaction of feeder-watching.

Mammals

About sixty species of mammals occur in the central prairies despite the fact that most are seldom seen due to their nocturnal habits. Beside habitat alteration, the greatest effect of European settlement in this region was the extermination of the bison, grizzly, and gray wolf, and the near complete elimination of prairie dogs. Prairie ecology had to adjust to those changes. Remnant prairie dog towns can still be found, much to the chagrin of some landowners. These communities host a variety of vertebrates, including burrowing owl, prairie rattlesnake, bull snake, badger, coyote, and ferruginous hawk. The black-footed ferret, a federally endangered species, was extirpated from Nebraska as dog towns were destroyed.

Bats are a poorly understood group of mammals, despite the fact that they are widespread. Some species are migratory, while others hibernate during the winter months. As darkness descends, bats become active and forage on a variety of insects. Perhaps the most common species is the big brown bat, which frequents both rural and

Badger   by Gary Lingle

urban areas, often turning up in attics, particularly in the fall.

Another group of insectivores is the shrews and moles. Masked shrews are the most abundant species, occasionally finding their way into households. The northern short-tailed shrew is unique among the mammals of Nebraska in that it is the only species that is poisonous. Its poison occurs in the saliva and is used to paralyze its prey, although it presents no threat to humans. Shrews are rarely seen alive, but a knowledgeable observer can find them trapped in discarded bottles littering the roadways. Eastern moles are widespread and their raised tunnels can be found throughout the region. Homeowners are not fond of moles inhabiting their lawns.

Nearly half of the mammal species of the region are rodents. This diverse and important group consists of everything from muskrats and beaver to mice and voles. Many species are fossorial (adapted for digging) and live underground, an adaptation well-suited for a region historically subjected to frequent fires. Their burrowing activity aerates the soil and redistributes minerals. Plains pocket gopher mounds can be found throughout the region. In sandy areas, Ord's kangaroo rat can be found. Their burrows are conspicuous. This species makes a fair pet, being very similar to a gerbil in captivity. Two species of ground squirrels are present, the ubiquitous thirteen-lined ground squirrel and the less

common Franklin's ground squirrel. Fox squirrels are the only arboreal or tree-dwelling squirrel found in this area. Occasionally, the black color phase may be found. Always surprising is to encounter a porcupine in the Sand Hills, miles away from the nearest forest. Yucca provides them with sustenance when they stray from the woodlands. Perhaps the most abundant rodent is the white-footed mouse and its cousin, the deer mouse. These tan colored mice with white bellies inhabit native tracts as well as cropland. The only exotic rodents found here are the Norway rat and house mouse, both species dependent on human habitation for their livelihood.

The carnivores, or flesh-eaters, form an interesting group of species. Perhaps most beleaguered and abundant among this group is the coyote. Despite over one hundred years of persecution, the coyote is thriving, unlike its larger cousin, the gray wolf, which was extirpated from the state by the turn of the twentieth century. Other canine, or dog-like, species found in the central prairies are the red fox and the rare gray fox. Only two native feline, or cat-like, species are found here, the bobcat and mountain lion. Bobcats are fairly common is some areas, preferring rough, dissected canyon habitat or wooded riparian zones. Mountain lions are rare, with increasing reports occurring along the Republican River drainage. The weasel family is made up of the following species: long-

White-tailed deer near Snake River   by Gary Lingle

Grouse Habitat located in Custer County, west of Merna, Nebraska   by Gary Lingle

tailed weasel, least weasel, mink, badger, striped skunk, spotted skunk, and river otter. Successful reintroduction efforts of river otters have bolstered their populations, especially along the Platte River. Raccoons belong to a unique family closely related to bears and are an important fur-bearer here. They can be found in habitats ranging from open prairies and riparian woodlands to underneath porches and attics.

Six species of ungulates, or hoofed mammals, occurred in the region. Most numerous but now extirpated was the bison, although captive herds are growing in popularity here. Wapiti and moose are accidental visitors here, occasionally wandering to Nebraska from more traditional haunts farther west or north. Pronghorn were common, but again were greatly reduced in numbers through habitat loss and market hunting. A few pockets of this uniquely North American species occur in the area, increasing in abundance in the western part of the state where they are hunted. Deer are the most popular big game species in the region and, therefore, are arguably the most important mammal economically. Two species are found here, the white-tailed deer and the mule deer. White-tailed deer favor wetland areas and river systems while mulies, as they are known locally, typically inhabit upland prairies. Deer populations have rebounded from near extinction in the early part of this century to levels now believed to exceed those prior to European settlement.

Herptiles

Amphibians and reptiles are those lowly, cold-blooded creatures collectively known as herptiles or herps. Thirty-eight species of herps are found in the region, far fewer than states south of Nebraska. Cold climates severely limit herptile distribution, thus species diversity drops off dramatically to the north. The tiger salamander is the only species of salamander found here, and it is uncommon. There are nine species of frogs and toads. Some are more often heard than seen. When the first ephemeral ponds occur in late March or early April, western striped chorus frogs fill the air with their courtship calls. Although they can be deafening, only the most astute observer can witness this

one-inch frog in the act of calling. Late spring and early summer deluges stimulate the emergence and mating of plains spadefoot toads. During dry years, they may remain dormant. The bullfrog has expanded its range westward into this region in recent years. Bullfrogs prefer the still water of lakes and ponds rather than the flowing water of rivers; thus, it is believed the construction of sandpits along waterways facilitated their expansion. This species is a voracious predator and, in some states, has been responsible for the decline of native species. Its impact here has yet to be determined.

There are twenty-eight species of reptiles in the region: six species of lizards, seven species of turtles, and fifteen species of snakes. Northern prairie lizards abound in the Sand Hills. Six-lined racerunners inhabit sandy areas associated with sandpits and uplands. Prairie skink are common in lowland prairies throughout the region. In late spring, female snapping turtles are often encountered along roadways as they seek sandy areas in which to lay their eggs. This relic from prehistoric times is sought by some for its flesh. Yellow mud turtles frequent the Republican River drainage. The males have a claw it the end of their tail and emit a foul-smelling musk when handled. Spiny softshell turtles, known locally as leatherbacks, inhabit all of this regions' rivers. The painted turtle is the most common and familiar aquatic turtle, while the ornate box turtle holds this distinction in the sandy upland prairies. The box turtle has been subjected to intense collecting for the pet trade, and concern over its future led to the recent passage of a state law limiting the collection of herps in general.

Undoubtedly, the most vilified group of terrestrial vertebrates is the Order Serpentes, or snakes. Only one species is poisonous to humans, the prairie rattlesnake. It is locally common near rocky outcrops and dissected hills. Due to its rather small size and timid demeanor, prairie rattlesnakes pose little threat to humans but can be a nuisance to hunting dogs. The black-headed snake has a mild toxin in its saliva that is used to subdue prey but is of no threat to humans. Without question, the most common snake of the region is the plains gartersnake. Its cousin,

Platte River wet meadow

by Gary Lingle

Upland Sandpiper nest

by Gary Lingle

Sandhill Cranes and a March moon   by Gary Lingle

the red-sided gartersnake, replaces the plains gartersnake along the drainages. Green racers, bull snakes, and western hognose snakes are prominent in the Sand Hills. The gentle hognose snake is fun to encounter. When threatened, it vibrates its tail and puffs up menacingly with its mouth agape. If that does not discourage a would-be intruder, it rolls over on its back and feigns death with its jet-black tongue hanging out. If placed right side up, it will resume its death-like posture. On the other hand, the widespread bullsnake commands respect. When threatened, it coils and vibrates its tail like a rattlesnake while hissing loudly. It does not hesitate to strike; however, it does tame rather easily and can make an excellent pet. Bullsnakes are excellent climbers and will depredate bird nests located in trees or on the ground.

Summary

The terrestrial vertebrates add to the richness and grandeur of the central prairie region, each in its own unique way. From the bubbling calls of a bobolink singing amongst a splash of flowers on a dew-laden June morning to the comical antics of a hognose snake feigning injury, life in this region demands subtle and patient observation in order to reveal its secrets and splendor. While the mountains and the ocean shores attract hordes of vacationers each year, the prairie, with its endless vistas and spectacular skies, offers tranquility to the slower-paced observer in a manner rivaled by no other. Although thundering herds of bison no longer stretch across the horizon, flocks of birds still darken the skies, and here one can find a pace of life reminiscent of bygone days. Our challenge is to allow natural processes to continue and to protect our natural heritage for our own enjoyment as well as for that of our grand-children's, so they do not lament the loss of those things we may take for granted today.

Selected**References**

Bleed, A. and C. Flowerday, eds. 1989. An atlas of the Sand Hills. Resource Atlas No. 5. Conservation and Survey Division, University of Nebraska, Lincoln.

Jenkins, A. and S.K. George, eds. 1993. The Platte River: an atlas of the Big Bend Region. University of Nebraska at Kearney.

Johnsgard, P. 1979. Birds of the Great Plains. Lincoln: University of Nebraska Press.

Jones, K., D. Armstrong, and J. Choate. 1985. Guide to the mammals of the plains states. Lincoln: University of Nebraska Press.

Lingle, G. 1994. Birding crane river: Nebraska's Platte. Gibbon, NE: Harrier Publishing.

Lynch, J. 1985. Annotated checklist of the amphibians and reptiles of Nebraska. Transactions of the Nebraska Academy of Sciences 8:33-57.

"The Covered Wagon"   Thomas Hart Benton

buffalo soldier
by charles fort

They were called buffalo soldiers
by the Indians and wore cowboy boots
with ivory holster and silver spurs
horsemen on hell's frontier carousel.

One can walk where they died
step into the tilted stagecoach
as the scarecrow floated in the field
and pointed its finger to the sky.

Were they shooting magic bullets
into sacred hoops and Indians
exhumed by a divining rod
and replanted on the battlefield?

The nurse amputated as they awakened
and the chief who had roamed the hills
expecting a last vision and rebirth
left his arrow burning in the earth.

HISTORYLAW

FORCES OF CREATION:

THE TRAGEDY OF THE PAWNEE

Mark A. Eifler, Associate Professor of History

According to the Skiri Pawnee, the world began with Tirawahut, the great power, who had everything that was and everything that would be. "I need helpers, "Tirawahut said, and he reached out his right hand, and his four fingers became four stars. He assigned these stars to the cardinal directions, to be known as the lodge poles of the heavens. After creating other helpers–clouds, winds, lightning, thunder–Tirawahut set out to create the world, composed of mountains and plains, plants and animals. After creating the world, the stars held a council, and decided to create people for their world. These first people, however, could only be created by the mating of the Morning Star and Evening Star. The Evening Star, however, protested that she did not want a mate, and called on Tirawahut to protect her. The Morning Star, however, called on the Sun, and was eventually able to mate with the Evening Star, creating the first people. At first, these new people had little knowledge of how to survive, but Tirawahut and the stars and their helpers instructed the new people.

Every year, the Skiri Pawnee recited this creation story, in order to remind the stars to bring new life to the earth. To the Pawnee, life on the central plains depended on their ability to learn from these forces of creation and to cooperate with a multitude of different helpers. To a remarkable degree, they were successful; the Pawnee were one of the first historic tribes to settle year round in the difficult environment of the Great Plains. They succeeded because much of their activities were engaged in collecting resources of two ecosystems–the riverine valleys and the mixed-grass plains–ordering them and redistributing them in their use. Yet to the Pawnee, the world only existed as it did because they had helped to create it through their ceremonies and rituals. Ironically, it was a world that collapsed when other peoples–particularly Dakota, American, and European immigrants–came to the region intent on creating their own world as well.

Of all the tribes that called Nebraska home when European explorers first arrived, the Pawnee had lived in the central plains the longest and were the only tribe living in the mixed-grass region of central Nebraska. The Pawnee were divided into two large groups: the Skiri (or Loup River Pawnee) and the South Bands, made up of the Chaui (Grands), the Kitkahaki (Republican Pawnee), and Pitahawirata (Tapage Pawnee). The

Skiri and South Bands were not always unified in their relations. The two groups spoke different dialects, maintained unique traditions and ceremonies, went on separate buffalo hunts, and occasionally fought each other.

The Pawnee and the Land

The relationship between the Pawnee and their land was never simple. The Pawnee lived in three different ecosystems: the tall-grass prairie, the mixed-grass plains, and the central plains river valleys. The Pawnee spent half their year in the river valleys. Here they planted crops and built villages. The broad, shallow, shifting river valley environments provided many of the resources they needed. Cottonwood, willow, and a few elm trees grew along the river banks and on islands in the river. Along the river banks and terraces, brush and tall grasses grew as well, many reaching farther into the more arid western plains than were common on the higher plains.

The Pawnee sought village sites that had available timber and fertile lands for their crops. Timber was needed for fire, which the Pawnee used for cooking, heating, making pottery, and drying their corn. Trees were also necessary for building earth lodges. The Pawnee prized oak and elm for their lodges, but often had to make due with cottonwood, which is not as strong or durable.

The Pawnee lived for most of the year in earthlodge villages. These settlements usually covered fifty to one hundred acres, were located on bluffs overlooking rivers for security, and were often surrounded by palisades and ditches. Surrounding the village were small garden plots, usually no more than three acres each, located near the river bottom or near tributary streams. After about 1714, most villages would also maintain a horse herd grazing in the vicinity.

The earthlodge itself was roughly sixty feet in diameter; the outer walls were six feet tall and the middle roof posts were twelve feet tall. In addition, the floor was usually excavated two to three feet. The wooden posts and beams were usually made from cottonwood and covered with a grass mat before being overlaid with sod. These lodges were warm in the winter, cool in the summer, and quite spacious. Pawnee lodges were originally square with rounded corners, but between 1500 and 1700 the shape became circular and the villages more compact. The change may have had to do with Pawnee religious beliefs, as the number and placement of posts within the earthlodge, its domed roof, and its overall orientation were dictated by Pawnee spiritualism.

Pawnee earthlodge villages were the center of Pawnee society, but were somewhat transitory structures. Lack of timber was a significant restraint on the tribe. Cottonwood

Nebraska State Historical Society

Close-up of Pawnee lodges

posts and beams were structurally weak, and the fuel needs of a village tended to deplete the area's resources of wood over time. As timber resources were used up, the Pawnee had to wander farther and farther from their village seeking wood. Therefore, the Pawnee abandoned their villages and built new ones roughly every twenty-five to thirty years.

Pawnee villages were surrounded by cornfields. Pawnee women planted corn, beans, melons, and squash. Plots were usually one to three acres each, and assigned by village leaders. Women used the same plot every year; the plot reverted to the village upon a woman's death. Plots were highly valued. The Pawnee used only sites where the soil was already disturbed by streams, along banks, creek bottoms, or the mouth of ravines, where the soil needed little hoeing and was more likely to be well watered. Such sites, however, were not always conveniently located; women sometimes traveled seven or eight miles from a village to find such lands.

The Pawnee favored flour corns, which were easier to grind. Plantings were on the same plot every year; the Pawnee did not practice rotation or fertilization. The crops the Pawnee planted were rather typical of north American tribes: corn, beans, pumpkins, watermelon, squash, and sunflowers. But they experimented very successfully with varieties of each of these crops, developing seven varieties of pumpkin and squash, eight varieties of beans, and ten

varieties of corn. They hoed only in corn hills, planted seeds only two inches deep. The Pawnee also mixed their crops, planting beans beside the corn. As both plants grew, beans used corn stalks as bean poles. Squashes were planted surrounding the corn-bean complexes, as their broad leaves kept down weeds. Generally the Pawnee planted patches of pumpkins, squash, and watermelons between the different varieties of corn, in part to inhibit cross-pollination. Entire plots were then surrounded with sunflowers, which were woven together as they grew in order to act as fences. During the summer, these plots were generally left untended, while the tribe was hunting.

The river valleys of the central plains provided other resources for the Pawnee also. Wildlife, such as beaver, waterfowl, and game birds, were common. Deer were common, too, though not numerous. The Pawnee did occasionally supplement their diets with deer meat, but such hunts made little sense on the central plains. Hunting deer would have taken the time and effort of many men, and likely yielded relatively few animals. Buffalo hunting farther west produced far more resources for the time involved. Deer hunting was practical at Grand Island, however, and the Pawnee usually stopped and hunted here on their annual trek to the high plains buffalo ranges. The river valleys also provided wild plants, which were more important to the

Pawnee than the animal resources of the valleys. The Pawnee were close observers of the natural environment and recognized many variations in wild plants, which they used for religious, medicinal, and magical purposes. Wild plants, such as the Indian potato, were also crucial to the Pawnee diet. They were harvested as the tribe moved to and from the annual buffalo hunt and during the days between planting and harvesting. These gathered plants were essential; if crops failed or if the buffalo hunt was unsuccessful, these gathered plants would be needed to sustain the Pawnee.

Annual Buffalo Hunts

During the summer, the Pawnee left their villages to hunt buffalo on the western plains. The Pawnee hunting range extended between the North Platte River and the Solomon River of Western Kansas. Though the South Bands sometimes cooperated in the summer hunt, the Skiri often hunted alone. During such times, the very old and very young might remain in the village, but the majority of the band would journey west. While hunting on the plains, the Pawnee lived in tipis. These were formed by erecting a number of poles and covering them with a buffalo hide. The size of the tipi, however, depended upon the length of the pole; before the Pawnee acquired horses, tipi poles tended to be small.

The Pawnee used the resources of the river valleys–including wild animals, plants, and their planted produce–to reach the plains to hunt the buffalo. Most of this food was dried and packed to carry on trips to hunting regions. In essence, they used the products of the valleys to reach the mixed-grass plains to hunt the buffalo. They largely ignored the tall-grass zones on their journeys; though rich in grass, they were poor in grazers. Buffalo did not live here in great numbers, but thrived in the mixed-grass and short-grass plains to the west. As the Pawnee moved to the West, buffalo usually began to appear about the 98th meridian (roughly the location of present-day Kearney).

During the seventeenth and early eighteenth centuries, hunting buffalo involved a "surround," a communal activity involving everyone in the tribe. Once scouts had located a buffalo herd, the majority of the band quickly formed and manned two broad walls, made up of brush and logs, while hunters tried to turn the herd into the avenue between these barriers. At the end of the avenue, lay a bluff, over which the buffalo would be driven, or a corral. More hunters waited here to kill injured or captured buffalo. These annual hunts were crucial to the Pawnee; buffalo made up over half of their diet and was also needed in a number of important Pawnee rituals.

Upon returning to their villages with the dried buffalo meat produced during the hunt, the Pawnee set out to harvest the gardens they had planted in the spring. The Pawnee harvested the squash and beans first, drying them for storage. Next they harvested some corn, while it was still green. This allowed them to get at least a partial harvest even if drought or insects later destroyed the rest. The Pawnee harvested their corn in a particular order. Small kernel corn was harvested first, and the best cobs were deliberately selected as seed corn for the following year. The Pawnee put great value on this corn.

Estimates of how much corn the Pawnee harvested annually are rough, but available evidence suggests that the Pawnee harvested about twenty-five to forty bushels per acre, and that the tribe planted about 1,400 acres each year, resulting in roughly 42,000 bushels of corn harvested each year.

Pawnee Religious Rituals

To the Pawnee, the success of their yearly planting, gathering, and hunting depended upon their ability to successfully carry out their religious ceremonies and rituals. There were religious differences among the Pawnee bands. Skiri religious views and practices were the most complex of all native Americans. Skiri authority was based on the movement of the stars, and the band practiced human sacrifice each spring in order to insure the successful cycle of the coming year–the only North American tribe that had such a practice. South band authority was based on animals, whom they believed were their helpers and intermediaries with the great power. The Pawnee also recognized fourteen sacred sites, places of pilgrimage and power. All but one of these lay between the Loup and Republican Rivers.

Power originated with Tirawahut, "the pervasive ocean-of-power investing the universe." In Pawnee cosmology, stars acted as intermediaries for Tirawahut. Tirawahut gave the stars the power to create humans and instructed the stars to give humans the medicine bundles. The symbolic soul of the Pawnee was the medicine bundle. The bundles themselves controlled the order of the seasons. Thus, the Pawnee had to handle them correctly to survive. Each warrior, lodge, dancing society, and village had their own unique bundle, and there was a definite hierarchy to the bundles. The most important bundles controlled Pawnee ceremonies.

Bundle ceremonies insured harvests and hunting success. In order for creation to work, the Sky had to vitalize the Earth; all Pawnee rituals were attempts to promote creation. Seed corn was kept in sky bundles and planted ritually in the spring. Rituals also dominated the buffalo hunt. The Pawnee regarded this not as following the seasons, but as ordering the seasons. They believed that they created the natural cycle through their rituals. Bundles contained a variety of items: buffalo skin, animal skins, wildcat skulls, stuffed bird skins, scalps, arrows, ears of corn, wads of buffalo hair, etc. These objects both symbolized and held sacred power.

Power flowed from Tirawahut to the stars to the bundles to the Pawnee. Only particular people could handle the bundles. These were the elite–stars on earth. Men passed their standing on to their sons–a hereditary elite. Chiefs were ranked according to birth, but the power of the Pawnee nation depended on the power of the chiefs to use the bundles correctly. Priests also used the bundles, and usually the chiefs and priests were one in the same. Priests needed to serve a long apprenticeship. The priest's bearing, conduct, and wisdom reflected that of the bundle. Pawnee chiefs thus had great power, much greater than most Indian peoples in North America. They could even proscribe the death penalty–a very rare power among tribes.

The significance of this power structure is that it was geared toward the redistribution of wealth, rather than the acquisition of wealth. Families gave their best crops and meats to family heads, who passed them on to society heads, who passed it on to Pawnee leaders; each person along the way was expected to give the best of what they had. Leaders were then expected to redistribute this wealth to the tribe. In doing so, they showed their generosity and made sure that food was distributed to everyone based on need, regardless of who had earned the most.

Expansion and Invasion

During the eighteenth century, Pawnee society flourished. The South Bands expanded farther southward: the Kitahaki established villages on the Republican River, and the Pitahawirata established villages on the Smoky Hill and Blue Rivers. Meanwhile, Pawnee traders and raiders extended Pawnee contacts even further. Pawnee warriors fought off Comanche, Apache, and Ute Indians who challenged their dominance of the Central High Plains buffalo hunting grounds. Though not a major trading tribe on the plains, the Pawnee did sometimes trade with the Arikara to the north, the Witchita to the south, and during the later eighteenth century, the Pawnee visited the isolated Spanish outpost of Santa Fe roughly every three years.

Yet, if the Pawnee felt themselves adept at harnessing the forces of creation on the central plains, other groups also looked to the region as a place where they could create a world of their own. Other plains Indian tribes rode onto the northern and central plains in the late eighteenth and early nineteenth centuries, followed by American fur trappers, missionaries, soldiers, and settlers. These invaders became increasingly forceful during the nineteenth century, upsetting the balance of resources that the Pawnee had maintained for centuries.

The initial invasion of the central plains, however, came not from these invading peoples, but from the invaders' unintentional allies: disease and horses. It is estimated that between 1500 and 1750, Pawnee population stood at about twenty thousand. During this time, the Pawnee probably maintained or

Pawnee men

increased their population. However, the Pawnee, like other Native American peoples, had no resistance to diseases carried to this continent by European explorers and settlers. These diseases passed from tribe to tribe, often spreading far inland to tribes that had never encountered a European. The effects of these diseases were devastating. Small pox, measles, and deadly strains of influenza struck the Pawnee in the 1750s and 1790s; during each epidemic, the Pawnee lost one-third to one-half of their population. Between 1800 and 1830, Pawnee population slowly began to recover. However, these diseases weakened the Pawnee just as their world was beginning to come under attack by outsiders.

While disease epidemics clearly weakened the Pawnee, the dangerous effects of the horse were more subtle. In fact, the horse at first seemed to help the Pawnee. Before the eighteenth century, horses were unknown on the plains. When Spanish colonizers established a settlement in Santa Fe, New Mexico, however, they brought their horses with them. Following the Pueblo Indian revolt in New Mexico in 1680, southwest tribes such as the Comanche quickly seized the colonists' horse herds. Over the following decades, horses were traded and stolen

between the various plains tribes and began to arrive among the Pawnee about 1714. Mounted on horses, Pawnee hunters could scout farther afield for buffalo, abandon the dangerous surround method of hunting, and carry more dried meat home to their villages each fall.

Yet, the horse brought a number of drawbacks to the Pawnee. Horse herds needed to be fed, and that further strained the limited resources of the river valleys where the Pawnee had located their villages. Horses sometimes broke into garden plots, making it more necessary to assign herders to Pawnee horses. In winter, the horses sometimes starved, unable to find sufficient forage. In response, the Pawnee initiated a winter hunting cycle, in which bands of Pawnee hunters took their horses west to hunt not only additional buffalo meat, but also to search for additional forage for their herds.

Worse still, horses increased the intertribal fighting on the central plains. Horses not only increased the hunting range of the Pawnee, but also of other tribes that had traditionally challenged the Pawnee on the western plains. The horse, since it was able to carry more dried buffalo meat, also made it possible for other tribes to move onto the plains year round, tribes such as the

Cheyenne, Arapaho, and the Dakota. Each of these tribes fought bitterly over the buffalo resources of the high plains, and also raided each other for more horses to increase their power. In these raids, the settled villages of the Pawnee were especially vulnerable to nomadic tribes. Weakened by disease epidemics and increasing warfare, the Pawnee found themselves hard pressed to continue their traditional lives on the plains. By the early nineteenth century, the Pawnee were trading with St. Louis-based fur companies, exchanging furs and hides for blankets, tobacco, and guns. Of these goods, guns were rapidly becoming the most important item of trade because of the increasing warfare on the western ranges. St. Louis traders welcomed the Pawnee trade, but often found it less lucrative than with other tribes. In part, this was because the Pawnee leaders effectively forbade the traders to traffic in alcohol among the Pawnee, an item which many traders depended on to make Indian tribes dependent on their goods.

Despite the growing challenges to the Pawnee world, the Pawnee were strong and confident throughout the 1820s. In fact, during the 1820s, Pawnee attacks on the Santa Fe Trail were so frequent that the governor of Santa Fe threatened to attack the United States if the United States did not control the Pawnee–something the United States was not in a position of doing! Then, during the winter of 1831-32, small-pox again devastated the tribe. Tribal population dropped from roughly ten thousand to less than six thousand. Since the last smallpox epidemic had hit around 1798, those under thirty years of age had no resistance. It was after this epidemic that the Republican Pawnee retreated back to the Platte River. In 1840, Pawnee population stood at only 6,244 by actual count.

The Dakota took immediate advantage of the Pawnee weakness. In the fall of 1832, the Dakota attacked the Skiri village, killing nineteen people. Dakota attacks came on two fronts, from both the Oglala and the Brule. At home, the Dakota struck Pawnee villages whenever possible, attacked women at work in distant fields, and stole horses. In the West, they sought control of the North Platte Valley, where the Skiri usually

wintered. By 1839, the Pawnee had virtually surrendered the North Platte River Valley.

United States Intervention

The Dakota were not the only people expanding to the West during this time, however. The United States had, over the previous four decades, spread from a new nation hugging the Atlantic coast to an expansive nation with continental ambitions. Initially, the United States had seen the central plains as a perfect setting for Indian peoples, so, in the 1830s, the government attempted to remove tribes from the eastern half of the continent to the plains. The relocated tribes–such as the Delaware– were settled on the southern boundary of lands claimed by the Pawnee, and these relocated tribes quickly came to compete with the Pawnee for the resources of the plains. In 1833, the Untied States approached the Pawnee (and other Nebraska tribes) about land cessions. Weakened by both smallpox and the Dakota, the Pawnee were in desperate shape. The chiefs made a treaty (not agreed to by the younger warriors) to give up all "right, interest, and title" to lands south of the Platte River (though they could still hunt there.). In return, the Pawnee were given $2000 worth of agricultural equipment ($500 worth per band) for five years; an education fund of $1000, and the services of two blacksmiths and two strikers. They were also promised protection from Dakota raiders. This amounted to selling thirteen million acres of land for roughly a penny an acre in money and services.

Between 1834 and 1839, Presbyterian missionaries John Dunbar and Samuel Allis visited the Pawnee–Allis with the Skiri and Dunbar with the Chaui. In 1837, they returned to the East, married, then returned to the Pawnee with their wives. In 1840, they built a mission on the north side of the Loup River at Council Creek. However, Dunbar and Allis, opposed by the Pawnee priests, found their efforts at conversion largely frustrated.

During the 1830s, the Rocky Mountain Fur Company used the Platte River Valley as a road to the central Rockies and the annual Rendezvous. Starting in the early 1840s, migrants began wandering through the valley,

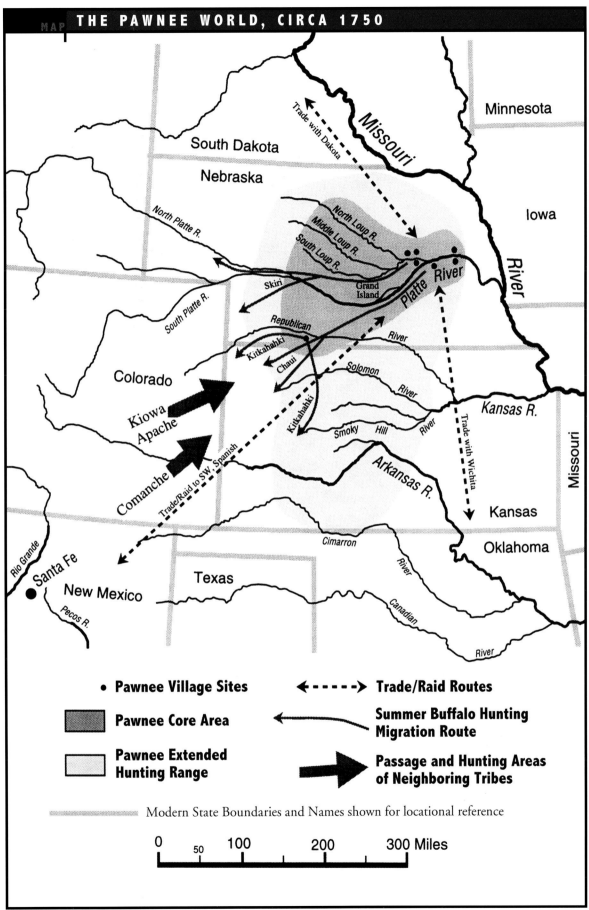

THE PAWNEE WORLD, CIRCA 1750

MAP

Minnesota

South Dakota

Nebraska

Iowa

Missouri

Trade with Dakota

Missouri River

North Platte R.

North Loup R.

Middle Loup R.

South Loup R.

South Platte R.

Skiri

Grand Island

Platte River

Republican

River

Kitkahahki

Chaui

Solomon

River

Trade with Wichita

Colorado

Kiowa Apache

Comanche

Trade/Raid to SW, Spanish

Kitkahahki

Smoky Hill River

Kansas R.

Kansas

Arkansas R.

Oklahoma

Rio Grande

Santa Fe

New Mexico

Pecos R.

Texas

Cimarron

River

Missouri

Canadian

River

• **Pawnee Village Sites**

Pawnee Core Area

Pawnee Extended Hunting Range

◄----► **Trade/Raid Routes**

◄───── **Summer Buffalo Hunting Migration Route**

Passage and Hunting Areas of Neighboring Tribes

Modern State Boundaries and Names shown for locational reference

0   50   100   200   300 Miles

Map by G.E. Bennett, UNK Geography

following the Oregon, California, and Mormon trails. These trails brought more pressure on the limited resources of the Platte River Valley, weakening the ability of the Pawnee to live off the resources of the central plains. At the same time, Dakota Indians continued invading from the north and west. The United States did nothing to protect the Pawnee or stop the Dakota; they refused to give the Pawnee guns, in part to keep fighting down on the plains. However, at the same time, the government supplied the Dakota with guns so that they would let the Americans cross the plains. Additionally, the Dakota acquired guns from the fur trade.

Some Pawnee bands then moved south of the Platte River for protection from the Dakota. However, the government argued that the Pawnee had broken their treaty to give up these lands. In 1847, the United States decided to build a fort in the area: Fort Kearny. Located between the villages and the buffalo, the government could then intercept the Pawnee on their way to the hunt. The following year, the Pawnee began to starve. In order to buy food, the Pawnee then sold Grand Island and the adjoining flood plain to the United States for less than two cents an acre.

The Pawnee were now in a quandary. Disease was devastating them. The United States demanded that they stay north of the Platte, but when they were there, the Dakota attacked. With the chiefs split over what to do, the Pawnee bands began to fragment, following different leaders. By 1839, the four villages had split into six small villages, one north and several south of the Platte. In 1843, five hundred Dakota boldly and cruelly attacked the mission village in broad daylight. Sixty-seven Pawnee were killed, two hundred horses stolen, and the village burned down. Now even the remaining northern Pawnee villages fled south of the Platte. But the Dakota attacked there, too, and by the late 1840s, with the California gold rush, huge numbers of migrants had ruined Platte Valley resources and spread cholera throughout the tribe. In the early 1850s, the tribal population was reduced to roughly four thousand. The tribe was so weakened that the six small villages regrouped into only two villages and

moved eastward to avoid Dakota attacks, just as settlers were beginning to push into Nebraska and the Government was planning to open the area up as a territory.

In 1854, the United States government, anxious to secure Indian titles to the land in order to build a transcontinental railroad, passed the Kansas-Nebraska Act. The government's goal was to force Indians onto reservations and restrict their annual hunting movements. This was very difficult for the Pawnee. In the mid-1850s, the Pawnee were still living south of the Platte, and still starving. In 1857, they made a treaty with the United States, establishing a Pawnee Reservation. The Pawnee wanted the reservation to be south of the Platte, but the United States insisted that it be north of the river. The Pawnee sold the remainder of their lands outside of the reservation for six dollars per person. The reservation was north of the Platte along the Loup River, west of the city of Columbus (what is today Nance County). Complicating matters, this site was already occupied by the Mormons, who had established the town of Genoa (population two hundred), planted one thousand acres, and built a saw and grist mill. The Bureau of Indian Affairs ordered the Mormons to leave, and turned the settlement over to the Pawnee in the spring of 1860. Thus, the Pawnee reservation had good lands, timber, rich soil, and was already improved. The Pawnee established three villages there: two Skiri and another village composed of the South Bands. By 1860, their population was only 3,400, but they were still able to field roughly 500 mounted warriors. The Pawnee started cultivating, and, at this time, there was little pressure on them from white settlers.

However, the Pawnee cultural world was crumbling. The deaths of leaders and priests also meant the permanent loss of many rituals, tribal lore, and knowledge. Before the nineteenth century, each of the bands had maintained separate customs and traditions, but with the breakdown and recombination of the bands, questions arose over which leaders and rituals took precedence. Furthermore, with the loss of their ability to go to the West to hunt buffalo, the tribe not only faced starvation but also the loss of important elements needed in their rituals.

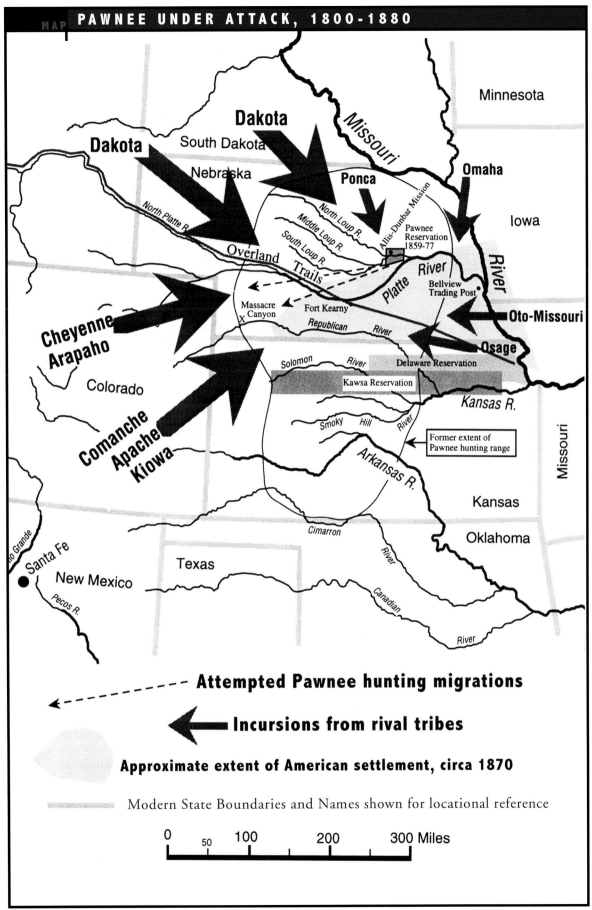

Minnesota

Dakota

South Dakota

Dakota

Nebraska

Ponca

Omaha

Iowa

Missouri

North Platte R.

North Loup R.

Middle Loup R.

South Loup R.

Allis-Dunbar Mission

Pawnee
Reservation
1859-77

Overland

Trails

Platte   *River*

Bellview
Trading Post

River

Oto-Missouri

Massacre
Canyon
X

Fort Kearny

Republican

River

Osage

Cheyenne
Arapaho

Colorado

Solomon

River

Delaware Reservation

Kawsa Reservation

Kansas R.

Comanche
Apache
Kiowa

Smoky   Hill   *River*

Former extent of
Pawnee hunting range

Arkansas R.

Missouri

Kansas

Cimarron

Oklahoma

Rio Grande

Santa Fe

New Mexico

Texas

River

Canadian

Pecos R.

River

- - - → **Attempted Pawnee hunting migrations**

← **Incursions from rival tribes**

Approximate extent of American settlement, circa 1870

Modern State Boundaries and Names shown for locational reference

0   50   100   200   300 Miles

Map by G.E. Bennett, UNK Geography

Nebraska State Historical Society

Pawnee lodges

Meanwhile, the Dakota stepped up their attacks. During the first year on their reservation alone, the Dakota attacked eight times. Dakota strategy was to wait until the Pawnee were on a buffalo hunt, leaving only the sick and elderly behind in the village; the Dakota found the villages virtually defenseless and could also destroy the Pawnee's crops. And, to the west, the Dakota burned huge sections of the prairie to drive the buffalo further to the west. This drew the Pawnee out further from their village base, leaving them more vulnerable to attack, as well as less likely to conduct a successful hunt, even if they were not molested.

The Demise of the Pawnee in Nebraska

During the 1860s, Pawnee population continued to decline sharply. By 1870, only 2,300 Pawnee remained. During this decade, the Pawnee did have a few good harvests and good hunts, and sometimes did manage to beat off Dakota attacks. But the Dakota were waging a war of attrition, which the Pawnee could not win, especially when coupled with a series of droughts and grasshopper scourges. Government payments to the tribe for lands were not enough, and a series of corrupt Indian

agents reduced this resource to the tribe even further. Dakota attacks on the Pawnee at this time were becoming especially brutal. The Dakota attacked to steal Pawnee horses and for revenge against Pawnee scouts for helping the United States Army. Also during this time, several railroads were built, bringing out buffalo hunters. As the herds began to disappear, there was more competition between the tribes for remaining resources.

Meanwhile, more and more United States settlers were beginning to enter Nebraska, and many of these settlers claimed that the Pawnee were "wasting" good lands that by right should go to United States settlers. Many argued that the Pawnee should be forced out of Nebraska altogether and relocated in the Indian Territory (now Oklahoma). In the early 1870s, the Pawnees were offered a choice: remove to Indian Territory or take up individual allotments of land, which would then open up the remaining lands within the reservation to white settlers.

Then, on August 5, 1873, one thousand Oglala and Brule Dakota trapped the Pawnee during their summer buffalo hunt in a ravine, where they slaughtered over seventy Pawnee while only losing two Dakota. After this attack in "Massacre

MEMORIAL DAY, THE SANDHILLS | by CHARLES **PEEK**

Canyon," near present day Trenton, Nebraska, nearly five hundred Pawnee decided to voluntarily leave Nebraska for Indian Territory. Over the next two years, the remaining Pawnee followed them. In 1875, the last of the Pawnee left Nebraska.

Oklahoma was not a land rich in buffalo nor capable of sustaining the horticultural traditions of the Pawnee, and so Pawnee population continued to decline. By 1885, only 1,045 Pawnee remained; by 1900, there were only 650. For centuries, the Pawnee had harnessed the forces of creation as they understood them to live a good life on the central plains. Ironically, during the nineteenth century, the Pawnee were destroyed by invaders who forced their own concept of the good life onto the central plains. The tragedy of the Pawnee was that they were ultimately destroyed by the forces of other peoples' creations.

Once I went to the Jannings family graves,
plotted with their progeny in mind.
It was not my family, but I admired
how the daughters planted, trimmed,
tucked everything neatly away.
They cursed the Sandozes as they worked
and seemed not uneasy there among the dead.

I have none to curse as I await my father's death
and I await not without anxiety.
I am prepared for him to pass,
and certainly he was ready long ago,
probably at least by the time he sunk into those silences,
broken by stares fixing you or what is right behind you,
one or the other.

But at each death, all the dead are raised,
some to judgment and some, I suppose, to approval.
At each death, the graves open a moment
and empty out their contents for a space.
Trim and tuck how we will, they find their way
back into the memories
that thought them laid to rest,
reminding us we are not so well preserved
as we would like to think,
that their remains do not disassociate
from what remains of us when they, or we,
all perishable goods,
are gone.

Selected **References**

Hyde, G.E. 1951. The Pawnee Indian. Norman: University of Oklahoma Press.

Weltfish, G. 1965. The lost universe: Pawnee life and culture. Lincoln: University of Nebraska Press.

West, E. 1995. The way to the west. Albuquerque: University of New Mexico Press.

White, R. 1983. The roots of dependency. Lincoln: University of Nebraska Press.

Wishart, D.J. 1994. An unspeakable sadness: The dispossession of the Nebraska Indians. Lincoln: University of Nebraska Press.

PRAIRIE VIEWS

Vernon L. Volpe, Professor of History

The prairie. Today's mind conjures up peaceful, perhaps prosperous, images of family farms, acres upon acres of cultivated fields or grazing livestock and charming if somewhat stagnant small towns. Except for the occasional state park or nature area, we experience mostly the remnants of the prairie, typically from the comfort of a motor vehicle speeding along the highway to some distant destination. If we are fortunate or wise enough, we may actually pause long enough to grasp the opportunity and contemplate a prairie landscape. Then we may experience the same sort of mixed emotions felt by the earliest visitors to the prairie. Our sense of satisfaction and, perhaps, wonderment may well be confused with feelings of insignificance if not dread, yet the desire to experience the prairie environment is hardly thereby diminished.

From the earliest Spanish explorers to those dispatched by the new United States government, the prairie engendered similar emotional responses, although conclusions about the prairie's ultimate appeal or usefulness have varied with the individual observer's preferences or prejudices. Today's prairie lands have barely withstood the onslaught of settlement and development, yet the prairie continues to fascinate and to inspire desire for further experience and greater knowledge.

The word prairie itself derives from the French and was originally meant to denote a small meadow. To the poet William Cullen Bryant, the prairie connoted "boundless and beautiful" land, "for which the speech of England has no name." Over time, the American usage has varied from a small, almost unusable clearing to an immense, almost overwhelming expanse of open, treeless land. Sometimes we confuse the term with the more specific designation of the Great Plains region, which extends from Texas to Canada between the Rocky Mountains and the 98th or 100th meridian. But the prairie has no specific boundary. Illinois may be the "Prairie State," but many states from Ohio to Colorado can likewise lay claim to containing large sections of prairie land. Some early observers of the prairie, especially west of the Missouri, suggested the region should be avoided.

Today no one would likely boast of hailing from the "Desert State," but many would take pride in being a son of the prairie (like Abraham Lincoln) or cherish the life of a girl who grew up in a little house on the Minnesota prairie. Yet, one suspects that today's notably nostalgic reflections on prairie life emanate more from the settlements and culture established on the prairie than from the natural environment itself. While our dread of the prairie environment may have eased as our ability to cross the land or derive income from it grew, we are not yet completely at ease with the land's desolation or its potential power over us.

From Coronado to Lewis and Clark

Coronado's men, searching for cities of gold on the Kansas prairies in the 1540s, first expressed a typical European response to this largely unknown land. Struck by the immensity of the landscape and the difficulty in crossing it, the Spaniards might be forgiven for their mostly negative reactions. Unprepared by their experience to navigate or, perhaps, to appreciate the prairie lands in the American interior, these brave, resourceful men, who had conquered the seas and great native cities to the south, retreated from the plains mostly disappointed and defeated. They had been reduced to marking their progress with buffalo dung while navigating with a sea compass; their reliance on comparing the land to the boundless ocean became a favorite metaphor for describing the open prairie to those not yet familiar with its seemingly endless horizons. Perhaps the first Europeans to be intimidated by the prairie, they would not be the last to find the challenge of surviving on the prairie, much less describing it, just beyond their means.

Natives had long inhabited the prairies and found this environment quite suitable to their needs. However, Indians did not possess the preconceived notions, or the desire to reap rewards, that the Europeans held in abundance. Indian populations, moreover, remained small enough to never quite overwhelm the prairie's ability to sustain life, while the region's river valleys and scattered groups of trees provided at least some respite from the prairie's occasional bad weather and unrelenting immensity. The Native Americans lived upon this land, and while they may have traversed it from place to place in order to survive, they did not have to reach for adjectives or develop metaphors to describe the land to those who had never witnessed it. However, this challenge immediately loomed for the early explorers, European and American alike, and, in a sense, it remains the task for modern writers who seek to capture the prairie's essence for those who may have seen the land but never really experienced it.

Coronado's men covered the plains on horseback; other early Spanish and French explorers could at least observe prairie lands while paddling a river in the comfort of a canoe. Under such circumstances, assessments of the prairie lands were likely to be much less harsh and, not surprisingly, more philosophical. Romantic notions emerge rather naturally while paddling a flowing stream. The great American explorers, Meriwether Lewis and William Clark, likewise presented mostly positive images of the prairies they encountered in 1804-1806 while paddling up (or just as likely walking along) the mighty Missouri on their quest to find a passage to the Pacific. These most observant captains noticed in particular the fertile soils and abundant wildlife along the Missouri riverbanks.

Garden or Desert

Following in the wake of Lewis and Clark's keelboat and canoes, those accompanying the path-breaking fur-trading enterprises into the Rocky Mountain West likewise remarked in passing upon the prairie's peculiar features. Most praised the Missouri River landscape, a practice recorded by Washington Irving, then America's most celebrated writer, but some noted the appeal of the Platte River country. In 1839, Philadelphia ornithologist, John K. Townsend, extolled the "rich and luxuriant prairies" lining the Platte and its "verdant islands." His fur trading party camped along the river among "a beautiful grove of cottonwood trees" and later embarked on the expected buffalo hunt. John Bradbury, a naturalist from England, joined the overland Astorians journeying up the Missouri in 1811. Bradbury, too, recorded the abundant growth of the prairie grasses and groves, predicted its certain fertility, and marveled at its wonderful beauty: "I have never seen a place, however, embellished by art, equal to this in beauty."

A most common reaction while ruminating on the region's nature was to note not only the desolation but also the unusual appeal of the nearly empty landscape. In 1811, Henry Brackenridge accompanied a fur trade enterprise up the Missouri. This young author described for eastern audiences the solitude of the boundless prairie that did not necessarily dull the mind, but allowed it to experience the "immeasureable immensity of the scene." Brackenridge testified to the inspirational powers of the prairie: "the intellectual faculties are endued with an energy, a vigor, a spring, not to be described."

George Catlin, famous as a painter and historian of the Plains Indians, traveled the region extensively in the 1830s. To Catlin, the vast prairie plains provided "a place where the mind could think volumes." Not

surprisingly, those who followed, mostly on horseback, painted a slightly different portrait of the prairie and its potential.

The first official observers of the American prairie beyond the Missouri came under the auspices of the U.S. Army. For a time a distinct corps, the Corps of Topographical Engineers embarked on its mission to survey the way westward while reporting on the region's natural features. Rather atypical military men, these Army engineers possessed excellent training and a zeal for scientific discovery, yet they, too, at first seemed bewildered by the prairie landscape. Zebulon Pike, later to meet a hero's death in the War of 1812, first set out overland in 1806 to explore the more southerly reaches of the Louisiana Purchase. Although he failed to ascend the Colorado peak named in his honor, and he suffered arrest at the hands of Spanish authorities, Pike further advanced knowledge of the American interior. Indeed, Pike first referred to the "sandy deserts" of the prairie region, helping later to instill the myth of the Great American Desert in at least some American minds.

In his 1820 expedition, Stephen Long would develop still further this unappealing picture of the plains region. The Long report, written with the assistance of his biologist Edwin James, fixed on the region the label of "Great American Desert," particularly upon the prairie lands south of the Platte River. Major Long and his team of scientists appeared qualified to render such judgements; indeed, for the first time, trained specialists had been dispatched to make careful observations of the western domain. The Long expedition, however, encountered numerous difficulties, perhaps motivating the harsh assessment that the region appeared "almost wholly unfit for cultivation" and even "uninhabitable by a people depending upon agriculture for their subsistence." Yet, the Long report was not unrelentingly depressing; in fact, it noted that the Platte country was "enlivened with great numbers of wildlife," in particular, "immense herds of bison." The report, infamous for its dreary portrait of the plains, recorded amusement in sighting the "unsightly figure and impolitic movements

Man hath no power in all this glorious work:
The hand that built the firmament hath heaved
And smoothed these verdant swells, and sown their slopes
With herbage, planted them with island groves,
And hedged them round with forests. Fitting floor
For this magnificent temple of the sky–
With flowers whose glory and whose multitude
Rival the constellations! The great heavens
Seem to stoop down upon the scene in love,
A nearer vault, and of a tenderer blue,
Than that which bends above our eastern hills.

of the bison," while it delighted at the "beauty and fleetness of the antelope" and the "social comfort and neatness of the prairie dog." The report, nonetheless, reached the rather illogical conclusion that this "barren" region seemed populated with far more wildlife "than its meagre production [was] sufficient to support."

Not all Americans were privy to Long's government report, but the critical assessment did have its repercussions. Early farmers of the eastern woodlands required sufficient quantities of wood and water to sustain their brand of agriculture. The nearly treeless, apparently arid prairie lands could hardly be seen as inviting. Indeed, the Long report had prophesied that the region provided the United States more a remote barrier from potential invaders than a region destined to be settled by family farmers.

Others saw the region's potential as a gigantic Indian reserve, allowing natives to be safely removed from the likely areas of white settlement to the east. Although the Long report might be dismissed for its failure to foresee the region's ultimate agricultural potential, its conclusions reflected the limits of current thinking and technology.

Long's report was not the only contemporary observation that viewed the treeless prairie as uninviting to America's restless farmers. The prairie's ominous nature appeared in influential literary accounts as well. Indeed, the famous American novelist, James Fenimore Cooper, relied on the Long account to construct his image of the western landscape in one of his most noted novels, The Prairie (1827). Besides drawing on the Long account for specific western scenes and landmarks, Cooper borrowed Long's depiction of a barren landscape to portray the prairie as nearly an overwhelming, primitive element in his novel. As the novel's main "character," the prairie loomed over the story and the human actors as an ever-present, dominant, and threatening force.

Although William Cullen Bryant's poem "The Prairies," published in the 1830s, proved more appreciative of the "encircling vastness" of the prairie, what he called the "gardens of the Desert," Cooper's narrative contributed to the Long prophesy that the western prairies would serve as both a barrier and a shield. Few would want to emigrate there while the region could ward off potential invaders.

Perhaps no force, not even the metaphorical power of the boundless prairies, could long stem the tide of American settlement westward. Pausing briefly to settle the Mississippi valley, this relentless surge of westering families stood prepared to leap both the Mississippi and the Missouri, waiting for the fur trappers and the government explorers to point out the proper path. Fur trapping enterprises, founded by such entrepreneurs as John Jacob Astor and William Ashley, led in the field by their hardy associates, such as Jedediah Smith and Jim Bridger, had scouted much of the plains and the passes across the mountains. This information, however, remained virtually secret in the hands of a few well-informed insiders. Although much had been written about the western landscape and its prairie borderland, many

TOPOGRAPHICAL MAP

OF THE

ROAD FROM MISSOURI TO OREGON

COMMENCING AT THE MOUTH OF THE KANSAS IN THE MISSOURI RIVER

AND ENDING AT THE MOUTH OF THE WALLAH-WALLAH IN THE COLUMBIA

In VII Sections

SECTION II

From the field notes and journal of Capt. J. C. Frémont,

and from sketches and notes made on the ground by his assistant Charles Preuss

Compiled by Charles Preuss, 1846

By order of the Senate of the United States.

SCALE — 10 MILES TO THE INCH.

Lithogr by E. Weber & Co. Baltimore.

North Fork

South Fork

SIOUX INDIANS

Longitude 102°

101°

REMARKS

1. The figures on the road indicate the distance in miles from Westport Landing.
2. Game — Antelope and Buffalo, the latter in inumerable bands.
3. Timber is extremely scarce, except on the islands. Some driftwood and buffalo excrement makes the fuel, as that of the camels does in the deserts of Arabia.
4. Good guard ought to be kept. Pawnees, if they do not kill, will at least take what they can from the travellers by force if they are strong enough, and by stealth if too weak to act openly.
5. With this section the prairie ends, and the barren sage (artemisia) country begins.

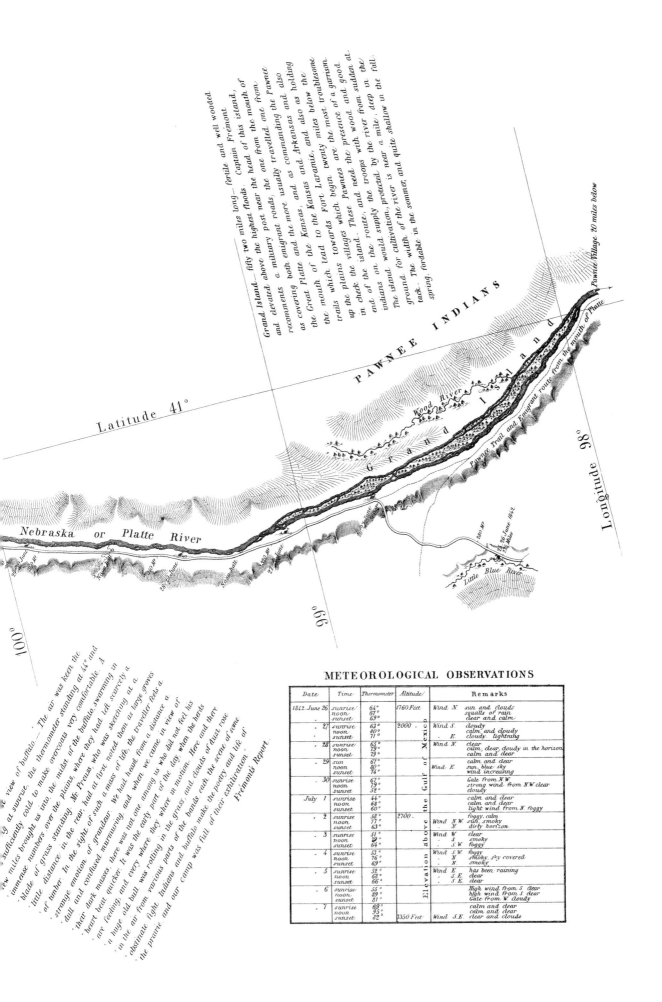

Grand Island — fifty two miles long — fertile and well wooded and elevated above the highest floods — Captain Fremont reconnents a military post near the head of this island, and elevated above the highest floods — the one from emigrant roads, the more usually travelled the Pawnee as covering both the Great Platte and the more usually travelled the Pawnee the mouth of the Great Platte and the Kansas and Arkansas and also holding the mouth of the Kansas and Arkansas, and also below the trails which lead to Fort Laramie, twenty miles below the up the plains towards Fort Laramie, twenty miles below the in check the island. These Pawnees are the most troublesome end of the island route, and near the presence of a garrison indians on the other supply, protected by the river from sudden at indians would supply, protected by the troops with wood, deep in the ground for cultivation, is near a mile, deep in the fall tack. The width of the river is near a mile, deep in the fall spring, fordable in the summer, and quite shallow in the

PAWNEE INDIANS

Latitude 41°

Nebraska or Platte River

Wood River

Grand Island

Pawnee Trail and Emigrant route from the mouth of Platte

Pawnee Village 30 mils below

Little Blue River

Longitude 98°

99°

100°

iew of buffalo. The air was keen the sufficiently cold to make overcoats very comfortable. A miles brought us into the midst of the buffalo, swarming in immense numbers over the plains, where they had left scarcely a blade of grass standing. Mr. Preuss, who was sketching at a little distance in the rear, had at first noted them as large groves of timber. In the sight of such a mass of life, the traveller feels a strange emotion of grandeur. We had heard from a distance a dull and confused murmuring, and when we came in view of their heart beat quicker. It was the early part of the day, when the herds are feeding; and every where they where in motion. Here and there in the air from various parts of the bands each the scene of some obstinate fight. Indians and buffalo make the poetry and life of the prarie, and our camp was full of their exhilaration and life of Fremont's Report.

METEOROLOGICAL OBSERVATIONS

Date	Time	Thermometer	Altitude		Remarks
1842. June 26	sunrise	64°	1760 Feet		Wind N. sun and clouds
.	noon	67°			squalls of rain
.	sunset	69°			clear and calm
. 27	sunrise	63°	2000		Wind S. cloudy
.	noon	80°		M	calm and cloudy
.	sunset	71°		E.	cloudy lightning
. 28	sunrise	65°		o	clear
.	noon	79°		f	calm, clear, cloudy in the horizon
.	sunset	79°			calm and clear
. 29	sun	67°		M	calm and clear
.	noon	80°		e	sun, blue sky
.	sunset	74°		x	wind increasing
. 30	sunrise	67°		i	Gale from N.W.
.	noon	79°		c	strong wind from N.W. clear
.	sunset	52°		o	cloudy
July 1	sunrise	44°			calm and clear
.	noon	68°		t	calm and clear
.	sunset	60°		h	light wind from N. foggy
. 2	sunrise	58°	2700.	e	foggy, calm
.	noon	77°			Wind N.W. sun, smoky
.	sunset	63°		G	N. dirty horizon
. 3	sunrise	51°		u	Wind W. clear
.	noon	79°		l	S. smoky
.	sunset	64°		f	S.W. foggy
. 4	sunrise	53°			Wind S.W. foggy
.	noon	76°		a	N. smoky, sky covered
.	sunset	69°		b	N. smoky
. 5	sunrise	52°		o	Wind E. has been raining
.	noon	68°		v	S.E. clear
.	sunset	66°		e	S.E. clear
. 6	sunrise	55°			high wind from S. clear
.	noon	89°		E	high wind from S. clear
.	sunset	81°		l	Gale from W. cloudy
. 7	sunrise	69°		e	calm and clear
.	noon	93°		v	calm and clear
.	sunset	82°	3350 Feet		Wind S.E. clear and clouds

John C. Frémont

Americans eagerly awaited a complete and more accurate picture before setting off on an overland migration of epic proportions. The situation was ripe for a man of action, and even better for an imaginative couple with a flair for the dramatic.

John Charles Frémont

Lieutenant John Charles Frémont of the Topographical Corps possessed few obvious advantages; illegitimate origins and no family fortune limited his prospects even in America's booming society. His future father-in-law, Senator Thomas Hart Benton of Missouri, initially preferred that his young daughter of seventeen avoid this young man with such meager prospects. But Jessie Benton defied her beloved father, hoping correctly that the powerful Senator would reconcile himself to the marriage once the couple confessed their love and their elopement. Both the Senator and his favorite daughter would advance the young man's career, helping to create a new American hero that almost brought Frémont to the presidency. Jessie, in particular, would assist John in preparing the official government reports of his overland travels along the Oregon Trail beginning in 1842. She would add colorful images of the prairie landscape and memorable vignettes of her husband's travels. Although pregnancy and

proper etiquette decreed that she remain home during John's travels, Jessie's help proved invaluable and quite remarkable. Unable to view firsthand the prairie lands west of St. Louis, her work would supplement her husband's records by relying on her knowledge of literary accounts and confidence in her creative talents.

"Everywhere the rose is met with, and reminds us of cultivated gardens and civilization," the Frémont couple wrote in 1843. "It is scattered over the prairies in small bouquets, and when glittering in the dews and waving in the pleasant breeze of the early morning, is the most beautiful of the prairie flowers." Such pleasing portraits of the prairie grasslands surely reflected Jessie's influence, although John, too, secretly admitted his preference for the prairie over all other landscapes. Long and his men had complained about the "inhospitable deserts of the Platte," and recorded that the monotony of the vast, unbroken plain proved as "tiresome to the eye and fatiguing to the spirit" as the ocean's dreary solitude. But the Frémonts answered, as some other writers had, that the prairie did not really tire the eye. Instead, the remarkable landscape invigorated the spirit: "The grand simplicity of the prairie is its peculiar beauty. . . .The uniformity is never sameness, and in his exhilaration the voyager feels even the occasional field of red grass waving in the breeze pleasant to his eye." Hardly akin to a desert, the Platte valley, in the Frémonts' view, "resembled a garden in the splendor of fields of varied flowers, which filled the air with fragrance." Along what would become the Great Platte River Road stretched prairies "of the richest verdue"; the islands in the Platte were "covered with dense and heavy woods" and surrounded by "a luxuriant growth of grass."

Frémont's travel along the region's riverbanks and during a favorable climatic period no doubt affected this judgement, but the couple's buoyant optimism and romantic nature likewise colored their memorable view of the prairie setting. In marked contrast to the Long report, the Frémonts concluded that the largely prairie landscape from the Mississippi to the Rockies was indeed "admirably adapted to

This [Frèmont] report proves conclusively that the country for several hundred miles from the frontier of Missouri is exceedingly beautiful and fertile; alternate woodland and prairie, and certain portions well supplied with water. It also proves that the valley of the River Platte has a very rich soil, affording great facilities for emigrants to the west of the Rocky Mountains.

agricultural purposes, and would support a large agricultural and pastoral population." Perhaps the Frémonts had not foreseen the ultimately harmful environmental impact of large-scale emigration, farming, and overgrazing, but their exhilarating images of the prairie better captured both the spirit of the land and its potential to provide succulence for both body and soul.

Published by the United States Senate and by several private printers, the report of Frémont's first two overland missions in 1842 and 1843-1844 did more than guide prospective pioneers to Oregon and California. These "best-selling" reports created a much more pleasing portrait of the prairie plains, helping to create an insatiable appeal for the entire West, the prairies and beyond. Jessie would later boast that from the ashes of her husband's campfires, great cities grew. Indeed, various government reports notwithstanding, eager pioneers eventually poured into the prairie regions, hardly waiting for the government to organize the territories or negotiate with the native inhabitants. Generous land policies, such as the 1862 Homestead Law, no doubt prodded the wavering, but so did such glowing accounts of the western prairie that the Frémonts and others provided an expectant populace.

In retrospect, the Frémont reports consti-tuted a key turning point in images of the prairie. Few observers or interpreters of the prairies would henceforth portray the region or its future in such stark, depressing terms as once had been more common. True, the prairie still awaited conquest by rails wrought of iron, tracks to transport pioneer families nearly as hardy, to settle the demanding landscape. And some novelists, such as

Norway's O. E. Rolvaag, might still resort to employing the literary device of showing nature's dominant power over insignificant human beings on the prairie. However, decades of both geographical and literary exploration had prepared those who would settle the land and otherwise experience the prairie region's peculiar attraction. The prairie's ability to overawe, even intimidate, may be diminished, but its ability to fasci-nate and inspire mere humans, hopefully, will never disappear.

Selected**References**

Jackson D. and M. L. Spence, eds. 1970. Expeditions of John Charles Frémont: Travels from 1838-1844. Vol. 1. Urbana: University of Illinois Press.

Thacker, R. 1989. The great prairie fact and literary imagina-tion. Albuquerque: University of New Mexico Press.

Thwaites, R.G., ed. 1904-1907. Early western travels. 1748-1846. Cleveland: Arthur Clark Co.

LAW AND ORDER

IN EARLY CENTRAL NEBRASKA

James N. Gilbert, Professor of Criminal Justice

Organized efforts to contain lawlessness within most central Nebraska counties began in earnest during the 1870s. Prior to this decade, few counties had either towns, population, or criminality extensive enough to warrrant peace officers or courts. When railroad expansion provided a means and motivation to settle the fertile prairie, towns and crime rapidly followed. The early towns of central Nebraska were not free from law violators. Despite media stereotypes which would portray only selected communities as "wild," cattle towns such as Dodge City, Kansas, or the booming mining towns of Tombstone and Deadwood, Nebraska communities also had their unfortunate share of felonious trouble.

Small at first, tiny railroad stops along the Platte and throughout central portions of the state developed into towns so quickly that by the 1880s, the vast majority of present day communities had been firmly established. It would be during this early period of rapid growth, from 1870 to 1890, that interpersonal violence and criminality in general would peak. Two basic population trends significantly contributed to the immediate need for law and order: transient drifters and cowboys employed to drive herds northward. Drifters of various sorts were common throughout the newly settled Great Plains communities. Mainly men, these rootless individuals were often trans-

plants from eastern or southern cities, but the majority were former ranch hands and homegrown criminals from throughout the western region of the nation. Attracted to the recently arrived immigrants and their savings, such individuals specialized in gambling, occasional robbery, and frequent theft.

Adding to the professional criminal population which centered upon vice activities came the hard-working but pleasure-seeking cowboy. Pouring into the Nebraska rail terminus towns, the cattle herders would come into continual conflict with stable, local citizens. Early Nebraska newspapers frequently reported the various crimes of the drifter and cowboy. Illegal activity among the cattle herders was so great that the term "cowboy" (unlike today's usage) was considered a negative, highly derogatory term. When used in any Western newspaper during the later nineteenth century, the term implied a criminal type, or, at the very least, an undesirable desperado.

In 1874, the dreaded "cowboy scourge" struck Kearney, culminating in criminal homicide. For months, herders had been riding through town, shooting indiscriminately at citizens and buildings. After firing upon the town Marshal, the cowboys were confronted by thirty armed citizens and driven out of town. Shortly thereafter, unsupervised horses belonging to the herders damaged a local man's crop and were held

Nebraska State Historical Society

Skinning a brand on a maverick, 1887   Butcher Collection

by the aggrieved party until damages were paid. A cowboy leader promptly shot and killed the Kearney farmer and released the horses. After an intense manhunt, the perpetrator was captured and sentenced to the penitentiary, narrowly missing "stretching hemp" by outraged Kearney citizens.

While cowboy-connected crime often resulted from excessive drink and celebration at the end of the cattle trail, other crimes were premeditated and committed by residents or transients who drifted between communities. Arrest records of the time demonstrate that most fined or jailed offenders were locals, who committed larceny or disturbing the peace offenses. The most infamous crime in 19th century central Nebraska was the 1878 mass murder committed by Samuel D. Richards. A drifter who befriended his victims, Richards brutally murdered four children and two adults in homesteads south of Kearney. Tracked and arrested in Steubenville, Ohio, by the Kearney County Sheriff and a private Pinkerton detective, Richards was returned and executed by rope before a large crowd in the southeast corner of Minden's courtyard.

As rough and tumble as Kearney was, Ogallala enjoyed a far more violent reputation. From 1875 to 1885, the community was often referred to as the "Gomorrah of the cattle trail." Due to strategic cattle loading pens established by the railroad, Ogallala

became the most popular cattle driving point in central Nebraska. Before economic conditions shifted the cattle drives elsewhere, Ogallala rivaled the infamous Dodge City in its frequency of homicide and vice, and was visited at various times by many frontier lawmen and gunmen, including Bat Masterson. During this same period, another notorious central Nebraska crime occurred near Broken Bow in Custer County. Two recently arrived homesteaders, Ami Ketchum and Luther Mitchell, shot and killed a deputy sheriff following an accusation of cattle theft. Both men were quickly captured, lynched, and their bodies subsequently burned. The 1878 "man burning" incident would, for many years, be utilized as a gruesome deterrence by large ranching interests against cattle theft by impoverished settlers.

Another notorious Custer County execution in 1888 involved a man who was purposely hanged twice for double homicide. Albert E. Haunstine was convicted of killing two deputy constables who were attempting to serve him with an arrest warrant for theft. Just prior to the execution, relatives of the murder victims rigged the hanging rope so it would break when first used. When the rope snapped during the first attempt, the sheriff replaced the rope and the trap door dropped a second time, resulting in a symbolic double hanging.

First Jail in Broken Bow, Nebraska   Butcher Collection

Early Nebraska Jails

While sensational crimes occurred with surprising frequency throughout the Platte river and central regions of the state, most crimes were far less life-threatening. For example, in 1875, the first criminal case in Pierce County accused a resident of illegally catching fish with a net. Similarly, Hall County's first court case involved a claim of mail tampering. Then, as now, the vast majority of those arrested were drunks and thieves. The fining of such individuals provided an early tax base for the emerging communities and necessitated the construction of crude county jails. The original jails were typically small. Frontier County's first jail building measured only eight feet square, less than a single modern prison cell. Often initially built of wood, most county jail facilities were eventually reconstructed of stone or brick. Many of the hastily erected wooden jails proved dangerous and sometimes deadly. The first jail in Saline County, a small wooden structure, burned in 1874, killing four inmates. When one or more of the prisoners attempted to escape by burning the lock off their cell door, a rapid fire developed, killing three alleged thieves and a woman accused of murdering her husband by lacing his apple pie with strychnine.

The Buffalo County jail was constructed

in 1876 of Kansas limestone and served for a decade as the most secure correctional facility within hundreds of miles. However, not all suspects would be transported to neighboring counties for confinement due to the absence of a local jail. In 1881, Valley county's first murder suspect, Neils Gotfreidsen, was "kept and confined" in an upstairs bedroom of Sheriff Herbert Thurston's home, as Ord had yet to construct a jail facility. Sherman County faced a similar problem when a local murder suspect was ordered by the court to remain restricted to his parent's home, as no jail was available in 1877.

The early jails of central Nebraska were normally built within or close to the county courthouse. Numerous legal executions were performed in the courtyard of county justice buildings, as state government in Lincoln did not assume responsibility for capital punishment until 1903. Typically, the condemned would be walked out to the gallows and allowed to make a short speech. Often the sheriff would construct a privacy fence around the execution site, but, in many instances, large crowds destroyed the barriers. In 1885, a convicted wife murderer in Polk county witnessed a sizable mob trample two fences constructed around his scaffold. This seemed to appease citizens,

D.O. Luce's underground stable for stolen horses near Anselmo, Nebraska, 1889

Crime in the city was punishment in the field
with the blindfelled crowd and a hooded
soldier at ease like a coiled serpent
taut as the bent cross on his armor.
The lunatic and depraved left the cry quarter
for the long march to circle the gallows
with the hanging judge who tore his bible
pruning the articles of faith and disorder
to soothe the heretic and bereaved.
Punishment in the field was crime in the city.
The rogue's bell swayed under the moon
as the helmsman carried a frayed noose
holy water and the triumphant blade.
Was it how we punished the wealthy
who plundered, robbed, and killed
or the poor and how many we killed?
The accused was tied to a quarter horse
for a gallop above the hollow ground
wearing her tar and feathers like a gift.
Crime in the city was punishment in the field
with quicksand and rope a foot too short.

from The Mississippi Review

as a local newspaper reported a "satisfied and orderly" crowd respectfully heard the murderer's speech, then witnessed his seven foot plunge through the trap door. Unfortunately, not all hangings within view of the courthouse were legal executions. An early Columbus mob lynched an accused murderer as he was walked back to jail from county court. The vigilantes utilized a large cottonwood tree directly in front of the courthouse. The fury of the crowd was satisfied only after the dead prisoner's body had been tied behind an ox wagon, dragged to the nearby riverbank, and thrown through a hole chopped in the ice.

Nineteenth Century Lawmen

Law enforcement in late nineteenth century central Nebraska modeled that found throughout other midwest and far west states. The positions of night watchman and town constable represented the bottom rung of frontier policing. Next came the various town marshals or, as they were also known, chiefs of police. The county sheriff followed, with U.S. Marshals possessing the highest status. While U.S. Marshals were more frequently employed in territorial regions, they often passed through central Nebraska or assisted local authorities in the investigation of federal crimes. Federal marshals and county sheriffs routinely patrolled vast areas of land. When "out on the scout," early lawmen would search shacks and soddies for fugitives or contraband whiskey, always prowling through ravines for stolen horses or cattle. Due to the nature of settlement within central Nebraska, city peace officers were often in place prior to the election of county sheriffs. When the population justified the creation of a county bureaucracy, elections were held for various county positions, including the office of sheriff. As the chief law enforcement officer of the county, the sheriff enforced laws throughout all unincorporated areas. In addition, the sheriff's office had responsibility for daily jail operations and often received substantial income from a fee system designed to contain and feed each county jail inmate.

Election to the sheriff's office was highly political, as successful candidates usually mirrored the dominant political party of the county. Eagerly sought after due to the profit potential of the position, the frontier sheriff spent much of his time collecting county taxes, receiving (as with his jail fees) a percentage of the total amount. Additional daily duties involved the service of court orders, selling delinquent tax property at public auction, and a host of miscellaneous chores, including brand inspection. Most central Nebraska counties have elected fifteen to twenty different sheriffs since their founding, most initially taking office in the early 1870s.

Despite the importance of the county sheriff, the majority of law enforcement activity was conducted on the town or village level. When early settlements grew large enough to necessitate a town charter, the selection of a peace officer was typically the first official appointment. Holding office at the pleasure of the mayor and city council, city marshals typically were aided by a small force of assistant marshals or town policemen. When emergency conditions warranted, both the sheriff and city marshal could deputize an unlimited number of citizens for assistance. Additionally, some early Nebraska communities had state militia units which were more frequently employed to battle criminal disorder than for military defense. Organized in 1873, the Kearney Guards were typical of such organizations. Comprised mainly of Civil War veterans, the forty-man militia group fought several gun battles with herders and was credited with freeing the city from its "cowboy reign of terror."

The duties of the city peace officer were sporadic and extremely varied. Naturally, public safety and law enforcement concerns came first, with service duties following. As there was little practical or financial value in arresting city residents, minor crimes were commonly ignored or settled with a warning. When an arrest was made, it was more often than not for larceny or assaultive behavior linked to excessive drinking. The offending party could be confined in the city jail, or simply fined. City officers were also responsible for a host of duties not associated with crime. These generally included keeping rubbish off the streets, monitoring excessive carriage speed, collecting license fees from saloons and houses of prostitution, and fire prevention.

The newly-established Nebraska town marshal commonly obtained a copy of Harlow's Duties of Sheriffs and Constables, a popular nineteenth-century manual published in California, which instructed frontier law officers on police duties and included copies of proper forms and a schedule of fees. As reflected within an official 1880s inventory, the equipment of city police was limited but highly utilitarian, including one water bucket, a tin cup, two slop buckets, one pair of handcuffs, and two blankets. Firearms were generally owned by the officers, although an ammunition allowance was furnished.

With the approach of the twentieth century, most Nebraska communities had gained a critical mass of rooted, law-abiding inhabitants. The changing demographics deterred much transient criminality, and the cowboys relocated elsewhere along with their herds. While sporadic law breaking continued through the early 20th century, reaching dangerous levels during prohibition and the gangster era, central Nebraska's truly lawless days were over.

Selected**References**

Bassett, S. 1916. Buffalo County Nebraska and its people. Chicago: S.J. Clarke.

Chaput, D. 1994. Virgil Earp: Western peace officer. Norman: University of Oklahoma Press.

Hollon, E. 1974. Frontier violence. London: Oxford University Press.

Howell, A. 1981-83. Tales of Buffalo County. Volumes 1-6. Kearney, Nebraska: Buffalo County Historical Society.

Jordon, P. 1970. Frontier law and order. Lincoln: University of Nebraska Press.

Lee, W. 1988. Wild towns of Nebraska. Caldwell, Idaho: Caxton Printers.

---. 1993. Bad men and bad towns. Caldwell, Idaho: Caxton Printers.

Nebraska Sheriff's Association. 1994. 100 years: A commemorative history 1894-1994. Dallas: Taylor Publishing.

Shirley, G. 1969. Law west of Fort Smith: A history of frontier justice. Lincoln: University of Nebraska Press.

Trachtman, P. 1974. The gunfighters. New York: Time-Life Books.

PRENTICE "PRINT" OLIVE

CATTLEMAN

Gordon J. Blake, Professor Emeritus of Economics

The Olives, especially Print Olive, became one of Nebraska's most famous, or infamous, citizens, depending upon one's point of view. At the end of the Civil War, in which Olive had been wounded, he returned to the family home near Taylor, in central Texas. Like many others, he and his father and brothers began to gather and brand wild longhorn cattle, a dangerous activity. The danger was not all from chasing wild cattle through brushy and difficult terrain. Some of the peril came from men who were in competition for the cattle; some came from rustlers who preferred to steal cattle already caught than to catch their own. The rustlers altered brands, and, if caught or suspected, gunfights frequently ensued.

As the situation grew more competitive and dangerous in Texas, the Olives decided that it would be in their interest to move north. They were in nearly open warfare with groups that they believed had stolen many of their cattle. The Olives had tried to secure redress through the courts, but believed that justice had not prevailed. Thus, they came north, harboring the belief that they could not depend upon the law and courts for protection from cattle thieves. It was an attitude that was to lead them into trouble in Nebraska.

In the Spring of 1869, Isom Prentice "Print" Olive helped drive a herd of cattle

from Texas to Fort Kearny. After arriving, Print Olive helped drive a herd of steers to Ash Creek range to the west of Fort Kearny and north of the Platte River. According to Harry Chrisman, who has written extensively about the Olives, Print Olive drove another herd from Texas to Abline, Kansas, arriving June 11, 1872. Upon arriving in Abilene, "most of the cows were cut out and sold to a Nebraska rancher on the Platte . . . going to Carter and Coe, at their new ranch operated under the name of John Bratt & Co." Because of these activities, Olive came to the conclusion that there was adequate open range in the area to accommodate new herds. He was also probably aware that the range farther west in the Panhandle of Nebraska and in Colorado and Wyoming was becoming crowded by the mid to late 1870s.

In 1877, the Olives moved to Nebraska and placed fifteen thousand head of cattle on the range along the Dismal river for a distance of twenty to thirty miles west of the current town of Dunning, Nebraska. In 1878, they moved farther south and opened a ranch on a school section four miles down river from what is now the town of Callaway, Custer County, Nebraska. The cattlemen thought that the area would never be settled by farmers. Most ranchers owned very little land, only purchasing enough for some corrals and several small buildings. They would establish a family residence in a nearby

The Olive residence in Lexington, Nebraska   photo by G.J. Blake

community, such as Lexington, then called Plum Creek. Sometimes, they also purchased land along streams in order to have assured access to water for their herds. Other times, they purchased land along streams in order to deny others access to water. Cattle would not stray very far from sources of water, so by controlling access to water, ranchers were able to control adjacent areas of range. Most of the land that they used was open range, unsettled land in the public domain, which belonged to the Federal Government or to railroads as a result of land grants, and could be grazed free of charge.

Custer County

In 1877, the cattlemen of the area organized Custer County because eastern counties had been trying to tax property in the unorganized area and because they thought that it would be a way to stop cattle and horse stealing. In fact, the sheriff of Dawson County supported the organization of Custer County because he thought it would have that effect. Cattlemen dominated the Custer County government for several years. However, a rapid influx of homesteaders caused the cattlemen to lose their majority on the Board of Commissioners by 1880.

The Olives had the largest herd in Custer County in the years 1879 and 1880, according to an estimate made by Frank Young,

who was the Clerk of Custer County at the time. He estimated that there were 64,758 cattle in the county. The Olives had a herd of 31,271, or 48 percent of the total. The second largest herd was held by Durfee and Gasman, who had a total of 19,070 head. Thus, the two largest outfits in the county accounted for nearly seventy-eight percent of the total. The Olive herd was probably grazing over 200,000 to 300,000 acres of land, nearly one fifth of that large county of 2,592 square miles.

Unlike areas in eastern Colorado and some parts of eastern Wyoming, much of the land used by the Olives and other ranchers was adaptable to row crop or mixed farming, especially along rivers and streams. As time went on, the influx of homesteaders and other settlers increased. These new settlers were farmers, not ranchers. Even though depicted otherwise in popular literature, farmers and ranchers did not invariably view each other as enemies. Of course, ranchers did view settlers who tried to farm on marginal land as interlopers and fools. However, many acts of individual kindness between the two groups have been recorded, such as instances of ranchers providing meat or loaning a cow for milking and of homesteaders providing ranchers with vegetables, milk, or butter.

Nevertheless, the potential for conflict existed. The Olives, as the largest ranchers in the area, were the most likely to experience difficulty. The problem was compounded when, on August 17, 1878, much of the range from the Dismal River to the Olive Ranch headquarters burned. This led the ranchers, including the Olives, to move their cattle eastward to adequate grazing areas, exposing their herds to areas partially settled by homesteaders. Some of these settlers were rustlers and thieves, but others were veterans of the Union Army and resented the very presence of Confederate veterans in Nebraska, especially those as successful as the Olives.

An especially troublesome area was on Clear and Muddy Creeks. The Olive cattle were not only in direct contact with homesteaders, but some of them were in Sherman County where the county government was very unsympathetic to the problems of cattlemen. Here, the Olives began to suffer heavy losses from cattle thieves. It was not in the nature of the Olives, especially Print Olive, to take these losses lying down. He was described by S. D. Butcher in his <u>History of Custer County</u> "as a good sort of man, and very generous and courteous to those with whom he was on good terms, [but] he was an implacable enemy and . . . adept in the use of firearms." His brother, Bob, was described as a "bad man when aroused." Bob Olive was using the alias of Bob Stevens in Nebraska, since we was wanted for murder in Texas, having shot his sister's abusive husband.

Print Olive assigned his brother, Bob, the task of ferreting out the thieves. A small rancher in the area of Clear Creek, who had also been losing cattle, informed Bob Olive that he suspected Manly Cople and Ami Ketchum. Many of the stolen cattle were simply killed, and their hind quarters skinned and sold as meat in Kearney and Grand Island. They referred to the beef as "slow elk." One guest of some settlers was served a meal featuring "elk," which he said tasted remarkably like beef to him. Some of the settlers probably believed that since the cattle were grazing on land that did not belong to the ranchers, they should have as much right to the cattle as the ranchers did to the land.

Ketchum and Mitchell

Of even more concern to the cattlemen than those settlers butchering their cattle were rustlers who were stealing large numbers and shipping them to markets with falsified bills of sale. Bob Olive found such a group in pens in Kearney. The falsified bill of sale was the work of Ami Ketchum, a blacksmith turning farmer and living with Luther Mitchell on Clear Creek, east of the present location of Westerville. Print Olive demanded that Sheriff Anderson of Buffalo County arrest Ketchum. Rather than seeing to the task himself, Sheriff Anderson deputized Bob Olive to do the job. Much speculation arose about the reason Sheriff Anderson deputized Bob, especially when everyone knew that a great deal of animosity existed between the Olives and Ketchum. Some contended that since Bob Olive was using the alias Stevens, the Sheriff did not know that Bob was an Olive. Others believe that the Olives bribed him since they had a poor opinion of law enforcement growing from their experience in Texas. In any case, on November 17, 1878, Bob Olive and two Olive cowhands, Barney Armstrong and Pete Beeton, went to arrest Ketchum.

When Bob Olive approached Mitchell's residence, Ketchum and Mitchell recognized him and knew that they were in trouble. A gunfight broke out, and in the conflict, Bob Olive was shot and wounded by Mitchell. Ketchum suffered a broken arm from a gun shot. Ketchum and Mitchell quickly fled to Loup City in Sherman County. There they sought the protection of a friend, Judge Aaron Wall, who hid them for a time. Bob Olive died of his wounds several days later. Evidently, he did not have the staying power of his brother Print, who had survived four gunshot wounds over the years.

Print Olive offered a reward of $700, about $6,600 in 1999 dollars, for the capture and return of Mitchell and Ketchum. A number of officers, including sheriffs Crew of Howard County, Anderson of Buffalo County, Gillan of Keith County, and Letcher of Merrick County, were anxious to capture Ketchum and Mitchell in order to collect the reward. Eventually, Mitchell and Ketchum were apprehended by Sheriff Farmer W. Crew of Howard County

Mitchell, Ketchum Sod House where Bob Olive was wounded

Posed hanging of Mitchell and Ketchum

and Sheriff William Letcher of Merrick County, who took them to St. Paul, Nebraska. A dispute arose among the lawmen as to who should receive the reward. Print Olive refused to pay the reward until the captives were delivered to Custer County. According to Solomon Butcher, "a proposition was finally made to Sheriff Anderson to take the men to Custer County, for which service the others agreed to pay him $50." This offer was "declined by Anderson unless he were [sic] paid enough to enable him to employ a sufficient number of men to guard the prisoners."

Finally, Sheriff Gillian, who held the warrant for the arrest of Ketchum and Mitchell, agreed to take them to Custer County. Gillian was a native of Texas who had been elected sheriff of Keith County with support of cattlemen. A friend of Print Olive, he was not sympathetic to the plight of Mitchell and Ketchum. Sheriff Gillian promised Mitchell's and Ketchum's attorneys that they would be notified of the movement of the prisoners and would be allowed to accompany their clients. Sheriff Gillian failed to keep his promise to the attorneys. He spirited the two prisoners out of Kearney, where they had been held, by train to Plum Creek [now Lexington]. Learning that they had been deceived, the Kearney attorneys telegraphed Captain McNamar, an attorney

in Plum Creek, and asked him to intervene. McNamar was unable to persuade Sheriff Gillian to wait, but followed him as he took the prisoners north toward Custer County. Nearing the South Loup River, not far from the Olive ranch, Sheriff Gillian turned the prisoners over to Dennis Gastrell, Pedro Dominicus, and Biron Brown, all Olive cowboys.

The prisoners were taken to a place called "Devils Gap," halfway between the Wood River and the South Loup River, about five miles southeast of the present town of Callaway. At that point, Mitchell was shot by Print Olive and Ketchum was lynched. Both bodies were left hanging from a tree. At some point, a fire was started beneath the bodies, and they were partially burned. They were later buried in a shallow grave. George Sanford, who first found the bodies on December 11, 1878, noted that they had been frozen into grotesque forms, having been forced into a very small grave. Also he noted that since the graves were so shallow, they had been partially uncovered and mutilated by wild animals.

The bodies were taken to Kearney, where H. M. Hatch, a photographer, photographed the bodies and sold hundreds of prints. The case became a media event and was reported in newspapers across the country. Print Olive and several of his ranch hands were arrested at the Plum Creek Post Office and were charged with murder. They were brought to trial at Hastings, Nebraska, in Adams County.

Trial of Print Olive

The trial was the biggest event to hit Hastings in some time. Opinions were sharply divided. Cattlemen in the area and to the west strongly supported Print Olive and his men, whom they viewed as heroes for attempting to drive cattle thieves from the country. In the eastern sections of the state, the Olives were branded as outlaws and scoundrels while Ketchum and Mitchell were described as "innocent settlers," as pure as the driven snow.

The trial was sensational and heavily attended by proponents of both sides. Many well-armed cattlemen were present in Hastings and attended the trial as well as many who wished to see Print Olive convicted of murder. Some voiced concern that the volatile mix would lead to violence in the streets and, perhaps, in the court room. Judge William H. Gaslin Jr., a politically ambitious judge, called in a detachment of Army troops to maintain order. Some critics of the Judge believed that his call for United States Army troops was more of publicity stunt than a response to a real problem. In any case, Print Olive was convicted of second degree murder and sent to the Nebraska State Penitentiary in Lincoln.

The Olives's attorneys, who were reputed to be the best in the state, appealed Print Olive's conviction to the Nebraska Supreme Court. The Supreme Court ruled that Print Olive had not been tried in the proper court, and they ordered his release in order to be tried in Custer County. He was released from prison after having served one year, seven months, and twenty days of his sentence. When he was brought to court in Custer County, no one appeared to bring charges against him, and he was released. Even though he was free, he had been so vilified in the press and among the growing number of settlers that he soon abandoned his range and moved to eastern Colorado. His move was also prompted by the loss of about one third of his cattle to severe winter weather in January of 1881. His brother, Ira,

stayed in the area, entering into banking in Plum Creek. Like most open range ranchers, the Olives had maintained a home in town for their families and spent only part of their time on the range. The departure of Print Olive signified the beginning of the end of large scale open range ranching in the mixed-grass prairie region of central Nebraska.

Selected**References**

Butcher, S. D. 1901. Pioneer history of Custer County, and short sketches of early days in Nebraska, with an introduction by Chrisman. Denver: Sage Books, 1965.

Chrisman, H. 1965. Ladder of Rivers. Denver: Sage Books.

Crabb, R. 1967. Empire on the Platte. Cleveland: World Publishing Company.

SOLOMON BUTCHER:

PRAIRIE PHOTOGRAPHER

Susanne George-Bloomfield, Professor of English

During the 1880s, when thousands of homesteaders poured onto the prairie in central Nebraska, one pioneer had the creative vision to record this historical event. "In the twenty years during which this portion of the Great Plains was being settled, Solomon D. Butcher pulled up his team, which drew his 'photographic laboratory,' and pitched his camp beside many streams and in many farm and ranch yards," states Harry E. Chrisman, editor of Butcher's <u>Pioneer History of Custer County</u>. "There was nothing too inconsequential for him to direct his camera upon." Because of his imaginative foresight, aided by his desire to strike it rich on the new frontier, his collection of photographs, as well as the stories of the people in them, re-create for modern readers what it would have been like to "hold down a claim" in Nebraska.

In 1880, accompanied by his brother, his brother-in-law, and his father, twenty-four-year-old Butcher traveled seven hundred miles from Illinois by wagon to the Nebraska prairie. According to John E. Carter in <u>Solomon D. Butcher: Photographing the American Dream</u>, Butcher and his father filed on claims in northeastern Custer County and set about constructing their sod homes out of "Nebraska marble." However, spending five years improving his claim, as required by the Homestead Act, did not appeal to Butcher, so he returned east,

attending the Minnesota Medical College briefly, where he married a nurse, Lillie Barber. Two years later, Butcher and his bride returned to Nebraska to live with his father, where he taught school until he had earned enough to purchase photographic equipment and set up a shop on the Middle Loup River west of Sargent, Nebraska.

When his business failed and he lost their sod home studio, rather than resort to the physically demanding life of a farmer, Butcher decided to produce a photographic history of Custer County. In 1886, after arranging with seventy-five homesteaders to have their pictures taken for his history, Butcher's father supplied his son with a wagon to travel the rutted roads of the prairie. Surviving on subscriptions and donations, trading food and lodging for photographs, Butcher created, in the next seven years, over fifteen hundred images of homesteaders and their families as well as painstakingly collecting family histories.

As Butcher took their pictures, he learned their stories and listened to their gossip. One photograph of "George Ankeney and Wife" is accompanied by the following Butcher comment: "Mrs. Ankeney was the wife of James Cumming who was killed in the well shown in picture in September 1885. This picture was taken in 1886. Mr. Ankeney was working for Mr. Cumming at the time of the accident." Other photographs continue the saga of Cumming's attempted rescue and "this most thrilling experience ever in Custer County." Another is of "Orson Cooley" whose "wife was a widow lady in Indiana [who] wrote an ad in a farm paper inquiring if a widow could come to Nebraska and make a living. Uncle Orson being a widower answered. They kept up the correspondence which ended by the widow and her two children meeting Uncle Orson at Ord and they were married. The little child in Uncle Orson's lap is their child which died."

About yet another portrait, Butcher commented, "Mr. York, one of the early settlers south of West Union in a debate on woman suffrage. One time he said he did not believe in ladies voting. He thought the dear ladies should not have to bother their brain about politics, just sit in their parlor in an easy chair and direct their housework. It is said he would follow his wife to the neighbors with a black snake whip and whip her home." Reading Butcher's comments, one understands the strength and closeness of community on the prairie, with both its advantages and disadvantages!

In the early 1890s, the drought and the nationwide depression hit Nebraska, driving Butcher and his family again from their home. Encouraged by the zeal of the Populist movement and his own economic straits, Butcher put up his camera and ran for Justice of the Peace and Clerk of the Election in West Union, Nebraska. He won, and for the next three years, he worked undauntingly to improve farm prices and to clear himself of debt. However, in 1899 his house caught on fire, and the family lost everything, including all of the photographic prints and stories he had collected from homesteaders. Fortunately, the glass prints of all of his photographs had been stored in the granary and were unharmed.

Uninsured, penniless, and with a family to support, Butcher decided to recoup his losses by rewriting his history and selling subscriptions for the lavishly illustrated book. The project floundered until Ephram Swain Finch, a wealthy cattleman and friend from his Populist days, came to his rescue with financial and moral support. In 1901, the first edition of Butcher's Pioneer History of Custer County and Short Sketches of Her Early Days in Nebraska, complete with two hundred engravings and four hundred pages of text, sold out before delivery, so he ordered a second edition to arrive in time for Christmas.

In the Preface to his book, Butcher wrote that it contained "thrilling stories of the founders of this county, their many trials ad[sic] hardships endured while braving the elements in the howling blizzards of winter, the sorching suns of the drought period and devastation by grasshoppers." He boasted, "All tend to make it a most remarkable book,

Solomon Butcher by his first Sod House

Solomon Butcher in his photographer's wagon near the Loup River, 1886

and everyone will have the satisfaction of knowing he is reading truth and not following the wild imagination of the novelist." For the first time, one of Butcher's ventures succeeded.

Excited by his success, Butcher moved his family from West Union to Kearney in 1902 and began planning photographic histories of Buffalo and Dawson counties. He invested one thousand dollars of his own money into the new enterprise and opened a studio in partnership with his son, Lynn. Always an adventure seeker, Butcher expanded his travels to other western states, such as Wyoming, Utah, and Colorado, and he and his son soon developed a thriving postcard business.

Unfortunately, Butcher did not capitalize on his success, but decided to work as a Texas land agent for the Standard Land Company. Intending to move to the southwest, he approached Addison Sheldon, who offered to buy his cumbersome collection for one thousand dollars for the Nebraska State Historical Society. However, controversy arose, and Butcher only received six hundred dollars.

When Butcher's Texas land schemes failed in 1915, he and his wife moved to Broken Bow, Nebraska, where she died after a long illness. Now in his fifties, without his long-sought fame or wealth, Butcher worked for a while documenting his collection for the Nebraska State Historical Society, remarried, and again began travelling, this time as a salesman for a grain and flour mill. As always, lured by "get-rich-quick" schemes, he abandoned his job to manufacture an electromagnetic oil detector and to plan a photographic journey to Central America for a series of travelogue lectures. Finally, he attempted to market a patent medicine he called "Butcher's Wonder of the Age," concocted mostly of alcohol. "Practicality and even common sense," explains Carter, "were not among his virtues. For all of his dreaming and planning, he was often barely able to make ends meet." In 1926, Butcher and his wife moved to be near his daughter in Greeley, Colorado, and he died there one year later.

Despite Butcher's economic ineptitude, as well as the tenuousness of a photography business in struggling prairie communities, he was able to endow future generations with an historical legacy of over four thousand prints and negatives that document the lives of pioneers who first settled central Nebraska. Although few of Butcher's actual photographs still exist, reproductions from his glass plate negatives are appreciated worldwide. His work is now being recognized by art galleries, museums, and historians for their narrative content, for the stories they tell about pioneer life. "What his pictures really deal with are states of existences," states Carter. "There is a pride here that comes not from the accumulation of wealth but rather from being a part of history in the making."

Most importantly, Butcher's photographs make the civilizing of the wild prairie, for better or worse, throb with life. The faces, postures, and possessions of ordinary people, whose lives were stripped to the essentials, show the heroic effort needed for survival. "The history that Butcher recorded was personal," states Carter, "one of individuals and not movements. . . . each homesteading experience was an individual drama."

Butcher's photographs also record the monumental changes that took place over his brief career as a photographer. Butcher's last photographs depict financially secure farmers and their families standing proudly in front of new Victorian frame houses, enclosed by gardens and trees, instead of sitting resolutely before barren sod shanties, dwarfed by the vast expanses of prairie. Cumbersome machinery has replaced horse-drawn equipment and the automobile has antiquated buggies. Towns have begun to throng with life, and political rallies, circuses, and chatuaquas crowd the brick streets and boardwalks of villages that once straggled across the plains. Ironically, Solomon D. Butcher, who stopped time with his camera, also recorded its passing.

SETTING OUT TO WALK A PRAIRIE

After all our talk,
now is the time to insert
curiosity's key
into the lock of silence,

to draw our minds
across these fields
*to hear **begin**.*
Believe me when

I tell you this:
antecedent
to all virtues
is the art of trying,

and one step
following another
is a kind of love.
It's precisely 10 a.m.

Why wait until
we're dead
to hear emptiness,
that long and lethal silence?

Why not set out
for our lives right now?
Begin, begin, begin!

DON**WELCH**

Selected**References**
Butcher, S.D. 1901. *Pioneer history of Custer County.* Ed. Harry E. Chrisman. Denver: Sage Books, 1965.

Carter, J.E. 1985. *Solomon D. Butcher: Photographing the American dream.* Lincoln: University of Nebraska Press.

Nebraska State Historical Society. 1986. *Solomon D. Butcher picture collection. Microfiche edition.* Lincoln: Nebraska State Historical Society.

STAND UP FOR NEBRASKA

The Farmers Alliance, The Populists, and Nebraska's Radical Political Legacy

Tom Frasier, Lecturer in History

"GET OFF THE GRASS," bugled the front-page headline of the May 24, 1894, edition of Lincoln's <u>Wealth Makers of the World</u> in mocking condemnation of the federal government. Promising to expose "The Rights of Americans Visciously Trampled On," the following article featured an extract from a speech delivered by Nebraska's William V. Allen. Elected as a Populist to the U.S. Senate in 1893, Allen, from rural Madison, stood on the floor to defend the quixotic vision of Jacob S. Coxey and his followers. The mainstream press had dubbed them, in derision, "Coxey's Army." In the spring of 1894, Coxey had convinced hundreds of unemployed workers and ruined farmers, victims of the depression that followed the stock market crash of 1893, to join him in a march on Washington to demand a massive program of governmental relief. Coxey proposed a national road construction project, financed by an issue of then nonexistent paper money. When Coxey led his Army of approximately twelve hundred protestors onto the grounds of the Capitol, Allen reported, "He was met with a mounted police force who used the baton, more properly known as the billyclub, and was beaten down and carried off the grounds." Arrested by Capitol Police, Coxey was found guilty of ignoring a "Keep Off the Grass Sign," fined five dollars, and incarcerated for twenty-five days. Theodore Roosevelt, remembered today for his progressive politics, suggested "taking ten or a dozen of their leaders out, standing them against a wall, and shooting them dead." "Why," Allen concluded, "were Americans thus treated?"

The Wizard of Oz

Six years later, L. Frank Baum, a Populist newspaper editor from Aberdeen, South Dakota, would immortalize Coxey's Army in his classic <u>The Wizard of Oz</u>. Baum characterized many of Allen's Nebraska costituents through the figure of the Straw Man. When another newspaper editor writing in the wake of Coxey's march on Washington, William Allen White, posed the question, "What's The Matter With Kansas?", he came to a simple conclusion: "the ragged trousers . . . the lazy, greasy fiddle" who made up the Populists, bent on giving "The prosperous man the dickens," lacked the intelligence to appreciate America's political system. Hence, Baum's Straw Man followed the Yellow Brick Road to the Emerald City with his companions, like Coxey's Army, in search of a brain. This path, paved with the gold money held by the Republican and Democratic parties as the only legitimate form of money, led to the heart of America's established political culture. Like Allen and Baum, many readers know the inside story of the plot. The Straw Man possessed a

Populist convention/nomination in Columbus, Nebraska, 1890   Butcher Collection

brain all along, one quite as capable as that of the all powerful Oz–a former circus performer from Omaha.

Derided by their opponents as "gibbering idiots," "hicks," and "anarchists," the men and women who made up the backbone of the Populist Party in Nebraska were members of the Farmers Alliance and Industrial Union, an amalgamation mirrored in both Coxey's Army and Baum's coalition of the Straw Man with the Tin Man. Allen wrote to the Secretary of the Nebraska Alliance, Luna Kellie (also the editor and eventually publisher of the official F.A. & I.U. newspaper), that "the Alliance is the cradle of the People's Party." The prominent place women played in this movement, illustrated by Kellie in Nebraska and Mary Lease in Kansas–who urged her neighbors to "raise less corn and more hell"–was cause for further scorn from their critics. Populist men, one editorial writer asserted, were henpecked "soaptails." One sure way of identifying a Farmers Alliance soaptail, he continued, was "by shaking hands with his wife. If her hands are covered with corns and have the appearance of having wielded the ax and held the plow, you may rest assured her husband is a genuine soaptail." Mollie Wells wrote to Kellie from Arapahoe in 1892 that she had received similar treatment from the wife of the local newspaper editor. "I am alone as far as having a lady friend who I can

talk with on the most important subjects," she lamented to Kellie. The editor's wife (a Republican), informed Wells that if she expected "to associate with the best families," they must not discuss the Alliance.

Although the men and women of the Nebraska Farmers Alliance represented a tradition of rural political dissent that reaches back to the founding of America, the Populists whom they supported posed the first serious agrarian challenge to the country's entrenched political powers. The message they conveyed was in stark contrast to the orthodoxy embraced by the dominant Republican and Democratic parties of the day. Kellie proclaimed in the Farmers Alliance "Declaration of Principles," published in <u>The Prairie Home</u> from her farm in Heartwell, Nebraska, that since "The farmers and laborers of this state will never secure 'the establishment of right and justice to ourselves and our posterity' under a competitive system we therfore resolve: To labor for a Co-operative commonwealth."

In Nebraska, by the time of Coxey's march, these were more than simply the sentiments of misguided farmers, unable to comprehend the realities of the American system. By 1893, Nebraska's legislative majority was Populist, Allen was a United States Senator, and two of Nebraska's three delegates to Congress–William McKeighan and Omer Kem–were Populists. Nebraska's

Omer Kem in front of his sod house, 1886

Congressman from District One, Democrat William Jennings Bryan, owed his election in large part to his appeal to Populist issues. The following year, Nebraskans elected a Populist Governor, Silas Holcomb. These Populists pushed through state laws securing the Australian (secret) ballot, relief for drought victims, the legalization of mutual insurance companies, the eight-hour day, free school text books, and the establishment of maximum railroad rates—issues that embraced the most radical political ideas of the era. Given the opportunity, the Straw Men (and women), it seems, were entirely capable of expressing themselves—and governing the state. In 1896, Bryan, running on the Populist ticket, came within four percentage points of capturing the American presidency.

Nebraska's Farmers Co-ops

Nebraska's Farmers Alliance activists created a cooperative culture apart from the political arena that has transformed the state's landscape—both physically and politically. The Co-op—still the business and social magnet of many of Nebraska's communities—first appeared through their efforts. In July of 1889, Omer Kem and his associates established the Custer County Farmers Alliance Purchasing Company, opening a store at

Westerville. Later that summer, the Cambridge Farmers Business Association developed a cooperative that constructed a stockyards and elevator the next fall. In the Sandhills, the Sheridan County Farmers Alliance was operating a co-op by 1894. H.F. Wasmund, president of the local Purchasing Bureau wrote from Rushville to Luna Kellie, requesting assistance in procuring suppliers: "We would like to have the help of the Alliance of the State to direct us to houses that will deal direct with the farmer and give them the benefits of the agents or middle men. We will need such goods and merchandise as farmers need in the house and on the farm including what they eat—ware and use for implements from a needle to a threshing machine. . . .We already have reductions from ten to forty percent in groceries and other things . . . The lowest bid catches our order. It don't matter where it comes from: and the merchants can't combine against us and Brake us . . . ."

Writing later that spring to advise Kellie on the progress of their cooperative efforts, Wasmund added that "It is time for us to be independent of our local merchants who as a rule are doing all in their power to keep us farmers down in business and politics." Wasmund's comments reflect the vitality of

Stand up for Nebraska.
In the center she lies.
The most valuable
jewel 'neath the fairest of skies.
So favored by nature, her vile man-made laws
we find of her poverty are the sole cause.
Let her own her own highways and a road to the south:
Stand up for Nebraska by your votes, not your mouth.

the cooperative enterprises created through the efforts of Farmers Alliance activists. John Minshull reported that the Farmers Alliance Co-Operative Association in Litchfield had successfully located suppliers for groceries, boots, shoes, dry goods, confectioneries, caps, crockery, and oil. "The only trouble we have now," he stated, "is insurance, as they (the local agents) refuse to insure our stock on account of us being cooperative." Minshull provided Kellie a list of wholesalers for use by other budding Alliance cooperatives. Among those requesting such information was the Farmers Elevator and Business Association in Funk, who had by 1894 already established a cooperative in grain, livestock, and oil.

The cooperative efforts of Nebraska Farmers Alliance even extended beyond the state's borders. Kellie corresponded with D.P. Duncan, Secretary Treasurer of the National Farmers Alliance and Industrial Union, discussing the exchange of agricultural products directly between the farmers of Nebraska and South Dakota. Kellie also maintained an ongoing correspondence with E.Z. Ernst, the editor of the Progressive Thought in Olathe, Kansas, concerning an even more radical cooperative effort–labor exchanges. Under these exchanges, farmers could store their commodities–especially grain–free of charge in warehouses, receiving notes negotiable with the local co-op in return, while they waited for the most propitious time to enter the market. In effect, they were establishing their own source of paper currency. "They are organizing a labor exchange in Bartley now," Ernst reported

in May of 1894, "and others will no doubt soon follow."

The cooperative activities of Nebraska's Farmers Alliance went hand in hand with their efforts to politically energize the countryside. The gains by the Populist Party in the state reflected the potency of their travelling campaigns, which often combined the most attractive features of the barbecue, band concert, and revival meeting. In the summer of 1895, W.A. Bates wrote to Kellie from Sheridan County about "the Alliance picnic at Clinton on the Second of June. There will be vocal and instrumental music and Speaking and a good time generally . . . our people are poor but without the Alliance would be poorer." The state Alliance employed a full-time lecturer, John H. Powers, who traveled the length of the state throughout the year delivering speeches, distributing Populist literature, and helping to organize local Farmers Alliances. Although his ostensible salary was two dollars per day, Kellie's records (she was also the Alliance

Omer Kem portrait

bookkeeper) indicate that he often worked for free. Power's speaking itinerary continued in defiance of Nebraska's fickle weather and often uncompromising roads.

Riley Watson's appeal from Humboldt was typical of the many requests for speakers Kellie handled for the state Alliance: "Send John H Powers, W.F. Dale and some other prominent speakers to the County [Richardson, in the southeast corner of the state] . . . our county campaigns last fall were largely attended and much interest Manifested." The state Alliance also maintained an extensive library from which it would loan or sell political tracts at a nominal cost. Kellie advertised a list of books in her paper, even offering to locate "any reform book not on our list." She maintained, "In the education of the masses lies our only hope for industrial freedom." C.B. Jones, an Alliance member and Secretary of the cooperative Polk County Mutual Farmers Insurance Company, wrote to Kellie concurring that "our success depends upon our education . . . and the nearer we can get to the people and get them to thinking."

Senators Allen and Kem

While the Populist Party was expressing the Farmers Alliance agenda through a vigorous demand for an active and expanded federal government, politicians like Senator Allen were involving themselves on a personal level with directly addressing

the needs of their Nebraska constituency. His papers at the Nebraska State Historical Society include dozens of requests from farmers in drought-stricken areas of the state for vegetable seeds to produce subsistence crops for their families. As spring approached in 1896, Emerick Post wrote from Newman Grove in Madison County: "Senator Allen, comrade; please send me some new kinds of garden seeds." Allen's loyalty with F.A. & I.U. allies extended itself to national conflicts. In the summer of 1896, Allen intervened on behalf of striking street car workers in Washington, who were attempting to organize a local of the Order of the Knights of Labor. John Hayes, the union's national secretary, personally thanked Allen for his "manly stand in behalf of our people."

Omer Kem, the first United States Congressman to live in a sod house, was a Nebraska Farmers Alliance organizer from Custer County re-elected three times to his congressional seat, twice after his district was reconfigured. William McKeighan, like Kem and Allen, found his political roots among the agrarian radicals whose political strongholds were Nebraska's most isolated communities. Voting studies have found little correlation between income and Populist loyalty, but a high correlation between low population density and Farmers Alliance/Populist success. In 1894, McKeighan wrote to the governing board of the state Alliance: "I feel that government ownership of the railroads is our only remedy . . . while our platform declared for government control, the ownership of the roads is the only way in which government can control them. Senator Allen, Mr. Kem, and myself are in hearty accord as to the best course to pursue in Nebraska."

In Congress, both Allen and McKeighan delivered speeches urging opposition to the repeal of the Sherman Silver Purchase Act—which they hoped would lead to inflation that would benefit farmers—and argued that "Paper money should be issued by the government and made full and complete legal tender." Allen's speech lasted over fifteen hours. Neither man ever abandoned his Populist principles. In a private letter written in 1895 to Luna Kellie and her husband marked "Not For The Public," McKeighan expressed his continuing sympathy with the agrarian movement. "My great ambition," he wrote the Kellies, "is to win a place in the hearts of the great Common people . . . My only fear is that life's thread will break before I shall see the delivery of the people from the Pluetark." In less than a year he would be dead. In 1894, he had expressed to Kellie his desire to "say to our republican and democratic friends, come stand with us for the great masses of the common people."

Following Bryan's defeat in 1896 by William McKinley–Bryan had raised $300,000 from his followers while McKinley managed, through donations like John D. Rockefeller's $250,000, to raise nearly $16 million–Nebraska's Farmers Alliance activists placed the blame for their national defeat on the shoulders of the Democrats. By "stealing" their candidate, they believed, the Democrats had tainted their great crusade. Bryan, the <u>Arapahoe Pioneer</u> declared, had betrayed the Populist Party and the F.A. & I.U.: "Having a platform demanding that the people should be a 'united band of brothers' the foundation principle of popular government . . . where free speech, free press, and a free ballot are found, and then supporting a democrat for president, and surely there was never a more unprincipled–or without principle worthless, partisan organization than the democratic party–is like professing religion and travelling the road that leads to hell. And Mr. Bryan claiming–as he did repeatedly during the campaign–to be a Jackson and Jefferson democrat, and yet upholding ALL THE CORPORATIONS, is so entirely inconsistent that I should not suppose any one would try to fool any people again that way."

Fusion with the Democrats

Among the Populists of Nebraska supported by the Farmers Alliance, fusion with the Democrats was seen as an attempt by a foundering, corrupt party to capture the energy of the agrarian revolt.

L.P. Cummins, an early Farmers Alliance organizer in Nebraska's Sandhills and a regular corespondent of Kellie, had seen the fusion movement coming and battled hard

to prevent it. Speaking of Democratic efforts to attract Farmers Alliance votes in his county, Cummins stated that "A lie will outrun the truth nine times in ten and the liars and the lawyers (little difference in sound and none in meaning generally) are in the lead in Sheridan county, and that too by the farmer." Despairing of his hope that McKeighan and Kem would be returned to Congress, Cummins worried that "Too many farmers are ignorant and childlike. Flattery, cigars, whiskey, etc. dealt out freely by a flippant and cunning lawyer will win hundreds to his side."

In the end, by forcing the mainstream parties toward real reform during the Progressive Era, the Populist movement, spurred on by agrarian activists like Nebraska's Farmers Alliance members, accomplished nearly all of its major goals. While its basic tenets were finally embraced by the urban middle class, these agrarian radicals who had precipitated a momentous shift in American politics were left behind. At the end of her life, Luna Kellie lamented: "I never vote [and] did not for years hardly look at a political paper. I feel that nothing is likely to be done to benefit the farmer in my lifetime. So I busy myself with the garden and the chickens and have given up any hope of making the world any better." At the end of Baum's novel, the Wizard complains to the Straw Man that "It was a great mistake letting you into my throne room," but the Straw Man remains to rule over the Emerald City. Once America's mainstream politicians had co-opted the Populist message, Luna suggested in contrast, they sent the messenger back to the corn field.

Selected **References**

Goodwyn, Lawrence. 1978. The Populist moment: A short history of the Agrarian Revolt in America. New York: Oxford University Press.

Hicks, John D. 1961. The Populist revolt: A history of the Farmers Alliance and Populist Party. Lincoln: University of Nebraska Press.

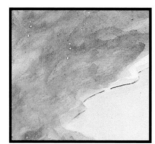

GEORGE W. NORRIS

THE VISIONARY NEBRASKAN

Larry Theye, Professor of Management and Marketing

Whose water is it anyway? Who has priority claims to the water flowing down the Platte and Republican Rivers?

Disputed claims to water rights have pitted irrigators, power companies, environmentalists, municipalities, and states against each other since the beginning of the development of water resources in the Midwest. No sooner has the long and expensive dispute over the relicensing of Kingsley Dam apparently been resolved than Nebraska finds itself a defendant in a lawsuit concerning water flows from the Republican River into Kansas.

Answers to the questions regarding priority claims to water have been elusive, but a historical and political perspective might provide insight into the problem. Certainly this debate would not be raging today had the water resources never been developed.

While many people were involved in developing irrigation and electric power in this region, one person–George W. Norris (1861-1944)–clearly stands out as the primary force in this effort, not only in Nebraska, but nationally.

Half a century after his death, many Nebraskans have forgotten George Norris, arguably one of the most effective Senators ever to serve in that august body, and probably the most prominent political figure in Nebraska's history. Even many residents of McCook, who are keenly aware that main street is named Norris Avenue, have never learned how the street came by its name. Clearly, the story of Norris's role in the development of water resources and electricity needs to be retold.

Overview of Accomplishments

George Norris's role in governmental management of water resources was but one of many national campaigns that he championed as Nebraska's voice in Washington for forty years, five terms each in the House (1902-1912) and the Senate (1912-1942). His perspective was always national in scope and his positions, frequently unpopular at the time, were consistent and predictable. Historians today regard Norris as one of the outstanding senators in our nation's history.

John F. Kennedy's <u>Profiles of Courage</u> praised Norris for taking on the Cannon-Dalzell Republican machine that had controlled Congress for twenty years. Appalled that partisan concerns overshadowed national interests, Norris led a Congressional uprising in 1910 that succeeded in reforming House rules to limit the Speaker's power. Kennedy also admired Norris's filibustering of a bill to arm the merchant marine–essentially a war resolution–in the Senate in 1917. Labeled a traitor for this extremely unpopular filibuster, he volunteered himself to a recall election, but regained support from his constituents as a result of a critical speech in defense of his actions. Finally, Kennedy approved of Norris's support of Al Smith, a Tammany Hall Democrat, a Catholic, and a "wet" against Herbert Hoover. As a Republican Senator, his endorsement and support for the Democratic nominee was considered treasonous and unforgivable by Republicans.

In a statement immediately after the election in 1928, Norris defended his position and outlined his political philosophy: "The real issues in the campaign were relief for agriculture and the preservation of our natural resources from the grasping fingers of the Power Trust. In the excitement over the artificial issues of religion and prohibition, farm relief was beaten and the Power Trust given the greatest victory it has ever achieved since it began the stealthy and secret attempt to control all the activities of our economic and political life."

His opposition to the Power Trust, the large holding companies that sought to control the generation, distribution, and sale of electricity, had become the theme of many of his speeches and much of his legislation. Considering that many of these occurred during the decade of the twenties, one of the most politically conservative eras of American history when big business dominated American life and politics ("What's good for General Motors [Electric] is good for America"), his leadership on the question of public versus private ownership

of utilities was especially critical.

Norris's greatest and hardest fought accomplishment as a Senator was, no doubt, the creation of the Tennessee Valley Authority. Twelve years of Congressional battles against some of the most powerful business interests, including Henry Ford, went into this bill. It was the forerunner of many smaller projects, such as Nebraska's Tri-County Irrigation Project.

In addition, Norris fought seven years for the Norris-LaGuardia Act, which was finally passed in 1932. Through this bill, he sought to correct abuse of the courts by great corporate wealth, which used the legal processes of injunctions and yellow dog contracts to oppress its workers. Passage of this bill led to new freedom and rights for American labor in the form of the National Labor Relations Act and made George Norris a national hero to organized labor–ironic for a senator from a state that has never been friendly to organized labor.

George Norris made other unique contributions. He almost single-handedly secured passage of the Twentieth Amendment to the Constitution, the Lame Duck Amendment that ended sessions of Congress after the elections. In addition, Nebraska's non-partisan unicameral legislature is the brainchild of George Norris.

1946

I became a storm center because it seemed to me that the development and conservation of these resources ought always to be under public control, public ownership, and public operation.

GEORGE**NORRIS**

Norris on his farm

George Norris's Vision for the Land

Norris's autobiography, <u>Fighting Liberal</u>, completed a few weeks before his death in 1944, provides an excellent insight into his philosophy and motivation. In it, he attributes the basis of his philosophy to his widowed mother in this poignant passage: "There was that warm spring afternoon when mother, who had been busy throughout the entire day, called to me to assist her in planting a tree. She had dug a hole, and she wanted me to hold the seedling upright while she shoveled the dirt in around its roots and packed it tightly. . .I said to her, 'Why do you work so hard, mother? We now have more fruit than we can possibly use. You will be dead long before this tree comes into bearing.' Her answer was slow to come, apparently while she measured her words. 'I may never see this tree in bearing,' she said, 'but somebody will.'"

Throughout his life, George Norris was guided by his vision for the future, working tirelessly for the generations to come. He was a friend to the farmer and the common man, reflecting the Populism of the area at the turn of the century. After farming the Ohio land where he was born, Norris moved to Nebraska in 1885 at age 24 to practice law, finally settling in McCook.

He immediately fell in love with the land and its possibilities. The fertile soil of the Beaver Valley, with its tall corn and absence of stones and stumps, seemed to him the ideal farming land. However, Norris resisted the urge to return to farming and practiced law as he had planned, and he became a judge before serving forty years in Washington.

Fortune did not always smile on Nebraska farmers as it did when Norris arrived in 1885. Lack of rainfall often destroyed crops before they reached maturity. As a farmer, Norris appreciated the value of irrigation, and as a politician, he envisioned how to provide it.

In a 1924 letter to Elwood Mead, Commissioner of the Bureau of Reclamation, Norris argued for the Tri-County Irrigation Project for Central Nebraska. Refuting a report by the Chief Engineer of the Bureau that a foot of water would be insufficient to raise a crop, Norris wrote: "I know from living in that country for more than thirty years, that taking one year with another, we would have been able to raise enormous crops if we had had but a few inches of moisture at the right time. It is not an arid country, and the majority of years, by the ordinary rainfall, the farmers are able to produce at least a fair crop. Sometimes this rainfall is sufficient to produce a large crop, and some years when they have absolutely failed they have had the finest possible prospects for a big crop to within a few days of its maturity, when one inch would have changed failure into a great success. If it is possible to store the moisture in the soil I can say from my own personal experience that there has never been a year during the last thirty years, that one foot of moisture would not have been more than sufficient to produce a big crop."

The source of the water, of course, would be the rivers–more specifically, the run-off during periods of excess rainfall. Norris's concept for irrigation was to combine it with flood control. Because rivers cross state boundaries, flood control projects must be the province of the federal government. Indeed, George Norris's vision for national flood control and irrigation projects was grand in scale, encompassing the entire Mississippi watershed.

Noting the millions of dollars in property damage lost annually due to flooding along the Mississippi and its many tributaries, the erosion of fertile soil that was extending the Mississippi Delta far out into the Gulf of Mexico, and the hundreds of millions of dollars Congress had appropriated for dike construction and rechanneling of rivers, Norris was convinced that he had a better solution. Why not build dams at the mouth of every natural reservoir in the Mississippi Valley? Not only would this control flood-ing, but it would retain the water to be released during dry seasons for irrigation.

While arguing for the harnessing of America's waterways for purposes of flood control, irrigation, and navigation, Norris was always intrigued and inspired by the potential to generate electricity as a valuable by-product. This vision is also described in his autobiog-raphy: "The snows of winter wrap the peaks of the Sierras gently in a deep white blanket or, in howling gales, fill the deep canyons with ice and snow. And then spring follows, and spring's warm sun, and snow water happily courses down the mountain side, gathering in tiny creeks which rush rapidly to the river, seeking the sea. Men may build dams to pile those waters back in lakes, avert-ing floods and providing cities with water and light. That is the miracle which embodies

the wisdom of an intelligent and competent people. It is the plan through which a modern world enters upon an electrical age."

The Vision Becomes Reality–the TVA

Why did Senator Norris choose the Tennessee River, which has no direct impact on his Nebraska constituents, as the test case of his vision for flood control, irrigation, and electricity? The answer lies in a unique combination of circumstances growing out of World War I. Nitrates used for the production of explosives and other military operations had been imported from Chile, but German submarines had interrupted their transportation, and the United States had to manufacture its own nitrates.

Abundant nitrogen exists in the atmos-phere, but to extract it requires vast amounts of electricity. Norway had demonstrated how to generate cheap electricity from dams on deep, swift streams, and, based on their example, Congress authorized the President to select a site for such a dam and a nitrate production facility. He selected Muscle Shoals on the Tennessee River, which became the site for Wilson Dam.

The war was over before Wilson Dam was completed, but the prospect of nitrates for peace-time use as fertilizer in this area where soil had become depleted kept the project alive. It was referred to the Agri-culture Committee, which was chaired by George Norris.

Because the federal government was already involved in building a dam and the project landed in his committee, Norris decided to expand it into a major flood control and navigation project in addition to generating electricity. It provided a great opportunity to begin implementing his vision for the entire Mississippi Valley. He viewed the TVA as a national model to demonstrate how an entire waterway system might be developed to maximize the benefits of water resources for navigation, electricity generation, and land reclamation, while at the same time control flooding and soil erosion.

Even with the favorable circumstances and opportunity, creation of the TVA was a long and bitter fight, primarily over whether

1946

Here was the place of all places where it seemed to me everything was designed for the happiness and prosperity of the farmer.

GEORGE**NORRIS**

such projects should be undertaken by government or by private enterprise. Power companies interested in selling electricity for profit fought the project successfully for twelve years. Norris finally prevailed with the argument that electricity is only a by-product, and no private company is interested in flood control projects. He twice steered the TVA through both houses of Congress, only to have it vetoed, first by Coolidge and then by Hoover. It was finally signed by President Roosevelt after its third passage in 1933.

Expanding the Dream–Irrigation and Electricity

The TVA makes no provision for irrigation, as rainfall is generally plentiful east of the Mississippi River. In all the regions to the west, however, irrigation is probably the most important consideration in the use of water resources. On this issue, Norris wrote in his autobiography: "Irrigation is a form of flood control, although generally unrecognized as such, and contributes very materially to navigation by the regulation of the tributaries of the Mississippi. The best and the most effective way to store water is in the soil itself. The water that piles up behind flood-control dams, and is turned out upon thirsty and parched soil, to a very great degree finds its way back to the stream; but in its return slowly and gradually, it alleviates those conditions which produce floods."

Norris was arguing for what we today call ground water recharge, a major benefit of the Tri-County project in Nebraska. But Norris is remembered more for his role in bringing electricity to rural America than for irrigation.

Norris saw the generation of electricity essentially as a by-product of dam-building, secondary in importance to irrigation in Nebraska and secondary to flood control and navigation elsewhere. There was little argument in the Senate that flood control and navigation are proper government functions, and that irrigators who receive the water should pay for it (although at a reduced rate when it is part of this larger system). But popular sentiment favored private development and sale of electricity. Norris was, at times, a lone voice in the

Senate when advocating for public electric companies, but he persisted and ultimately prevailed.

Norris played an active role in expanding, as well as implementing, the government's involvement in flood control and irrigation projects, and in generating electricity. In a 1929 letter to McCook Daily Gazette editor Harry D. Strunk, Norris traced his efforts on behalf of irrigation and electricity. He offered an amendment to a bill providing flood control on the lower Mississippi, which would also provide half the funding for irrigation dams, and he proposed to build two storage dams on the Platte River for irrigation and development of electricity. Both narrowly failed because no other member of the Nebraska delegation supported them, prompting Norris to comment in the same letter, "I was working for [irrigation and electricity projects] when I stood almost alone. I stood for these propositions when they were not understood by the people and when it was not popular."

In Norris's grand vision for the country, the entire Mississippi watershed, and perhaps the Western slope as well, would be developed and controlled by hundreds of government-built and government-operated water storage dams. Through a federally coordinated system, water flows could be stabilized the year round for enormous public benefit in terms of flood control, irrigation, improved navigation, and inexpensive electricity. While a project of this scope would be enormously expensive, dovetailing all these activities lessens the cost of each and makes economically feasible what would be impossible under any other system.

The REA–Lighting the Farms

Generally attributed to George Norris, the Rural Electrification Administration was actually created by an executive order from President Roosevelt in 1935. Norris introduced a bill in the Senate in 1936 to make it permanent and to effect some changes in its operation. Using the TVA as a model, Norris intended through the REA to create a national system of similar projects on all streams of the country where it was practical to preserve and protect the natural resources effectively and economically.

1946

We should commit an economic sin, a folly, if we built large dams to control floods or improve navigation or irrigate the fertile soil of the western plains without utilizing the water to produce electric power.

GEORGE**NORRIS**

Norris was motivated by what he perceived as the unfairness of the system that provided affordable electricity to cities and towns, but not to farms. He knew the drudgery of farm work, and he also knew that it could be alleviated by labor-saving electrical devices. Writing in his autobiography, Norris explains his reasons for introducing the REA: "I had seen the cities gradually acquire a night as light as day. Anyone giving extended study to electrical developments in America could come to no other conclusion as a simple matter of equity, justice, and progress than that the farmers of the United States should have the benefit of cheap electricity to the same extent and in the same way that villages, towns, and cities would possess it under the TVA Act. . . . I therefore regarded the REA not only as a necessary twin development of the TVA, but as a step which would extend the blessings of electricity to agriculture throughout the nation." The bill was opposed by the private utilities, who had done little to provide electricity to rural areas because the cost of constructing lines and maintenance were prohibitive.

The provisions of the bill called for the establishment of public power districts in rural areas following logical lines of geography. These districts would construct necessary transmission lines and create distribution systems to deliver electricity directly to every farm home within the district. While districts could build their own generating plants, the bill intended for districts to purchase electricity at wholesale rates from either private or public generating plants, re-selling it at retail rates to pay for the transmission lines.

United States government loans would provide the money to any organized district in order to build the system. The loan rate—whether it permanently remained less than or more than three percent—became a major stumbling block. Abuse of this loan program later became a problem.

George Norris undoubtedly considered the electrification of rural America his major achievement. Just before his death he wrote: "After nine years, the REA has developed into a wonderful success. . . . Now the REA constitutes one of the largest organizations of a governmental nature ever undertaken in the United States. Its benefits to the rural population have been of mammoth proportions and will grow constantly as electricity is carried to thousands more of farms in all areas of the country."

The Little TVA

The Tri-County Irrigation Project in Nebraska, which Norris called "a little TVA," had slowly been taking shape during the 1920s. With the passage of the TVA in 1933, he began to devote increased attention to this project. The centerpiece of this project was a large dam on the North Platte River near Ogallala, which would feed smaller reservoirs downstream with enough water to irrigate the entire Platte River Valley of central Nebraska. The Upper Loup would also be harnessed for both irrigation and electricity.

While farmers were the principal beneficiaries of both water for irrigation and cheap electricity through the REA, municipalities along the Platte River Valley also benefited from the Tri-County Project through ground water recharge, keeping their wells productive year after year.

Although Norris didn't use the term "ground water recharge," this was part of his plan from the beginning. In a 1924 letter to Commissioner Elwood Mead of the Bureau of Reclamation complaining of lack of support for the project from the Bureau's chief engineer, Norris wrote: "I think the chief difficulty with him is that he does not understand and has never comprehended the theory involved in this Tri-County Project in Nebraska. He seems to be thinking entirely of arid regions where no calculation whatever is made upon the rainfall; and in addition to this, he does not take into consideration the fact that in the Tri-County Project, the principal object will be to store water in the soil for future use. He apparently has no idea of the nature of this soil and of the possibility and practicality of storing water in it."

It would be misleading, however, to imply that George Norris fought alone in the efforts to bring water and electric power to Central Nebraska. Such attempts had begun in the 1880s and continued intermittently until 1922 when depressed farm prices

1946

Why not build reservoirs high up on tributaries which would hold back such floods as, in rolling down the Mississippi, had carried millions of tons of rich silt, had built a great delta extending far out into the Gulf of Mexico?

GEORGE**NORRIS**

If you ask me if I think electricity is the most important part of it, I'll answer you frankly, no. In Nebraska, the most important part of this matter is irrigation. Down in the lower Mississippi Valley the most important thing is flood control. All over the system a very important proposition is navigation, and everywhere—that is, wherever storage dams are built—the by-product, electricity, becomes extremely important.

revived interest.

Two men who were particularly instrumental in these efforts were Charles W. McConaughy (1859-1941) and George P. Kingsley (1865-1929). McConaughy was a grain dealer, mayor of Holdrege, and lobbyist in Washington for the project while Kingsley, a Minden banker and lumber yard operator, organized local support. They formed the Tri-County Supplemental Water Association, which in 1922 became the Central Nebraska Public Power and Irrigation District.

McConaughy served as president of the organization; Kingsley was its vice-president. Both men worked closely with George Norris to secure federal funding for the project. Although their specific concern was irrigation for Phelps, Kearney, and Adams counties in south-central Nebraska, they became involved in the national debate over reservoirs on the tributaries of the Mississippi, as they needed to justify the project as part of the flood control program for the lower Mississippi River.

McConaughy and Kingsley are now familiar names to most Nebraskans, as the lake and dam on the North Platte River bear their names. Less familiar today, but also prominent in the Tri-County project, were R.O. Canady, James L. Clark, and Clark E. Mickey, Chairman of the Department of Civil Engineering at the University of Nebraska. The Hastings Chamber of Commerce, under the leadership of P.L. Johnson, also actively and effectively promoted the project.

In his autobiography, George Norris wrote of the Nebraska project: "I spent enormous energy on those projects. I fought days and months against opposition. Now they are taking form. In my own valley, against heavy odds, only the Republican remains for incorporation in the program of conservation of natural resources. On several occasions, I rescued it from the dump heap. I had been accused of a deeper concern for the Tennessee valley than for my own homeland. Strangely, I had also been accused of seeking "pork" for my own state. But in the revival of these ancient river valleys, in the security and stability which irrigation provides, and in the cheap electricity of the years ahead, I am sure this river plan will justify itself."

His efforts also led to flood control projects on the Republican River, but he did not live to see the fruits of this labor. Through his editorials in the <u>McCook Daily Gazette</u>, Harry D. Strunk, inspired by a devastating flood along the Republican Valley in 1935, became instrumental in the Republican River reclamation project.

Public vs. Private Development

Throughout his political career, George Norris not only resisted political partisanship, but actively fought it. Although he was a Republican, he was often the most effective voice in the Senate to oppose the Republican agenda. In his re-election campaigns in Nebraska, he normally received

Norris in his office

1946

The Tennessee

Valley Authority

does produce,

in my judgment,

the maximum

benefits which

come from

the proper

development

of an entire

waterway

as one system.

GEORGE**NORRIS**

George W. Norris portrait

stronger support from Democrats than from Republicans. In fact, he was elected to his final term in 1936 as an Independent.

It is not surprising, then, that Norris took great precautions to protect the TVA and REA from partisan political appointments. Boards of Directors are elective and non-partisan, and all employees are hired on the basis of merit, not political patronage.

The major controversy involved in the TVA project, and which delayed its passage for twelve years, was the question of whether it should be developed by private companies or by the federal government. Originally, Congress seemed to assume that private development was the only option, and in 1922 accepted Henry Ford's bid to lease Muscle Shoals. George Norris was at first a lone voice of dissent in the Senate, arguing that private companies would be interested only in selling electricity, as there would be no profit in flood control and conservation. He later wrote in his autobiography: "From the beginning to the end, there was that irreconcilable conflict between those who believed the natural wealth of the United States best can be developed by private capital and enterprise, and those who believe that in certain activities related to the natural resources only the great strength of the federal government itself can perform this most necessary task in the spirit of unselfishness,

for the greatest good to the greatest number."

A national coalition of holding companies that generated and sold electricity, which Norris always referred to as the "Power Trust," strenuously opposed all federal reclamation projects for which Norris labored so persistently. He spelled out his reasons for opposing them in 1929 in a heated letter to Strunk, who had argued editorially for private development of electricity: "I contend that when we have built these dams from public funds and have stored flood waters belonging to the Government, it would be an economic sin, after we have used the money of the people to do all this, to let the electricity so developed be turned over to private corporations for private gain, to be sold back to the people who originally owned it . . . . You want to give to this Trust the property belonging to the people and let it have the privilege of selling it back to the people at exorbitant profits. I am opposed to this, and that is where our paths diverge."

In many speeches on the Senate floor, Norris supported his arguments for public control of electricity by showing comparisons of electric rates charged by municipally owned plants and rates charged by privately owned plants. Today Nebraska is the only state whose electric utilities are totally public owned, and its electric rates have remained among the lowest in the nation.

Norris leaves no doubt about his distaste for the Power Trust; in his autobiography, he referred to it as "the greatest monopolistic corporation that has been organized for private greed." This coalition opposed his efforts, not only to promote municipal ownership of electricity, but also his projects for flood control such as the TVA, the Tri-County Project in Nebraska, and the Bonneville and Grand Coulee dams. Norris strongly believed water to be a God-given natural resource intended for use by the people, not a commodity to be exploited for profit.

George W. Norris has unquestionably left a legacy, not only for Nebraskans, but for the entire country. While some in Nebraska accused him of showing more concern for the Tennessee Valley and Pennsylvania coal miners than for his home state, others in Washington accused him of seeking "pork" for Nebraska. By an objective account, however, he was a senator for all Americans, he had a grand vision for the future, and he possessed the political skills and courage to implement it.

Certainly everyone in central Nebraska who uses water and electricity is greatly indebted to Norris's foresight and unrelenting efforts to develop the water resources, not only of this area, but throughout the western two-thirds of the country. His concept of combining flood control, irrigation, ground water recharge, in-stream flow maintenance, land reclamation and reforestation, and electric power generation into a single giant effort was possible only through the federal government, and it required a lifetime of dedicated effort on his part to bring it about.

The only use of projects such as Nebraska's Tri-County Irrigation Project that Norris apparently didn't envision was recreational boating and camping on the reservoirs— perhaps because "recreation" may not have been in his vocabulary. It certainly wasn't in his routine, as he normally worked sixteen to eighteen hour days throughout his life.

While listening to the arguments regarding water rights today, it is enlightening to review George Norris's vision of water development. Originally, he no doubt envisioned irrigation as the top priority, and that has remained a high priority for the past fifty years. While Norris often referred to conservation as an important function of the projects, he was clearly referring to water and soil conservation. Wildlife conservation was not a priority during his lifetime, but it seems clear from his concern for preservation of natural resources that he would have added conservation of fish and wildlife to the critical benefits of water control projects.

As we weigh the competing claims to the waters of the Platte and Republican Rivers, we will do well to remember the contributions of George Norris. Except for him, there likely would be no water held in reserve for which to compete, and we would all be the poorer for it.

When we turn on the switches to light our homes and to drive the wheels of industry with affordable electricity, when we turn on the water taps in our homes or open the gates of irrigation ditches, when we read about floods around the country while our own homes remain protected by up-stream reservoirs, we need to keep in mind that all these are among the many gifts of George Norris.

Selected**References**

Center for Great Plain Studies. 1991. Norris from Nebraska. George W. Norris Committee of the High Plains Historical Society: Lincoln.

Norris, G. W. 1924, June 3. [Letter to Elwood Mead, Commissioner of bureau of reclamation] Manuscript Record of Nebraska State Historical Society, Lincoln, NE (MS2999).

Norris, G. W. 1928, Nov. 9. [Public statement issued by Senator Norris] Manuscript Record of Nebraska State Historical Society, Lincoln, NE (MS3298).

Norris, G. W. 1929, Dec. 14. [Letter to H. D. Strunk, Editor of McCook Daily Gazette] Manuscript Record of Nebraska State Historical Society, Lincoln, NE (MS2999).

Norris, G. W. 1940, April 8. Comparison of electric rates between municipally owned and privately owned plants. [Speech in the Senate of the United States]. Congressional Record. Washington, D.C.: Government Printing Office.

Norris, G. W. 1946. Fighting liberal: Autobiography of George W. Norris. New York: MacMillan.

"Cornfield with Pumpkins" Marion Smith

where wildness has such precarious space
by charles a. peek

no question now
the sumac in red splendor
our only vagrant and unruly sign,
sole comfort to some eastern sense of color,
of beauty, of well-being.

no doubt its brilliance looms much larger
in those microscopes we have evolved for eyes,
to raise the small to newer definition

but we esteem the sumac most
because its glory will be brief

this the schrift we grant
to things that by their being run heretic
to our orthodoxies:

difference here must pay the price
of seeming same.

ARTCULTURE

WRITING HOME NEBRASKA

Charles Peek, Professor of English

Pause over the works of those who have sought to capture the life of this place. It will not matter if their images are formed of words or drawn in paints, created by the most contemporary computer graphics or patterned in the ancient arts of tapestry. Nor will it matter if you are pausing over early Whitman or later Westerfield and Welch, over Cather or Cleary, Kloefkorn or Koozer. Possibly you will be looking at a Catlin or Benton; possibly at Marc Hoffman, Joan Sheen, Jeff Justensen, or Todd Smith. Perhaps you recall the "lieden" from the old German song clubs or are listening now to Libby Larsen. It will not matter. All that matters is that the image maker, the dream catcher has paid the place, in Wallace Stegner's words, "that human attention that at its highest reach we call poetry," and without which it is "no place."

Pause as poet Don Welch bids, and you will see that the common feature of all their works is a love-hate relationship with this place. Together, theirs is the art of ambivalent feelings. Some may express their ambivalence by following the beauty in the violence of our weather, others by finding a feeling of freedom in the ordered rows of our crops, the straight lines of our streets. It's all the same story, a story of what belongs to whom, who belongs where, and why our place produces for us such paradoxical passions. It is not a matter, as Stegner

assumed, of one person being placed and another displaced; here those terms describe one and the same person. They describe us all.

In places like Nebraska, space is the primary feature of our landscape, the only thing we have in abundance. Something about the meaning of place appears in the history of those old, sad warriors who gathered on these plains over a century ago now, the Indians and the cavalry whose battles youngsters used to re-enact. There and then, in the closing events of the unfortunately labeled "Indian" Wars and the subsequent closing of the frontier of that equally unfortunately labeled "free" land, "the world," Willa Cather lamented, "broke in two." Cather's phrase was at once belated and prescient, a half century after the fact but a half century before its recognition in contemporary studies. In any event, after the closing of the West precluded resolving its issues, those who inhabited the old prairie region would never again know quite where they were.

Crazy Horse

Even now, we can't ever quite feel like we belong where we are. The passage from Ian Frazier's <u>Great Plains</u>, where he recounts the death of Crazy Horse, captures and explains our dis-location. Frazier writes, "What I return to most often when I think of Crazy Horse is the fact that in the adjutant's office

Indian Camp at Pine Ridge, 1891   Butcher Collection

he refused to lie on the cot. Mortally wounded, frothing at the mouth, grinding his teeth in pain, he chose the floor instead. What a distance there is between that cot and the floor! On the cot, he would have been, in some sense, 'ours': an object of pity, an accident victim, 'the noble red man, the last of his race, etc. etc.' But on the floor Crazy Horse was Crazy Horse still. On the floor, he remembered Agent Lee, summoned him, forgave him. On the floor, unable to rise, he was guarded by soldiers even then. On the floor, he said goodbye to his father and Touch the Clouds, the last of the thousands that once followed him. And on the floor, still as far from white men as the limitless continent they once dreamed of, he died. Touch the Clouds pulled the blanket over his face: 'That is the lodge of Crazy Horse.' Lying where he chose, Crazy Horse showed the rest of us where we are standing."

The extraordinary aptness of his mother's name, "Touch the Clouds," sets the scene in ironic relief. Together Crazy Horse and Touch the Clouds confounded the sense of what was land, whose it was, and where we are. They pretty much displaced all of us who live here now and suggest the dispossession of many who do not. Crazy Horse's act, Touch the Cloud's epigram, resonate here, to be sure, but resonate equally whereever people feel out of place in their own place, a feeling being expressed by more

and more people, as, increasingly, difference encounters the driving forces of what we have preferred to call destiny. Poet Tino Villanueva aptly captures this feeling in his description of the character Sarge in the movie Giant. Villanueva writes of the irony:

that Sarge, or someone
like him, can banish you from this

Hamburger joint; from the rest of your
Life not yet entered; from this Holiday
Theater and all sense of place.

Crazy Horse's death–in its resonance through much of our history, many of our lives–provides ample evidence of how traumatic loss not only destroys romantic illusions but also creates a sense of things being out of place. Even now, as Gertrude Stein later put it of our own century, "nothing much agrees with anything else."

Dislocation and Loss

The events that brought about the settlement of our region ironically wrote an obituary to belonging. We know we don't belong here, that we are suffered here only by some "amazing grace." Possibly that's why we love it and, too, why we're such a suspicious lot. The cultural heritage that shaped the current life of this place arose right where we finally could no longer deny that loss is the nature of nature, hope the habit of any inhabitants who hang on. It

Southwest Custer County farm scene, 1892   Butcher Collection

Go back to
your homes
and work
on your eyes,
bring back a
sight which
can co-create
meaning.

DON**WELCH**

arose among those discovering that they would forever have to cope with the loss of the right to claim our own discoveries, embrace our own experience, name for ourselves the place where we live, where even our stories are written by absentee wordlords.

These are not the losses the world notes. Today, for instance, others are noting not simply the loss, but the hemorrhage of our population. And even we ourselves have not quite grasped how this experience links us, the current occupants of this region, with our predecessors in this place. But, our poetry, as before it their legends, discerns in the face put here on loss a trait others don't easily discern, a trait drawn, no doubt, from our sense of how weak are the vessels in which our lifeblood courses. It is the trait of taking pride in the absence of those things people elsewhere convince themselves they have to have. We take pride even in the absence of those others whom demographers further absent by referring to them as a "population."

This pride is enacted in "Nebraska" where Don Welch embraces the state as "a woman of spare beauty." To outsiders, our acceptance of "spare beauty," even of absence and deprivation, spells unhappiness. Thus, in the same poem, Welch allows the woman's voice to ask: "Why do you keep imagining me in other places and states? / And why do you keep assuming our children are unhappy?"

The striking thing, of course, is that we aren't any more unhappy than anyone else, possibly even less so. Adrian Louis, amidst the most horrible scenes and icons of reservation life on the Pine Ridge, continually captures the sense of irony that undergirds our acceptance of lack with a flair for hilarity.

In his novel, Skins, Louis writes: "Rudy got up out of his chair and walked over to where his brother was sitting. He shook his hand. Shaking hands was something Indians were extremely fond of doing. Someone once told him that when the first white men came here and shook their hands, the Indians found the act so hilarious that they fell to the ground and laughed for hours about it. It was such a pleasingly funny act that they kept doing it, and still do it each and every opportunity they get."

Paradox of Geography

Starting from the undeniable geography of these plains and from their inevitable brokenness, such writers show us how to find the way into a whole other country: by accepting both moments hilarious as a handshake and moments deep as the death of Crazy Horse, moments on the surface of the earth but at once at the heart of a new civilization. We learn to live in constant paradox, or we don't learn really to live at all.

And, in that paradox is the truth that here something urges us forward toward freedom,

HOW TO LIVE IN BUFFALO COUNTY

by DON**WELCH**

Bless the wind.

Listen to at least
three languages:
the county's, the township's,
your house.

Love distance like
a loon, read stones,
make wild flowers
familiar.

Live in this place,
hoping to get there.

freedom from much we might have accumulated, much we might even have cherished, but freedom, too, from let and hindrance. Where our hemorrhages are not overlooked, and above all not hidden or denied, our condition proves to be treatable after all. Bleeding sites heal, places bled into can be relieved; we can, in Twyla Hansen's lines from her poem "Blue Herons," "take inventory of threatened senses, / pick ourselves up above the dark water, / to rise, to rise."

Some call us a calculating people. If we are calculating, it is because we have always to juggle the equation, to make the finer distinctions, to find a place where we can have some space without that spaciousness leaving us no place, nothing that is really place. We are always seeking a way from mere material, mere plains, to that whole other country Texans claim to have already found but that would really be a country where human society could be great and human beings could be whole.

Where will that be? I am drawn to the closing lines of State Poet Bill Kloefkorn's poem, "Crazy Horse, Final Reflection, Number 7":

It does not matter where his body is,
for there is grass;
but where his spirit is,
there it will be good
for all of us to be.

Perhaps, however, that would be a wholly other country, one where, to be sure, we truly belong–but where it seems none of us can yet live.

Selected**References**

Frazier, I. 1989. Great plains. New York: Penguin.

Hansen, T. 1995. Wellsprings. Ed. S. K. George. Kearney, Nebraska: UNK.

Louis, A. 1995. Skins. New York: Crown.

Sanders, S. 1995. Wrting from the center. Bloomington, IN: University of Indiana Press.

Stegner, W. 1992. Where the bluebird sings to the lemonade springs. New York, Penguin.

Villanueva, T. 1993. Scene from the movie Giant. Willimantic, CT.: Curbstone Press.

Welch, D. 1975. Dead horse table. Lincoln, Nebraska: Windflower Press.

THE HAPPINESS AND THE CURSE

LITERARY VIEWS OF THE NEBRASKA PRAIRIE

Susanne George-Bloomfield, Professor of English

When American pioneers packed their belongings into their wagons and headed west, they not only brought along their hoes, quilts, kitchen chairs, and the family china, but they also imported preconceived ideas about what the Great Plains would be like.

In "The Prairies," poet William Cullen Bryant echoes the sentiments of his time and adds fuel to the westering movement when he describes the grasslands as "boundless and beautiful," calling them the "gardens of the desert." He compares the undulating grasses to waves on the ocean and declares the prairies God's most magnificent work: "The hand that built the firmament hath heaved / And smoothed these verdant swells, and sown their slopes / With herbage, planted them with island groves, / And hedged them round with forests." Further inspired by the belief that it was their "Manifest Destiny" to transform the wilderness into an American Garden of Eden, American and immigrant settlers set about to create a democratic utopia where everyone would have an equal chance to achieve the American Dream. Soon, however, these settlers discovered that although the soil was rich and the land free, the environment could be harsh and cruel. The reality of droughts, grasshoppers, and prairie fires, made more unbearable by the economic depression of the 1890s, caused some settlers to reassess their belief in the

"fruited plains" and to consider the hostile landscape as an American Desert. Many repacked their wagons and either returned to their families in the East or headed further west. Those who stayed, according to Mary Austin in <u>The Land of Little Rain</u>, had to learn to adapt to the reality that "the land sets the limits."

Western American literature has played a significant role in recording the facts of the settlement of the West. Native Americans Zitkala-Sa, Charles Eastman, and Luther Standing Bear recorded their lives and times before and during this discordant period on the Nebraska prairie. Other Nebraska writers, like Bess Streeter Aldrich, Mari Sandoz, Willa Cather, John Neihardt, Elia Peattie, Kate Cleary, Nellie Snyder Yost, and Mollie Sandford, have given us firsthand accounts of what life was like for the newly-arrived European inhabitants on the prairie, exploring the beliefs and emotions of the pioneer men and women as they began different lives in a new country. Of these writers, Willa Cather and Kate Cleary epitomize, through their lives and their writings, the love/hate relationship many pioneers experienced with the prairie landscape.

Willa Cather

Willa Cather, internationally acclaimed author of <u>O Pioneers!</u>, <u>My Antonia</u>, <u>A Lost</u>

Mary Miner, Willa Cather, and Douglass Cather in Red Cloud, Nebraska

Lady, One of Ours, and countless other stories about the Nebraska prairies, arrived in Webster County, Nebraska, from Virginia in 1883. She was nine years old. Cather grew up on the dusty streets of Red Cloud, meeting the immigrants who came to town for supplies and exploring the rich farm lands bordering the Republican River as well as the grassy prairie along the Divide, the broad plateau of land between the Little Blue and Republican Rivers. These were essential years for her as a writer. In a 1921 interview, she stated: "I think that most of the basic material a writer works with is acquired before the age of fifteen. That's the important period: when one's not writing. Those years determine whether one's work will be poor and thin or rich and fine."

Cather entered the University of Nebraska at Lincoln in September 1890 and graduated in 1895. Three years later, at age thriry-three, she became managing editor of McClure's magazine, one of the largest and most prestigious magazines in America. However, editing other authors' works did not give her time to do her own writing, so in 1909, Cather moved to a Greenwich Village apartment in New York City. Realizing that her childhood memories of the Nebraska prairie were her most important, she wrote O Pioneers! in 1913 and My Antonia in 1918, beginning a long line of successful novels and collections of short stories. All of this time she had to deal with critics who said: "I don't give a damn about Nebraska no matter who writes about it."

Later in her life, Cather described her ambivalent response to the vast Nebraska prairie: "This country was mostly wild pasture and as naked as the back of your hand. I was little and homesick and lonely and my mother was homesick and nobody paid any attention to us, so the country and I had it out together and by the end of the first autumn, that shaggy grass country had gripped me with a passion that I have never been able to shake. It has been the happiness and the curse of my life."

Kate Cleary

Kate Cleary, born in Canada, was raised in New Brunswick, Philadelphia, and Chicago. In 1884, she came as a twenty-year old bride to the newly established town of Hubbell, with its "brand new buildings, many in process of erection, straggling across riven cornfields," situated in south-central Nebraska, about fifty miles east of Cather's Red Cloud. Soon, thanks to the mushrooming growth of the new community and materials from her husband's lumber business, the Clearys were able to construct a new, two-story Victorian-style home where Cleary did much of her writing.

The Nebraska years produced an eclectic assortment of works by Cleary: domestic articles published in <u>Good Housekeeping</u>; humorous sketches and poetry in <u>Puck</u> magazine; naturalistic short stories about the West for the <u>Chicago Tribune</u> and <u>Belford's Monthly</u>; and children's stories and poems in <u>St. Nicholas</u> and the <u>Youth's Companion</u>. In 1893, she was honored by having two of her poems read in the opening ceremonies for the Nebraska Building at the Chicago World's Fair. Cleary's second novel, <u>Like a Gallant Lady</u>, 1897, was set in fictional Bubble, Nebraska. The romantic plot, enlivened by realistic descriptions of prairie life, both rural and urban, involves an insurance scam in a tiny frontier community.

In 1898, the Cleary family returned to Chicago when her husband's health worsened and his business faltered due to the general Depression of the 1890s. There, she began writing her strongest realistic short stories, most of them about the people and places in Nebraska, many of them humorous and satirical.

Cleary, like Cather, had conflicting emotions toward Nebraska. In the first stanza of her poem, "To Nebraska," which prefaces <u>Like a Gallant Lady</u>, she describes Nebraska as "a land of toil and pain" and a place "Where high hopes are buried low." However, in the opposing second stanza, she predicts that it is "a land that yet shall be / Fair and fertile, proud and free." The poem's conclusion illustrates her mixed feelings about her life on the Nebraska prairie, a place that "Harboured bride, and slave and guest, / Has been kind to–has been cruel– / And has given worst–and best!"

Both Cather and Cleary reveal in their writings the range of opposing emotions they experienced towards the plains as well as reflecting the diverse experiences and attitudes of their neighbors. Neither saw Nebraska dialectically, either as a hopeless, unyielding Desert or a promising, fruitful Garden, but realistically recorded in their works the complex interplay of men and women with the land, which allowed some to succeed while forcing others to fail. In these women's most successful works, a tension exists within the stories as the characters struggle with the realities of the land.

Cather's "Earth Mothers"

In <u>O Pioneers!</u>, Cather describes the struggles pioneers faced in trying to domesticate the grassy plains. John Bergson, after working the land for eleven years, laments that he "had made but little impression upon the wild lands he had come to tame." He compares the fertile grasslands to "a horse no one knows how to break to harness, that runs wild and kicks things to pieces." He had an idea that "no one knew how to farm it properly."

Bergson's daughter, Alexandra, inherits the land and the responsibility of surviving on it. Her father also passes down to her his American Dream of living in freedom and with self-reliance on his own land. One day, as Alexandra drives from the rich bottom-lands along the Republican River to her farm on the prairies of the Divide, she realizes that she had never known before how much the country meant to her: "The chirping of the insects down in the long grass had been like the sweetest music. She had felt as if her heart were hiding down there, somewhere, with the quail and the plover and all the little wild things that crooned or buzzed in the sun. Under the long shaggy ridges, she felt the future stirring." Because Alexandra is able to accommodate her belief in the Garden Myth to the realities of the land, she succeeds in transforming the wild grasslands into fertile croplands– "the country had become what she had hoped."

Antonia Shimerda, from Cather's <u>My Antonia</u>, serves as another strong woman who helps the prairie bear fruitful harvests. Antonia loves the prairie, but her father, who can not endure the harshness and isolation of the New Frontier, commits suicide. Cather describes the love of Antonia and Jim Burden, her friend and neighbor, for the grasslands: "As far as we could see, the miles of copper-red grass were drenched in sunlight that was stronger and fiercer than at any other time of the day. . . . The whole prairie was like a bush that burned with fire and was not consumed. That hour always had the exultation of victory, of triumphant ending."

In the end, Antonia triumphs in her pastoral Eden. No longer does she have to subsist on "some potatoes that had been frozen and were rotting," for her new fruit

Isolated Thayer County farm wife in the doorway of her log house, 1890s

Community of women in early Hubbell, Nebraska

Kate Cleary, her son, Gearld, and her mother in downtown Hubbell, Nebraska, 1891

cellar overflows with barrels of pickles and shelves of canned vegetables and fruit, the barn stores sacks of wheat flour, and the orchard, "grown up in tall bluegrass," boasts rows of fruit trees that Antonia loves "as if they were people." The once outcast immigrant woman fulfills her Bohemian grandmother's dream of finding happiness and success in the New World.

Ennobled by the land, both Alexandra and Antonia serve as symbolic and mythic Earth Mothers in the American Garden of the West, personifying the goodness and fertility of the grasslands and portraying the strengths and passions of many of America's early settlers. This connection with the land is not achieved without cost, and Cather creates tension in the text by depicting other settlers, like Alexandra's brothers, Antonia's father, Pavel and Peter, Crazy Ivan, and Frank Shabata, who fail in domesticating the wilderness.

Cleary's Protagonists

Cleary, too, creates characters that personify differing views of the western experience. In "An Ornament to Society," she describes a mother's and daughter's opposite responses to life on the Nebraska prairie. Mrs. Harrowsby "had been the model of all the hard-worked farmer's wives around" through her "unceasing labor." Because of her harsh and isolated life on the farm, Mrs. Harrowsby had three wishes. She coveted a black silk dress, a house in town, and a different life for her only surviving child, Cleopatra, a young girl upon whose capable shoulders heavy farm work had often been placed.

One of Mrs. Harrowsby's dying wishes was for her daughter to become "an ornament to society," a lady with white hands and a proficiency in embroidery and china painting, a lady who "never does any work except play on the pianny–or the organ if she hasn't a pianny." Unfortunately, Cleo's hands were more skillful in "handling the reins from the seat of a harrow, or even when gripped confidently around plow handles."

When Cleo dislocates her shoulder breaking a young, black stallion, her father decides to send her to a convent to continue her career of feminine culture. She rebels and returns, living "almost all of her waking hours in the open air." She exults in life on the prairie with "those crisp, yellow, autumnal days, whether walking miles and miles or skimming over the good, hard Nebraska roads on her bicycle her father had bought her, or shooting quail and prairie chicken along the short cuts and seldom used prairie ways."

The tale concludes with the marriage of Cleo and the hired man, and their move to a farm of their own where they will till and harvest the crops together. In this story, a man and a woman work together as equals, sharing their respect and love for the land as well as the work, despite family opposition. A fulfilling life on the farm, Cleary concludes, is often a matter of temperament.

Cleary also analyzes mixed emotions toward the prairie in her novel, Like a Gallant Lady. She narrates the story through the consciousness of Ivera Lyle, a sophisticated young woman from Chicago, who comes to Nebraska to solve the mystery of her fiancé's disappearance. Ivera arrives in Nebraska with preconceived, eastern notions of the land: "It is different from what I imagined. I've always thought of Nebraska as level. I find its prairies are like the waves of a subsiding sea." She, too, compares the prairie to an ocean, admiring its "billowy undulations all plaided with the dull amber of cornstalks, the vivid green of winter wheat, the delicate daffodil of withered grass." Her brother, Rob, humorously responds, "It is level, in spots . . . This doesn't happen to be one of the spots."

Ivera's first response to the grasslands is positive: "It was an idyllic morning, the sky blue and luminous, the earth wearing a fresh-washed face, the air crisp and caressing. There were shifting, silvery hazes on the distant bluffs, and to one city bred the absolute absence of sound was by contrast strangely restful." Later in the novel, after Ivera has spent the winter with her brother in a little shack on the prairie, that same silence overwhelms her: "The plains stretched away, boundless and mysterious. The sky, frigated with whitish clouds, loomed low and light. Between these crept the silence, the awful, oppressive, over-whelming silence of the prairies. It seemed to close around the girl standing there in gigantic coils that crushed out individuality–almost extinguished identity. An impulse to scream as if in a nightmare frenzy–anything to break the spell, came to her."

Cleary compares the silence of the plains to a monstrous snake, personifying the abstract fear felt by many homesteaders when confronted by Nebraska's vast and empty grasslands. The physical isolation of the open prairies creates in Ivera what Diane Quantic, in The Nature of the Place, terms a "psychological entrapment" that produces "an acute sense of displacement," causing individuals to withdraw from normal human society or try desperately to escape.

When Ivera visits the farmers' wives in their rude log houses and dugouts, she observes their feelings of hopelessness, and it reinforces her negative viewpoint of the prairie: "Such isolation! Such monotony! Such drudgery! And the hopelessness of ever escaping from these conditions accentuates the horror of them." One of the women homesteaders Ivera meets compares her life on the homestead to that of one of Rudyard Kipling's fictional characters, Marrowbie Jukes, who tries to escape from the plague pit: "We are like that here," she said. "When those accursed creatures tried to scale the walls that bounded their living grave, the sand sifted down on them, destroying their foothold. We try to escape, and there is the drouth one year out of three, sometimes oftener. In the odd years of prosperity the price of grain goes down, until the most a man makes after all goes but a short way toward paying the indebtedness incurred dur-ing the years his land yielded him nothing."

Here Cleary ironically depicts the grass-land, stretching unbroken from horizon to horizon, as a prison, from which there is no escape.

The tension in Cleary's works often is not only between characters, one viewing the land as benevolent and another as antago-nistic, but the struggle also exists within the characters themselves. Cleo must muster up enough courage to resist her mother's dying wish and her father's guilt in order to return to the farm, breaking sod and breaking horses. Ivera must reappraise the mythic baggage she brought from Chicago when she discovers that Nebraska is "different from what I'd imagined."

In O Pioneers!, Cather writes, "But the great fact was the land itself." Once the pioneers unpacked their wagons and built their sod houses, they had to confront the prairie. As they attempted to survive in the new country, their experiences with its bounty as well as its adversity forced them to reassess their mythic preconceptions. Those who were unable to adapt to the land's demands saw the prairie as a curse. Those who endured and became one with the sea of grasses discovered, like Antonia, what it was like "to be dissolved into something complete and great."

Selected **References**

Cather, W. 1918. My Antonia. Boston: Houghton Mifflin.
---. 1913. O Pioneers! Boston: Houghton Mifflin.

Cleary, K.M. 1897. Like a gallant lady. Chicago: Way & Williams.

---. 1899. "An ornament to society." Ed. S.K. George, 1997.

George, S.K. 1997. Kate M. Cleary: A literary biography with selected works. Lincoln: University of Nebraska Press.

Quantic, D. 1995. The nature of the place: A study of great plains fiction. Lincoln: University of Nebraska Press.

Woodress, J. 1987. Willa Cather: A literary life. Lincoln: University of Nebraska Press.

art culture

WORDS AND MUSIC:

CATHER AND LARSEN, "THE MARGARET SONGS"

Valerie Cisler, Associate Professor of Music and Performing Arts &
Anne Foradori, Assistant Professor of Music and Performing Arts

The Margaret Songs, written by contemporary composer Libby Larsen, are three songs that comprise a character sketch of Margaret Elliot, a character in the chamber opera, Eric Hermannson's Soul. This opera, which premiered at Opera Omaha in November, 1998, is based on a short story by Willa Cather by the same title, published in 1900. The Margaret Songs were commissioned by the Nebraska Music Teachers Association and first premiered at a concert of Libby Larsen's works at the 1996 Nebraska Music Teachers Association State Convention.

The story of Margaret Elliot is a compelling one–a young woman whose life is inexorably changed by a trip to the West. The landscape of the prairie, with its tall grass, open spaces, endless horizons, and magnificent sunsets become a metaphor for Margaret's life–a fresh canvas onto which she paints the landscape of her life, changed to a new and heightened awareness by love and by the immense beauty of the prairie. Willa Cather's words hold a significant message for those who have experienced the prairie and been transformed by its wonders.

The Emerging American Voice

The depiction of "American life" has held a fascination for both American and European composers since the late nineteenth century. Stage and orchestral works, as well as art songs, have explored themes of Americana, patriotism, and the mythical Wild West. New England composer Charles Ives infused all genres of musical works with quotations from patriotic songs, hymn tunes, and popular melodies, weaving the old and familiar with new musical ideas. Ferde Grofé's orchestral work, Grand Canyon Suite (1931), painted a vivid picture of a journey through the west, borrowing melodies and rhythms from folk and cowboy songs. Douglas Moore's opera, The Ballad of Baby Doe (1958), tells the story of the rise and fall of a mining empire in Colorado in the late 19th century. The West even inspired Italian composer Giacomo Puccini to write an opera based on American playwright David Belasco's play, The Girl of the Golden West. The result was La Fanciulla del West (1907), a western story, complete with sheriff, outlaws, and a saloon maid, sung in Italian!

American musicals from the "Golden Age" of Broadway, like Oklahoma (1943), Annie Get Your Gun (1946), and Paint Your Wagon (1951), helped to perpetuate the tales of the Old West by depicting these larger than life characters in real and imagined dramatic situations. As American composers searched for their musical identities, they began to broaden their vision, moving from the East and traditions of the European masters to the West–a land of rugged landscape, tales of adventure, and new traditions. More than any composer of his generation, Aaron Copland sought to incorporate western themes in his works. From his opera of the prairie, <u>The Tender Land</u> (1954), to western ballets, <u>Rodeo</u> (1942) and <u>Billy the Kid</u> (1938), Copland celebrated the American West. In addition to these stage works, Copland arranged a dozen <u>Old American Songs</u> (1950, 1952), which have become a repertoire staple in American Art Song literature.

The American Art Song has evolved from a rich and varied legacy: written classical traditions of nineteenth century German Lied (Schubert, Schumann and Brahms); French mélodie (Fauré and Debussy); and oral traditions of folk song. These have become a wellspring of ideas for melodies and texts, forming and shaping the development of the American Art Song. Poets like Walt Whitman, Langston Hughes, and Carl Sandburg, who addressed "The American Experience" in their verse and found the rhythm of American life in common parlance, became a significant influence to a new generation of American song composers.

During the 1920s and after World War II, young composers traveled to Europe to study with French composer and pedagogue Nadia Boulanger. Celebrated American composers Aaron Copland and Leonard Bernstein were among her pupils. Boulanger did not so much teach a specific "style" or "school" of composition as encourage her students to create a mélange, borrowing from many traditions (including popular music) to formulate their own "American sound."

In the last half-century, American composers have looked beyond poetry for sources of text. Poetic prose, essays, and diary entries, as well as the use of poetic fragments, became new sources of rich literary material. The absence of verse form, strict meter, rhyme, and academic English, and the focus on larger forms, free verse, and vernacular English with its abundance of short and descriptive words, enabled composers to make musical choices that more closely followed and complimented their individual styles. Composers crafted not only musical portraits, but also shaped a literary image through careful and thoughtful selection of fragments from a larger work.

The trend in contemporary American Art Song appears to be the shaping and creation of dramatic persona in song. Calling their compositions monodramas, character studies, or cycles, recent works by American composers have renewed the popularity of the art song. <u>The Margaret Songs</u> by Libby Larsen is one such example.

Libby Larsen

Libby Larsen (b. 1950) is one of America's most prolific, successful, and influential composers of her generation. She has a

Libby Larsen   Courtesy of Libby Larsen

Music is a language, influenced by the spoken language, and both represent the soul.

LIBBY**LARSEN**

and Publishers (ASCAP), the American Symphony Orchestra League, and the National Endowment for the Arts. In addition, she is a guest lecturer at colleges, universities, and conventions throughout the United States.

Larsen and the Art Song

When asked to describe her musical style in a September 25, 1996, interview for the Terre Haute Tribune-Star, Libby Larsen said, "I do have a style, but the style is not recognized in the consistent use of a harmonic language . . . My style can be recognized by its rhythm more than anything else. I believe that music springs from language of the people. I am intensely interested in how music can be derived from the rhythms and pitches of spoken American English."

During an October 17, 1996, lecture for the NMTA, she explained, "I am interested in finding the rhythms and language and tempos by which we live in this country. With each piece I try to find the kind of musical language to communicate to contemporary audiences–some of whom would be very knowledgeable and some of whom would not be particularly knowledgeable. Every piece in one way or another is a search to find out who we are."

Since the late 1970s, Larsen has found a real interest in American English, which is very different than working with translations from German, French, or Italian. She specifically looks for texts that are American English. Larsen has, in fact, based several song cycles on texts of the American West, including Cowboy Songs (1979) and Songs from Letters: Calamity Jane to her daughter Janey, 1880-1902 (1989). The texts of The Margaret Songs are drawn from three different works by Willa Cather, two poems, "Going Home" and "The Hawthorn Tree," and the short story, "Eric Hermannsons's Soul."

Cather and Music

Perhaps Larsen was drawn to the works of Willa Cather because of their intrinsic musical cadence, for Cather not only captured the rhythms of the American and immigrant voices, but aspired to transform readers to the very essence of artistic expression, that which communicates itself above

remarkably varied compositional output, ranging from solo repertoire to small and large vocal and instrumental chamber works, to works for the theatre and dance, and finally, the most extensive, for orchestra and opera. Her music is prized for its contemporary American, at times humorous and also deeply moving, spirit.

Ms. Larsen's awards and commissions are of national and international significance. Her music is widely performed and recorded by major artists and orchestras, such as the Baltimore Symphony, the Los Angeles Chamber Orchestra, and the London Symphony on labels such as Decca, Koch International, Angel/EMI, and others. Her "Sonnets From the Portuguese" were featured on a 1994 Grammy-Award-Winning CD. Ms. Larsen has received commissions from Saint Paul Chamber Orchestra, the Cleveland String Quartet, the Minnesota Opera, the Charlotte Symphony, and the Colorado Symphony Orchestra.

In addition to her active life as a composer, Ms. Larsen has, perhaps, made an equally significant contribution to music through her active role as an arts advocate. In 1973, she co-founded the Minnesota Composer's Forum, now the American Composer's Forum. Ms. Larsen has also served as advisor to several important organizations, including the American Society of Composers, Authors literal content. To Cather, explains Richard Giannone in <u>Music in Willa Cather's Fiction</u>, music was the pre-eminent art form, "the condition toward which other significant forms aspire." Edith Lewis writes, "I think no critic has sufficiently emphasized, or possibly recognized, how much musical forms influenced her composition and how her style, her beauty of cadence and rhythm, were the result of a sort of transposed musical feeling, and were arrived at almost unconsciously, instead of being a conscious effort to produce definite effects with words." Cather freely called the essential appeal of a play or poem the "music of a work."

Music was a true passion for Cather during her entire life. As a child she took piano lessons, but seemed more interested in listening to the stories her teacher would tell of his experiences of his European life and studies with the famed Anton Rubinstein. While in Pittsburgh and New York, she regularly attended the opera and recitals and had several musician friends, including Yehudi Menuhin and Myra Hess.

Throughout her literary works, music is used both directly through characters and indirectly through symbolism and metaphor. In "Eric Hermannson's Soul," the main character, Eric, a violinist, struggles between religious inhibition through deprivation of his natural impulses (the violin was considered a devil's instrument) and the inner belief that music was "his only bridge into the kingdom of the soul." That a composer has set Cather's texts to music serves to enshrine her work on a level she considered a pre-eminent art form, with universal communicative powers. In a May 12, 1900, article for the <u>Courier</u>, Cather terms music as "the speech of the soul." Cather and Larsen share a fundamental view of the process of their work—the artist serving as a medium for art, not as art serving as a vehicle for the self.

Margaret Songs

Margaret Elliot is one of two principal characters from Willa Cather's short story "Eric Hermannson's Soul." Larsen has set three songs as a character sketch, depicting the story from Margaret's point of view—her experiences on an adventurous journey by

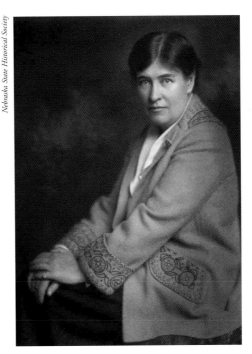

Willa Cather

train to the west in "Bright Rails;" her transformation of inner spirit as she becomes aware of the shallowness of her city life in "So Little There;" and her reaction to having found her one true love, Eric, in "Beneath the Hawthorne Tree." The texts of <u>The Margaret Songs</u> are drawn from three different works by Willa Cather; only the text of the second song, "So Little There," is derived directly from an excerpt of "Eric Hermannson's Soul." Larsen employs but three lines of the original text—the first and last lines of the song, and the phrase "Oh, it is all so little there!" The remainder of the song's text is constructed from impressions and images—dramatic license which captures the heart of the scene based on Cather's lengthier narrative. The two poems, which frame the set ("Going Home" [Larsen's "Bright Rails"] and "The Hawthorne Tree" [Larsen's "Beneath the Hawthorne Tree"]), were chosen for their depiction of particular sentiments or moods rather than of story line.

Margaret Elliot

Margaret Elliot is the toast of New York Victorian culture. She grew up in a world of affectation, wit, culture, and language, and she has mastered all the arts and manners of her culture. She is engaged to a fellow from her same class and status, but before she's married, she wants to take "the tour."

I must have music!

WILLA**CATHER**

GOING HOME
(BURLINGTON ROUTE)

How smoothly the trains run beyond the Missouri;
Even in my sleep I know when I have crossed the river.
The wheels turn as if they were glad to go;
The sharp curves and windings left behind,
The roadway wide open,
(The crooked straight
And the rough places plain).

They run smoothly, they run softly, too.
There is not noise enough to trouble the lightest sleeper.
Nor jolting to wake the weary-hearted.
I open my window and let the air blow in,
The air of morning,
That smells of grass and earth–
Earth, the grain-giver.

How smoothly the trains run beyond the Missouri;
Even in my sleep I know when I have crossed the river.
The wheels turn as if they were glad to go;
They run like running water,
Like Youth, running away . . .
They spin bright along the bright rails,
Singing and humming,
Singing and humming.
They run remembering,
They run rejoicing,
As if they, too, were going home.

from April Twilights and Other Poems by Willa Cather.
Copyright 1923 by Willa Cather and renewed 1951
by the Executors of the Estate of Willa Cather.
Reprinted by permission of Alfred A. Knopf, Inc.

Although most nineteenth century travelers visited the great cities of Europe, many set their sights on the West. An adventurous spirit, Margaret decides not to go to Europe, but to go west with her brother Wyllis.

Margaret and Wyllis take the train across the West and cross the Missouri River; their destination is Rattlesnake Creek, Nebraska. As Margaret arrives in Rattlesnake Creek, she is absolutely captivated by her journey and charmed by the quaintness of the people around her, who are equally charmed by her wit and polished manner. She has come to gather stories of the Wild West to share at dinner parties back east.

I. "Bright Rails"

The text for the first song is an excerpt from Cather's poem "Going Home" ("Bright Rails"), from April Twilights and Other Poems, 1923. It was written by Cather in recollection of her travels west to visit family in Nebraska. Rich in imagery, the poem evokes the spirit of the journey by rail, an emotional state that Larsen finds befittingly expressive of Margaret's similar state of mind en route to Nebraska. There are some small, but significant differences between Cather's original verse and Larsen's adaptation. The change from "the trains run beyond the Missouri" to "the train runs beyond the Missouri" personalizes the journey for Margaret. She is no longer speaking in the abstract, but of her own experience– the journey by rail and of the heart. Repetition of the first line of text at the end of the poem gives the song a cyclical feeling–a sense of seamless continuity, like the wheels of the train that turn without ceasing until the destination is reached at journey's end.

"Bright Rails" captures the true spirit of the art song through its marriage of text and music. It is framed by a mezmerizing accompaniment evoking the motion and sounds of a train. The music enhances the text through a variety of repetitive rhythmic and overlapping intervallic patterns–the smallest note values in the upper voice, like the wheels turning fast; the middle voices in two-measure ostinato (repeated pattern) groupings, suggesting the equi-distant breaks in the track; and the long pedal tones in the bass, heavy and persistent, perhaps representing the body and weight of the train itself. Above the sounds of the train, the voice sings in long, smooth tones, as if depicting the scenery from the eyes of a

Prairie Windmill

passenger. The eyes move slowly along the horizon, gazing over the vast landscape, only periodically becoming aware of the sounds of the train itself.

In the tradition of the art song, Larsen effectively uses the music to "paint" the words of the text. Margaret sings, "even in my sleep I know I have crossed the river," as the accompaniment comes to the foreground. She becomes aware of the change in sound of the clamoring wheels on the open track, while the breaks in the track become more pronounced. Larsen creates an effective color contrast as Margaret sings, "They spin along the bright rails" through a sudden harmonic shift to a higher, brighter palette of sound. A dramatic moment occurs when the continuous motion of the train wheels comes to a stop as Margaret sings, "they run remembering, they run rejoicing." She seems to become unaware of her surroundings and relishes the inner experience of looking out at the miles of bright rails with a heightened sense of freedom and adventure. Margaret sings of "going home" as the music returns to its "home key." While the train takes its passengers to their homes, it is also a metaphor for Margaret's personal journey of the heart.

II. "So Little There"

The text for the second song is based on an excerpt from the second part of Cather's short story, "Eric Hermannson's Soul." "So Little There" is a scene of transformation in which Margaret begins by controlling the situation. She sings of the social gestures which make up the fabric of her life as an upper-crust Victorian New Yorker–teas, dances, invitations, gloves, and gossip. She tells her brother Wyllis that she hasn't been so happy in years, and likens this new adventure on the plains to their childhood fantasies of exploring Troy. But the Great Plains of Nebraska give her a profound and disturbing new perspective on herself. For the first time in her life, she experiences the horizon, the sunset, and the immensity of her surroundings– she is overwhelmed by powerful emotions that she simply cannot control. Margaret's transformation mirrors Cather's own experience of traveling West to Nebraska as a child. In a 1913 interview in the Philadelphia Record, she explains, "As we drove further and further out into the country, I felt a good deal as if we had come to the end of everything–it was a kind of erasure of personality."

The musical setting of this text is evocative of the great differences between life in New York City, depicted by fast, articulate rhythms, and a vocal line that resembles a patter in its limited range–in direct juxtapo

I haven't been so happy
since we were children discovering the ruins of Troy
and here we are!
Just like when we were children, Together!
Away from New York City and its endless details.
So many small things in the city!

Teas and dances. Invitations.
Thank you notes. Gloves and gossip.
Small things
Oh, it all is so little there!

Minutes filled to the brim with detail.
Hours enslaved by fashion.
Days, months and years
a calendar of manners. Always manners!
The wind has swept that all away.
Here at the edge of the world, when I lift my foot
I feel I could step through the sunset into heaven.

Artists in the galleries of New York
portend to paint the mysteries of clouds
writers and poets have only words to tell us about the
light of dawn and dusk,
the smell of May, the sound of summer,
the silence of snow.

Actors and singers play the stage
They make believe that love finds itself in words,
I used to think it natural that two minds could love,
even if the hearts do not.
When ev'rything else is so small,
Why should I expect love to be great! . . .

Margaret Songs: Three Songs from Willa Cather
Music: Libby Larsen (b. 1950)
©1996 Oxford University Press, Inc.
Used by permission.

herself to question her belief system, she becomes more detached from the patter, the pace of her New York life. She realizes, as she catalogues all the things about her east coast life, that the things she has mastered and loves are really small and do not define true emotion.

Margaret's transformation is communicated musically through an augmentation of musical elements, most noticeably through tempo, but also through an extended range in both voice and piano and an increase in harmonic tension. Ascending vocal lines in phrases mirror Margaret's awakening, her search for answers, her search for true love. She ends the song by saying, "When everything else is so small, why should I expect love to be great." The postlude ends in a question, the tension musically depicted through harmonic dissonance.

III. "Beneath the Hawthorn Tree"

The final song is a verbatim setting of Cather's "The Hawthorn Tree," from April Twilights, 1903. Although the words are unrelated to the story line of "Eric Hermannson's Soul," Larsen's artistic license in selecting this poem is based on the composer's primary concern for relaying the overwhelming intensity of Margaret's having found her one true love. The words of Cather's early poem eloquently express the passion of true love and are ideally suited to Larsen's portrayal of the character's profound experience with this fundamental and universal sentiment.

In Cather's story, Margaret meets Eric Hermannson, a fellow who doesn't speak English very well, but who speaks with every part of his being, in a silent, strong, and very profound way. Margaret and Eric understand one another without words. It is through Margaret's music that Eric is released from his artistic suppression and

sition with Margaret's impressions and emotional experience of the Great Plains and of her growing self-awareness, which are depicted by long pedal tones with sweeping scales, legato lines, and freer, recitative-like rubato rhythms. The tempo contrasts move from fast and animated to sections with markings such as "as if suspended in time." She says, "when I lift my foot here, I feel as though I could step through the sunset into heaven." As Margaret allows

THE HAWTHORN TREE | by WILLA CATHER

Across the shimmering meadows—
Ah, when he came to me!
In the spring-time,
In the night-time,
In the starlight,
Beneath the hawthorn tree.

Up the misty marsh-land—
Ah, when he climbed to me!
To my white bower,
To my sweet rest,
To my warm breast,
Beneath the hawthorn tree.

Ask me of what the birds sang,
High in the hawthorn tree;
What the breeze tells,
What the rose smells,
What the stars shine—
Not what he said to me!

from April Twilights. 1903; 1923; 1933.
(Reprint 1903 ed.) published by University
of Nebraska Press, 1990.

returned to the language of the soul. "The Hawthorn Tree" is rich in imagery and metaphor, evoking the spirit of Margaret and Eric's "one great moment" on the night of the dance, their one and only night together. "Margaret gets her one great moment in this song of rapture, but it's her rapture," states Larsen during the NMTA lecture. "It is not to be shared at any dinner table party in the East; in fact, when she returns to the East coast, she knows that she won't be telling any tales of quaint Norwegian dances—she won't be talking about this at all."

The musical fabric of this song is marked by an ostinato (repeated) pattern in the middle register with rhapsodic, colorful "splashes" of sound in the upper register and long tones in the lower register. Larsen's effective use of word painting is evident in numerous ascending vocal lines. Phrases like "starlight," "up from the misty marshland," "when he climbed to me," and "starshine," evoke an image of uplifted motion. Margaret sings of "shimmering meadows," the tall prairie grasses that appear to dance in the wind. The "splashes" of sound are heard in the moonlight sparkling on the river, the twinkling stars on a clear summer night, the birds in the Hawthorn tree.

An extraordinary, inner transformation takes place in this story. Libby Larsen has tried to convey this transformation of Margaret in just these three songs. The set does not comprise a scene from the opera, but rather a character sketch. Together the three songs are meant to give the listener an idea of Margaret's character in the opera. In the tradition of art song and opera aria, Larsen's selection of these three texts by Cather serve to express the character's richly varied emotional reactions to her circumstances. As Margaret expresses,

"I think if one lived here long enough one would quite forget how to be trivial, and would read only the great books . . . and would remember only the greatest music."

Selected **References**

Balensuela, M. "Composer emphasizes rhythm in her music." Special to the Tribune-Star. Terre Haute, Indiana, 25 September 1996.

Bohlke, L.B., ed. 1986. Willa Cather in person: Interviews, speeches and letters. Lincoln: University of Nebraska Press.

Cather, W. 1970. "Eric Hermannson's soul," Willa Cather's collected short fiction 1892-1912. Ed. V. Faulkner. Lincoln: University of Nebraska Press.

---. 1923. "Going Home." April twilights and other poems. New York: Alfred A. Knopf.

---. 1903. "The Hawthorn Tree." April twilights. Ed. B. Slote. Lincoln: University of Nebraska Press, 1968.

Giannone, R. 1968. Music in Willa Cather's fiction. Lincoln: University of Nebraska Press.

Larsen, L. Lecture at Nebraska Music Teachers Association State Convention. Hastings, Nebraska: Hastings College. 17 October 1996.

---. Letter to authors, 26 June 1998.

---. 1996. Margaret Songs. New York: Oxford University Press.

a r t c u l t u r e

PRAIRIE RECLAMATION PROJECT

THE POETRY OF TWYLA HANSEN AND DON WELCH

Steven P. Schneider, Associate Professor of English

American poets have long held a fascination with the prairies. In <u>Specimen Days</u> (1882), Walt Whitman wrote that the vast stretches of buffalo grass and wild sage in the country's midlands are "North America's characteristic landscape." The "pure breath, primitiveness, boundless prodigality and amplitude" of the prairies inspired several poems that appeared in <u>Leaves of Grass</u>, including "The Prairie States," "The Prairie-Grass Dividing," "Prairie Nights," and a "Prairie Sunset."

Over one hundred years after the death of Walt Whitman, the prairie landscape still figures prominently in the work of contemporary Nebraska poets. Although much of the original prairie of this region, described by Whitman and later by Willa Cather in lyrical terms, has been plowed under, planted over, or blown away, contemporary plains poets such as William Kloefkorn, Ted Kooser, Roy Scheele, Don Welch, Carol Ann Russell, Twyla Hansen, Linda Hasselstrom, Nancy McCleery and Kathleene West, to name but a few, continue to reclaim the prairie as an important landscape for their poetry.

Indeed, there has been something of a renaissance of prairie poetry in the last twenty-five years, with several anthologies devoted to it. Two of the more interesting anthologies, <u>As Far As I Can See</u> (1989, Windflower Press, ed. Charles Woodard) and <u>Wellsprings</u> (1995, University of Nebraska at Kearney,

ed. Susanne K. George) were both published in Nebraska, a veritable breeding ground for poets today who feel deeply connected to the prairies. Moreover, a number of small presses, among them The Slow Tempo Press and Sandhills Press, have published some very fine individual collections. Mark Sanders, editor of the Sandhills Press, has long been a champion of prairie poets, and his series of chapbooks has been especially influential in introducing readers to the newest work of these writers.

Two of the most compelling figures in this resurgence of contemporary prairie poetry are Twyla Hansen and Don Welch. They represent two different generations of writers among contemporary plains poets. Hansen, a horticulturalist at Nebraska Wesleyan University, is a member of a younger generation of prairie poets that would include J.V. Brummels and Barbara Schmitz. Don Welch, who taught at the University of Nebraska at Kearney for thirty-nine years, is a member of a more senior generation of Nebraska poets, which includes William Kloefkorn and Ted Kooser. Hansen and Welch, through their poetic careers and their poems, represent an on-going engagement with the prairies. Their hard-won knowledge of its flora and fauna testify to the legacy of the prairie in the literary imagination of two different generations of contemporary American writers.

Walt Whitman

Before examining the prairie poetry of Hansen and Welch, however, I would first like to pause and have you consider some of Whitman's remarks and writings about the prairie, for he provides us with an historical context for contemporary poetry that reclaims the prairie. As early as 1871, in Democratic Vistas, Whitman had speculated that the nation's future capital could be refounded in the nation's heartland. In his prairie poems, Whitman celebrates the open and sunlit landscape of the prairies–"with the far circle-line of the horizon all times of day." In his expansive vision of inland America, he discovered an analog for his own expansive consciousness and for his idealized conception of Americans living free of constraint.

Whitman, of course, lived prior to the agricultural development of the region and could not foresee the development of the land in ways that Willa Cather suggested in her novel My Antonia and addressed in later prose essays. Whitman, in his prairie poems, also makes little mention of the Native Americans of the region or the buffalo. He seems much more interested in the virtues of white farmers and pioneers, whose spirit and strong work ethic he admired. Although, according to Ed Folsom, author of Walt Whitman's Native Representations, Whitman did take some interest in Native American culture and made efforts to use Native

American names like "Paumanok" for Long Island, he has been criticized by contemporary Indian writers Simon Ortiz and Maurice Kenny for his seeming acceptance of Manifest Destiny.

In his poem, "The Prairie-Grass Dividing," Whitman praises "those of the open atmosphere, coarse, sunlit, fresh, nutritious." His romanticized description of those who lived in the prairies reflects his faith in inland America. "The Prairie-Grass Dividing," however, is a remarkable poem, not because of its praise of the landscape and its inhabitants but because of the striking parallel Whitman draws between the prairie grass and his vision of male companionship, which he called "adhesiveness." Whitman's insistent repetition of the imperative "demand" near or at the beginning of lines two, three, and four in the first stanza of the poem suggests the sense of urgency the speaker feels.

The prairie-grass dividing, its special odor breathing,
I demand of it the spiritual corresponding,
Demand the most copious and close companionship of men,
Demand the blades to rise of words, acts, beings . . .

Just as the short and tall prairie grasses grow close together, so, too, did Whitman envision the "close companionship of men." In this poem, the prairie grass is both an image and a metaphor, the landscape out

NINE-MILE PRAIRIE, MID-MAY

out here on a hilltop
you discover
how brief sunset lasts
watching the red ball
sink into the dust
shadows paling
the flat-chested hills
now knitted in green

down in the gullies
cool willows and elms
thicken with gnats
birds scatter
bedding down the day
the gradual loss of light
slowing all things
to still-life

toward moonrise
deer step out of hiding
owls sweep their prey
bullfrogs chant in mud
in step with the breeze
bluestems rise and fall
cottonwoods rattle
wild indigos bloom

each day the repetition
of sun and wind and sun
you feel it breathe
from the bottom
of its deepest roots
this tallgrass relict
exhales its stored-up heat
back to the stars

(from Heartland)

TWYLA HANSEN

Twyla Hansen   Photo Courtesy of Twyla Hansen

of which an audacious and lusty race has emerged and the sweet-smelling perfume of copious manly love. The poem both seeks and manifests a "correspondence" between the landscape or geography of the plains with the human body, between Whitman's love of the land and his fellow Americans. "The Prairie-Grass Dividing" is a key poem in Whitman's canon. It echoes the sentiment that the westward plains states, with their vast expanses of prairie, are the seat of a vigorous and healthy manhood.

Twyla Hansen

Twyla Hansen, author of two collections of poetry, <u>How To Live in the Heartland</u> (Flatwater Editions, 1992) and <u>In Our Very Bones</u> (Slow Tempo Press, 1997) finds, like Walt Whitman, the prairie to be both an image and a metaphor, the landscape where-in one rediscovers a sensual relationship with the earth. Her poems often encourage the reader to discover the inherent but frequently overlooked beauty of a prairie. They serve as a guide into the much forgotten and neglected landscape. In one of her signature poems, "Nine-Mile Prairie," the speaker provides a set of instructions to the reader on how to experience the prairie. "Note the sun," she tells us, "how it has tipped the grassends / to tangerine." The poem works through a set of

instructions from the speaker to the reader. By the end of the poem, the reader has been led through a series of experiences that includes hiking, observing a hawk, and pulling at the switchgrass. All of our senses have been led in such a way as to optimally experience the pleasures of the prairie landscape. Hansen's aesthetic appreciation for the prairie is consistent with both landscape paintings of the region and earlier romantic lyrics by Whitman, such as "Prairie Sunset," which relies heavily upon color and sensory appeal.

In "Nine-Mile Prairie, Mid-May" and in "Standing on Nine-Mile Prairie Watching the Lunar Eclipse," Hansen evokes the pulsating diversity of life on a prairie at the same time she observes larger rhythms of nature. "Nine-Mile Prairie, Mid-May" begins like so many of Hansen's landscape poems, "out here on a hilltop" amidst prairie grasses and wild flowers. She registers an impression-ist's view of the scene, blending many colors in an evocative and painterly manner. But the moment she chooses for this "still-life" is twilight. Hansen's prairie poems are riddled with wild flowers and many different types of prairie grass, and this one, with its bluestems, indigos, and tall grasses, is no exception.

In this particular poem, Hansen is as much interested in cosmic cycles of nature as she is in observing the prairie around her. She discovers a cosmic cycle in the "repeti-tion / of sun and wind and sun," and when the tallgrass breathes it exhales "its stored-up heat / back to the stars." One cannot help but hear the echo of Whitman's line from "Song of Myself": "I believe a leaf of grass is no less than the journey-work of the stars."

Hansen's seemingly simple landscape poem uncovers one of the more profound insights of American visionary poets, the way in which natural processes connect earth to sky, grass to stars, and thus bridge the cosmic gap between seemingly disparate elements of creation. Curiously, she chooses the word "relict" to account for the tallgrass around her, a term which suggests that the prairie grass itself has become a remnant of an other-wise extinct flora. It is what remains after other parts have disappeared, suggesting both the devastation of the prairies and, at the same time, the need to reclaim them.

While rarely making explicit environmental statements, her poems embrace the prairie and all that can be observed in and from them and, thus, reclaim the prairie landscape as part of our heritage.

In her poem "Standing on Nine-Mile Prairie Watching the Lunar Eclipse," she is up to her "armpits in bluestem and indigo." This poem, like the previous one, relies upon color and kinesthetic movement. And like the other poem it, too, records a transitional moment, the disappearance of the moon and its reappearance during a lunar eclipse.

Standing On Nine-Mile Prairie Watching the Lunar Eclipse

on a summer night that is learning now
to let go, the steady breeze warm-cool-

warm, as up from the wooded ravines
stirrings of autumn already started,
the city spread below, studding Salt Valley
with its nightlights, cornfield to creek

to hayfield and I out on the west ridge
up to my armpits in bluestem and indigo,

nocturnal cacophony of crickets
drowning almost the whine of jets,

while above us the luminous globe
we once knew as moon glowing fat,

hanging dim-orange, until it all moves,
earth on its axis, rare alignment tilting,

bringing back the familiar flat disk,
lighting again the tipends of the grasses,

raising my skin and what's underneath alive,
rolling back the umbra toward tomorrow.

(from Heartland)

For Hansen, the moon-struck, prairie poet of post-Cather, post-small farm Nebraska, the lunar eclipse presents her with an important occasion to register her playfulness with language. The "moon glowing fat" hangs "dim-orange" as a result of the lunar eclipse, but in the single word, "until," she signals the shift of the world back to normalcy, "bringing back the familiar flat disk" which both lights and lights up the landscape and herself. This poem, like the preceding one, also places heavy significance upon a single word ("umbra") toward the end of the poem. The momentary darkness caused by a solar eclipse creates a shadow region over the

earth's surface, which is called the umbra. During a lunar eclipse, the moon near its full phase passes partially or wholly through the umbra of the earth's shadow. Although clearly conscious of its scientific connotations, Hansen suggests in her last line the psychological dimension of the term "umbra," suggestive of when the source of light disappears from our lives and darkness ensues, sometimes momentarily but at other times for long phases, "until," of course, it is rolled back toward tomorrow. The poem ends on this characteristically hopeful note.

In other poems, such as "When the Prairie Speaks" and "Love Poem from the Prairie," Hansen evokes the erotic and sensual nature of the landscape. Hansen, unlike Whitman in "The Prairie-Grass Dividing," engenders the prairie in her poems as a seductive female. In "Love Poem from the Prairie," the speaker invites her male lover into her hair, which she describes as "gold-tangled indiangrass." Through a series of powerfully inviting verbs, "come," "nest," and "take," the other is literally invited into the prairie-lover and all that she has to offer. Hansen invokes here the tradition of love poetry best exemplified by Solomon's "Song of Songs," in which the female body is described in terms of the landscape. Phrases such as "taste my rosehips" and "nest in my wildrye" are, of course, deliciously sensuous in ways reminiscent of the Hebrew love poem.

In "When The Prairie Speaks," she also engenders the prairie as a seductive woman. The hillside with its swaying prairie grasses and "golden wild underthings" awaits discovery and exploration: "laid out, it whispers I'm yours." She has reclaimed the prairie in these love poems in an unfashionable way, as a female and as a lover, but then again, the prairie itself has never been all that fashionable a place.

Don Welch

Don Welch, a native Nebraskan, in his poems encourages readers and visitors to Nebraska and the Great Plains to work on their vision. In the first stanza of his poem "Advice From a Provincial," he addresses the experience so many newcomers to Nebraska have when out for a ride in the country.

WHEN THE PRAIRIE SPEAKS

it whispers I'm wearing
my purple red dress, my red slip,
now my golden wild underthings;
oh, can you recall, how

on that autumn afternoon in a
slant of sun, the breeze called
you out of that stone life, how
you and your love took flight,
skyward like startled pheasants;

it says I'm the distant hillside,
patient, waiting for you,
discovery in every season;
laid out, it whispers I'm yours;
be listening.

(from Heartland)

TWYLA**HANSEN**

Don Welch   Photo Courtesy of Don Welch

Advice From a Provincial

When you drive down our river-road,
spare us your talk about our backwardness,
of how mile after unrelieved mile dispirits you,
of how there is nothing, simply nothing to see.
Go back to your homes and work on your eyes,
bring back a sight which can co-create meaning.
Then notice at sunset how our river is on fire,
a long burning vowel running westward,
back to the mountains, those granite consonants
which thrust themselves at the sky.
Slow down. Colorado can wait.
Skiing, of course, will make the cold warmer,
but think of this river, frozen in winter,
as a long silent scream.
To the settlers who waited it out,
who felt their sodhouses thaw,
who survived this place and were scarred,
pay a momentary tribute.
And in spring, if you're the right kind,
catch the wind with its invisible fingers
making love to the water.
You'll never read it in a brochure,
but the only worthwhile rivers
are those which simplify lives.

(from The Platte River)

Welch, a native of the Sandhills and a long-time resident of the Platte River Valley, knows the folly of seeing "nothing" in a landscape whose rhythms and curves and inhabitants he knows as well, if not better

than, any contemporary Nebraska poet. Welch has learned the important lesson that all American visionary poets teach: that it's not the place that makes the poet, but the poet who makes the place. Like Walt Whitman and Wallace Stevens before him, he prizes vision and understands that perception and experience of the world is constructed through individual consciousness. He employs all his senses to reclaim a region often derided for its lack of beauty. His advice from a provincial is to "go back to your homes and work on your eyes / bring back a sight which can co-create meaning." Meaning, of course, is not simply a visual function, but involves the brain and requires interpretation of what we see. Welch prides himself on being an interpreter of a landscape many simply cannot see, or refuse to see, or simply don't know how to see.

In stanza three of his poem, Welch discovers the language of the country, replete with its long vowels and harsh consonants. He notices how the sun sets the Platte River on fire, "a long burning vowel running westward." He pays tribute to those who have survived here and who reap the reward of catching "the wind with its invisible fingers / making love to the water." Like Twyla Hansen in her poem, "Nine-Mile Prairie," the speaker provides advice on how to experience the prairie landscape. Welch, however, introduces irony in the mocking gesture of the title in which he refers to himself as a "provincial." The irony, of course, is that he reverses this in the text of the poem so that by its end, the outsider to whom the poem is addressed becomes the "provincial" and the speaker the worldly-wise "insider."

As an insider, Welch knows a dark, fierce side of the prairie, subject to periods of drought, sudden blizzards, wind storms, and freezing cold nights. In his poem, "To a Californian about the Prairie," he ends with an allusion to the cold and emptiness: "black prairie nights when all the stars in the sky fall out . . . and the air is as stark as enamel." In two more recent prairie poems, "Drought, 1934" and "Blowout," he evokes the darker side of the landscape that devoured the likes of Mr. Shimerda in Willa Cather's novel <u>My Antonia</u> and that even today causes one to ask, in the middle of a driving snowstorm,

<table>
<tr><td>

SUNSET AT THE WILLA CATHER PRAIRIE

</td><td>

by DON**WELCH**

</td></tr>
</table>

"what am I doing here?"

His poem, "Drought, 1934," speaks more than dozens of newspaper reports can about the severity of long climactic dry spells, when "dust strung taut as wire / hums sterile songs." It is a landscape with "signatures of strain / and thin-lipped laughter." Although Welch knows that vision is necessary to reclaim the forgotten landscape of this region, he also knows that vision and our other senses can be affronted by the severity of the physical landscape and its climate.

Like most visionary poets, Welch also understands well the connection between the external landscape and our own interior one. In "Blowout," from The Plain Sense of Things, he likens an unusual geological formation called a "blowout," to the dark side of human experience and the psyche.

In this poem, Welch draws an analogy between the ever-increasing "gape" in the otherwise whole landscape and the way in which fault lines develop in our own psychic lives. Welch pushes beyond the surface of the landscape to discover here a dark ray of connection between an unusual geological formation and human life. Like Thoreau, he discovers a connection between scientific fact and our humanity, albeit in this case, a rather gloomy one.

It would be a mistake, however, to end on such a note when considering the poetry of Don Welch. For although he knows well the shadowy terrain of the prairies, he also praises its wonders in poem after poem. Perhaps his poem, "Sunset at the Willa Cather Prairie," testifies to this as well as any other. In this poem, Welch praises what he knows is hardest of all to do in this landscape, to take root here, to stay, to endure, even to triumph. "Staying is hard," he writes. "It's like the big bluestem: You'd think the grass / would never survive, but it does." The balance of the poem pays tribute to this prairie grass which lights up field after field with its "greenness." And what the speaker of the poem admires most is its resilience, its refusal to bow down, to give in, to capitulate.

Like the big bluestem out on the Willa

Look, the big bluestem holds on,
its wan roots going down,
its stems green as bones,
thin with reasons.

You'd think the grass
would never survive, but it does.
In fact there are years
when it riots.

Getting out of our cars, in field
after field we can see a greenness
pursued, a thing bobbing
and weaving, refusing

to go down, in round
after round something coming at us,
half-earthen, half-human,
tough as a lug.

Cather prairie, Welch's poetry comes at us, round after round, refusing to give in to blindness or weariness. It is there for the reader to experience, season after season, its words and figures of speech going down into our hearts and minds. As a poet, he has managed to survive in a time hostile to poetry, in a region suspicious of aesthetic form, in a landscape where terror can strike in the form of a sudden storm or a long, dry drought.

Both Twyla Hansen and Don Welch represent what is best in recent poetry about the prairies. Each poet is willing to take a realistic look at the landscape, to enter it not as a tourist but as an inhabitant rooted in its rich human and natural history. Moreover, each of these writers transcends the local, by discovering in the prairie landscape metaphors for human experience. The "well-springs" they discover nourish the terrain of our very being.

Selected**References**

Hansen, Twyla. 1992. *How to live in the heartland*. Lincoln: Flatwater Editions.

Sanders, M. Ed. 1997. *The plain sense of things: Eight poets from outstate Nebraska*. Grand Island: Sandhills Press.

Scully, B. and H.W. Blodgett. Eds. 1973. *Leaves of grass. Walt Whitman*. New York: W.W. Norton & Co.

Welch, D. 1992. *The Platte River*. Kearney: University of Nebraska at Kearney.

Whitman, W. 1882. *Specimen days*. Boston: D.R. Godine, 1971.

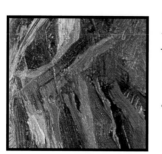

THE ART OF EMERGING NEBRASKA ARTISTS:

LIFE ON THE PRAIRIE-A LOVE/HATE RELATIONSHIP

Marsha Hewitt, Associate Professor of Art

Frequently beautiful, the prairie also can be harsh and cruel. On the prairie, the open space, immense vistas, big sky, and subtle colors of grasses and fields of crops seep into our consciousness, affecting how we think and feel. Life on the prairie is not for the weak at heart; those living here must find strength from inner resources.

This article will showcase the art of five emerging artists of Nebraska, who have chosen to create work that visually describes their relationship to the land. All of the artists' works evolve organically out of the nature of "place": a state of being and a state of mind.

All five artists were born and raised in Nebraska, or close to its borders. The land and the relationship to it is not only the subject for these artists' works, but their inspiration. Some of these artists have lived on the prairie for several generations. They know this land: the extremes of its seasons, the structures that surround them, and the history, myths, and stories of its settlers. For each of them, the land is in their blood, at the very fiber of their being. It colors their consciousness: how they see the rest of the world, how they think, and how they live. To a large extent, the prairie has determined who they are. Their artwork is a reflection of not only the physical geography of the prairie, but also the emotional and spiritual geography of their hearts and minds.

Sometimes one's relationship to the land is one of peace and pride in place, a place to go when there is a "need to feel calm and comfort," in Pat Wiederspan Jones's words. Her paintings investigate the immensity of the landscape and the sky, as well as the "feelings of peace and solitude" that the prairie evokes.

Marc Hoffman quite literally follows the violent weather patterns, tornadoes, in particular, that have threatened prairie inhabitants for generations. Marc photographs severe weather patterns and then creates paintings on the computer that portray his fascination with these powerful forces of nature.

Always living close to the land, Joan Sheen grew up on a farm and married a farmer. In order to see her surroundings from a different perspective, Joan floated above the prairie in an airplane and translated those visions into a series of tapestry weavings that express the energy and vitality of the land.

For some, the connection to the land is a love/hate relationship, a "sometimes loving and sometimes cruel master" in Jeff Justesen's words. His paintings express the duality of man's relationship with the land and its resources. "We breed our cattle to be strong and beautiful and when they are at their physical peak, we sell them into slaughter. . . . This situation is typical of all of mankind's relationships. We have a tendency to love and destroy all in the same breath."

Todd Smith's art is a powerful expression of the struggle of generations for the survival of the family farm. He draws on "the everyday battles of the farmer against the weather, government, family, and the simple physical limits of being a mortal human."

Torn between familial expectations and obligations to continue farming and his desire to paint, Todd works out these strong emotions in his art. The land is part of his whole being. It is the life blood of his family, a blessing and a curse. "I sometimes wonder whether my connection (to the land) is an addictive curse, or if it is a cathartic cure."

The work of these emerging artists points us to the sensuality of the local, the immediate. Eloquently demonstrating their continuing love for the land in a frequently harsh environment, these artists simultaneously invite us to appreciate the beauty and the wonder of the physical geography of the prairie and question the spiritual and emotional geography of our own hearts and minds.

Pat Jones's Statement

When I paint, I almost always choose to paint the landscape of Nebraska. I have struggled to identify why I am so interested in this subject matter and have concluded that I find a solace and serenity in the horizontal structure of our surroundings.

Having lived in this area of Nebraska nearly all of my life, I associate the landscape with a feeling of home. When I was a young girl, my family lived in several small towns. As a family, we would go for drives in the country for recreation. I would accompany my father on fishing and hunting outings, or we would travel across the state to visit relatives on weekends. Looking out the window on these drives, I would watch the Nebraska landscape go by. Nebraska is a state of changing seasons and changeable weather. The same location, no matter how many times we passed by, was never the same twice. Now, as an adult, I still associate seeing the landscape with the feelings of security and happiness as a child with my family.

As a trained artist, I have learned to see the landscape in terms of line, shape, color, texture, value, and space: the elements of art. This gives me a way to organize that which I see, a way to make sense and order out of what is there. The farmers who settled this vast open plain also were striving to create a sense of order, and they did so by planting trees in rows, by laying out fields and roads in geometric grids, by erecting buildings in line with each other. Our highways and railways were laid out in east-west, north-south directions. I am fascinated by recurrent, repetitive motifs, and I believe I find a reassurace in recognizing the attempt for order.

"Hog Shed"   Painter, Pat Jones

In my landscapes, I also am interested in the horizontal features of the prairie, which are inescapable because of the huge amount of open land and our ability to see the horizon from almost anywhere. We relate everything to the horizon. And as I look toward the horizon, I see layer upon layer of color and texture as the ground recedes to the distant horizon line. These layers show up as horizontal stripes in my paintings.

I like to look for regularly repeated motifs or patterns in fence rows, treed shelter belts, rows of hay bales, rows of grain bins, even regularly placed doors and windows in farm buildings. In the painting "Big Bales," I was interested in the positioning of several round bales of hay as a repetition of the spiraling, circular shape of the front end of the bales with variety in the placement. The negative space in the painting is treated with the repetition of horizontal linear forms: the clouds, the trees along the horizon line, and the horizontal patterns in the field and grasses of the foreground.

The painting "Hog Shed" is an example of my observation of man's attempt to conform to the needs of the prairie. This building is long, low-slung, very horizontal, and constructed with repeating motifs, creating a sense of pattern and beauty on a very ordinary, utilitarian structure. I purposely made the space very horizontal and panoramic to emphasize the horizontal quality of the building, and included very little detail in the foreground or sky because of the beautiful patterning occurring on the building itself. Even the roof is a series of repeating shapes, and the rust adds a lovely color.

Because of the vastness of the space here, and the relatively low population, I think one can feel a great sense of isolation. Sometimes this can feel elegiac, even lonely, but usually I feel a peaceful solitude when I am alone in the country. In each of the paintings mentioned, I painted the landscape on a background of grey paper. This color helped to project a unified lonely feeling. However, there is a difference between being lonely and being alone. I feel a oneness with the land and the sky, and I find that being there creates a feeling of belonging. When I am upset, a solitary drive in the country will set everything right again. It restores my priorities and puts the significance of life into perspective.

For these reasons, the landscapes that I paint are self-portraits of where I have been, who I am, and what I would like to be.

Biography

Pat Wiederspan Jones was born in Kearney, Nebraska, and grew up in several south-central Nebraska communities, including Pleasanton, Stratton, Beaver City, and Hastings. She holds a B.A. degree in Art Education from Hastings College and a M.A. degree in Art Education from the University of Nebraska at Kearney. With a background of teaching art in the public schools and working for several years in the advertising business, Jones is now serving as adjunct faculty at UNK. Pat has exhibited her work in the Nebraska Art Educators Association juried competition at Nebraska Wesleyan University, Lincoln, Nebraska, at Kearney Public Library, and "Art in the Park," Kearney, Nebraska. She was a presenter on a "Visual Poetry" panel at MONA in conjunction with Nebraska Women's Caucus on Art. She resides in Kearney with her husband and son.

"Big Bales"   Painter, Pat Jones

"I-80 Bales"   Painter, Pat Jones

Left image, "You are Going the Wrong Way"
Right image, "No Trespassing"

Artist, Marc Hoffman

Marc R. Hoffman's Statement

I have always been strangely drawn to weather patterns. Not to sound too eccentric, but the more severe the weather pattern, the better I liked it. The darker the clouds, the bubblier the clouds, the more movement contained within the clouds–in short, clouds that would make any normal human being run for cover–these are the clouds that I have always liked. And for the areas in which I live, Julesburg, Colorado, and Kearney, Nebraska, summertime tends to bring in the most striking examples of these weather patterns. Once I spent three years trying to get lightning on film. When I finally succeeded, I was extremely excited! My mother was quite relieved afterwards because she would always worry about the danger.

I remember the first time I captured a building thunderstorm on film. I was on top of an overpass just outside of my hometown of Julesburg, and I used a whole roll of film shooting these beautiful forms. Since then, I have taken many pictures of thunderstorms. I am disappointed when winter rolls around because the clouds during the winter are flat and boring. They do not capture my interest nearly as much as in the summertime.

My next "big thrill" to catch on camera was the elusive tornado. These formations, as deadly as they are, are very interesting to me. One look at a tornado is enough to convince anyone that weather is highly organized. So many factors come into play in the formation of a tornado, making it a finely tuned machine consisting of power

and beauty. I have only really seen one tornado in my entire life, and that was about thirteen to fifteen miles away from me. I didn't have a camera at the time, and since I bought my 35mm camera, I have been unable to capture a tornado on film. Strangely enough, I have had many dreams about being near enough to a tornado to snap a few pictures.

The tornado and lightning have been two of my favorite themes in my computer paintings. Perhaps the best way to describe my technique is to draw an analogy to a traditional painter. A painter uses oil paint to create pieces of artwork. Instead of using oils, watercolor, or acrylic, I use the computer. The computer becomes a kind of "hi-tech" paintbrush in which colors can be applied to a work of art as never before. Color can be mixed, blended, made transparent, or opaque. Masks or stencils can be applied to the artwork–and all of this can be done without the clean-up work of using traditional media! This is not to say that computer art is here to replace the traditional media of artistic creation. On the contrary, I value my training in the traditional media highly, and in fact I am able to transfer what I have learned from my traditional art education to the computer. I have even applied my love of these clouds to a kind of science-fiction theme of the creation of nebulous formations that could exist in outer space. But, the one theme that stands clear in my art is the cloud. And out here on the plains, we have a grand view of these beautiful formations.

Left tapestry, "Dynamics of the Land: Energy & Vitality I"
Right tapestry, "Dynamics of the Land: Energy & Vitality II"

Artist, Joan Sheen

Biography

Marc Hoffman was born and raised in Julesburg, Colorado, which is located in the northeastern corner of Colorado about three miles from the Nebraska border. The landscape of the area is very much like the Nebraska landscape: rolling hills, prairie, and, of course, the best views of thunderstorms in the West. Hoffman attended McCook Community College in McCook, Nebraska, where he studied with a master landscape painter, Don Dernovich. He received his Bachelor of Fine Arts degree in Studio Art at the University of Nebraska at Kearney, where he was awarded a graduate assistantship at UNK in the fall of 1996. Marc has received awards in art shows held in Italy and Finland (Bit.Movie in Riccione, Italy, Pixel Art Expo Roma in Rome, Italy, and Jazz.Bit in Finland). He also writes magazine articles on computer art, which have been published in <u>Amazing Computing for the Amiga</u> and <u>AmigaWorld</u>.

Joan Sheen's Statement

There is part of the Creator in me. The first sentence in the Bible declares: "In the beginning God created the heavens and the earth." Man is made in the image of God; therefore, man has the capacity to create. All people are to some degree creative. I draw closer to the Creator when I focus on the earth, something He created out of nothing but His spoken Word. Our human boundaries require creating from something that has already been created. The Creator is my God,

his Son is my Savior, may I glorify them.

The land with its contour, texture, fiber, and organic qualities intrigues me as a motif. These inherent qualities are the real nature of the land and are not dependent upon external circumstances. This recurrent thematic element is seen in my tapestries. I choose to portray only what I know and understand.

The process of creating begins for me by first seeing, then making a quick sketch in pencil. As the composition develops, watercolor paintings will emerge, with an eye always toward a possible design for fiber. I always work in a fluid form before addressing the media of fiber in a tapestry. The choosing of wool and cotton as the final media also has connections with the earth, as they are natural fibers. Cotton is from a seed pod grown in the soil. Wool is a fiber originating from sheep.

I have narrowed my subject matter to the land only, with no regard to sky, horizon line, or clouds, which led to the thought of flying above the surface of the earth. The actual experience of hiring a pilot and airplane and then flying over the Platte Valley, the Platte River, and the hills on either side, allowed me to photograph several aerial views of the land. These photographs provided visual cues for a series of watercolor paintings that showed the intrinsic qualities of the land. Simple contour lines of the topography of the land became the essence for the creative process. These organic shapes were reduced to minimal abstractions

"The Temporal Dreams of the American Farmer II"

Artist, Joan Sheen

and served as a point of departure. As the dynamic land qualities in the weaving emerged, the feelings of energy were derived from the vigor which occurs when using opposites, such as organic shapes within geometric shapes. The high value contrast and diagonal composition increased the feelings of vitality and limitless might. I chose colors with reference to their placement on the value scale and their ability to provide a sense of intensity of expression and emotional involvement.

My livelihood depends upon the land and its yearly ability to produce income. Likewise, my art is dependent upon the land. Knowing my subject matter so well, I need to describe it in visual terms with tapestry.

Biography

Joan Sheen's love for the land was first developed on the family farm near Loomis, Nebraska, and has continued into married life on a four-generation family farm west of Kearney, Nebraska. Using the land as an art form began with continuing education at UNK, where Sheen earned a B.A. in Art Education in 1973. Later with completion of an M.A.E. in 1992 from UNK with an emphasis in fiber, the land continued to be a source of inspiration. Sheen taught fiber construction, surface design, and loom weaving at the University of Nebraska at

Kearney from 1992-1999.

Sheen's creative work has been exhibited in the following juried shows: 1992 and 1993 Fiber Directions, Witchita, Kansas; 1993 Topeka Competition 17 in Topeka, Kansas; 1992 and 1994 Honorable Mention at the Association of Nebraska Art Clubs; and 1995 Surface Design exhibit in Milwaukee, Wisconsin. One-man shows include: Kearney Library, 1993; Thesis Exhibit at the Walker Gallery on the UNK campus, 1992; and Phelps Gallery in Hastings, Nebraska, 1998.

Sheen currently resides in Kearney, Nebraska, and is designing with living art in her landscape and greenhouse business, Dove Hill Gardens.

Jeff Justesen's Statement

The earth is in many ways our greatest asset. From a place to build our home to the way we raise the food we eat, it is involved in every aspect of our lives. It is, in essence, of what we are made. Most people take the land for granted; they fail to think of it as anything more than what they walk on or sell to make a profit. But it is much more. It is our life giver, our dwelling place, and for some, God.

As a child growing up on a farm in rural Nebraska, the land was always a provider. In my youth, I rarely, if ever, thought of it

Left, "The Loving Master"
Right, "The Brutal Master"

Painter, Jeff Justesen

in any other way. I know now that it is much more than merely a provider; it is now to me my home and my inspiration. It took several years of farming on my own to realize what a wonderful muse the land and the occupation of farming would be. I struggled through many phases in my growth as an artist, never really finding that one element that brought both love and contemplation to my work. As I matured, I started to look at what I did as a source of inspiration, and I found that the land and farming, in general, were just what I longed for.

I remember riding in the tractor with my father in the spring when I was a child, breaking ground for the year. The intoxicating smell of newly broken ground is my most clear recollection of the land. As I became older, other smells of the earth came to me: the smell of an approaching thunderstorm, the cool breeze felt just before a storm hits, the smell of a field of growing corn at sunrise, and the smell of fall when the crops start to mature and become ready for gathering. Harvest especially brings the satisfaction of knowing that the year's hard work and long hours all come down to this moment, and that the dormancy of winter is approaching when the land will rest and wait for another birth in the spring. The memories

of my life with the land drive me. And I am lonely without her.

The dualities of this life intrigue me. American farmers breed and raise their cattle, lovingly care for them, and slaughter them when they reach their most perfect state. It is this relationship that I want to convey in my paintings, "Loving Master" and "Brutal Master." A similar duality of man's relationship to the land and its resources can be seen in how we set aside land to protect from development, but we put up fast food billboards and souvenir shops to clutter its beauty. It is our nature to produce and destroy, all in the same breath, regardless of beauty or worth. This sense of duality and mankind's relationship with the land inspires my paintings.

My love for the land increases daily, as does my longing for it. I feel as though the pavement smothers the land and blocks my merging with it. When I stand alone looking out at the land, I think, "This is permanent, and I am not. These hills and valleys have seen more and have known more than I will ever see or know. I am but a flash in the pan, and the land is the fire beneath it."

Biography

Jeff Justesen grew up on a farm in St. Paul, a small community in central

"Schism" oil/enamel on masonite

Painter, Todd E Smith

"Ripe" oil on canvas

Painter, Todd E Smith

Nebraska. As a farmer's son, he had many daily chores, and, other than public school and church, little contact with others. He believes that this instilled a strong sense of self-reliance and individualism within him. He attended Hastings Colllege for two years and then transfered to the University of Nebraska at Kearney. It was at UNK that Justesen really started to cultivate his skills as an artist. He also met his wife in one of his art classes. After receiving a BFA in Studio Art, Justesen was awarded a Graduate Assistantship at UNK, and for one year, taught Art Structure, while taking several graduate classes. During that time, he found that he greatly enjoyed teaching and plans in time to pursue graduate school with the hope of becoming a college professor in drawing or painting.

Todd E. Smith's Statement

I consider my art to be influenced by the original Expressionist idea that art must go beyond the subjective and attempt to give the psychological and deeply personal side of painting a higher status than the visual. What separates me from these great artists is that my trials, when compared to the disastrous miseries that the Expressionist artists experienced early in the twentieth century, are trivial.

Expressive art must come from experience, otherwise it lacks the truth necessary for it to exist. The experiences I draw from are the everyday battles any farmer wages against the weather, government, family, and the simple physical limits of being a mortal human. Farming is the most elemental of occupations, but the relationships (as well as the technological aspects) inherent in a family farm are quite complex.

Family farms are usually stressed from the inside, with a family battle for control always in progress. When one member is unable to continue farming due to age or other restraints, another younger and less experienced member waits in the wings. This power struggle is always a painful experience. Often one person has sacrificed his life for the farm and now must hand it over to someone whose loyalty is unproven.

My two paintings, "Schism" and "Ripe," concentrate on the family, the land, and the good of the farm. "Schism" is a large painting influenced by a family fight between my father, grandfather, and me. It is a visual fit of anger, insecurity, love, and respect. I painted this with the idea that I would destroy the painting when completed. I just let the intensity of my feelings at the moment, not the compositional elements, decide the outcome.

The figure in the corner of "Schism" represents me, encapsulated in a box from which I cannot escape. The figure opposite represents my father in a business suit, and the smaller figure in the background is my grandfather. The story told in this painting is one of my love and respect for my grandfather and all that he has endured and survived with the farm. It is also a story of my fate concerning the farm, my deep-seated problems in relating to and pleasing my father, that I am sure nearly every son goes through at some point in his life.

"Ripe," I suppose, is a second chapter to the tragedy. It is a painting about my realization, as well as my family's, that I am ready to assume a large role in the future of the farm. Instead of the turmoil of "Schism," "Ripe" portrays peace and acceptance of my fate.

The land of western Nebraska is part of my whole being. I am as much a part of it as the old Elm tree with its roots in Lodgepole Creek. That mud on my feet is my livelihood, and that cloud in the west on a hot July day determines my success today, just as it will tomorrow, making things grow where they couldn't without my sweat, blood, and love of the land. I sometimes wonder whether my connection to the land is an addictive curse or if it is a cathartic cure.

Biography

Todd Smith lives outside of Chappell, Nebraska, with his wife, Laurie, and son, Brayden. He is a farmer, an artist, and a part-time volunteer fireman and EMT for the town of Chappell. He graduated from UNK with a B.F.A. in Studio Art in 1995.

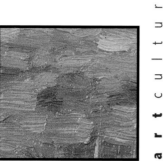

A PATCHWORK OF QUILT LEADERSHIP

Carol Bosshardt, Lecturer in English

When Grace Snyder published two original quilt designs in the Kansas City Star, she dreamed of making the best quilts in the world. At the time, she probably didn't realize how much her contributions would add to national recognition of Nebraska's quilters. More than fifty years later, Snyder remains one of only thiry-one members of the national Quilter's Hall of Fame, but men and women with whom she exchanged ideas continue to lead the United States in quilt research and design.

Snyder's "Return of the Swallow" and "Semi-Circle Saw" patterns remain relatively unknown, although her Return of the Swallow quilt appeared in an exhibit at the Furguson House and at the Sheldon Memorial Art Gallery in 1974. Mary Ghormley and other Lincoln Quilt Guild members remember Snyder fondly, as do people like Hazel Carter and Joyce Gross from the Quilter's Hall of Fame and American Quilt Study Group. But few people realize how Snyder and her sister quilters contributed to Nebraska's current reputation as a leader in quilt research and development.

One early Nebraska quilter, Maria Suhr, appliqued and quilted Floral Wreath in 1895, copying a family quilt. Even earlier, before the Nebraska Territory was opened to settlers, Martha Hollis probably received the fabric and pattern for her wedding quilt from her family members in the East, who shared them with women who had no fabric store nearby.

Grace Snyder

Although pioneering conditions often made life in rural Nebraska primitive, pioneers like Snyder, Suhr, and Hollis maintained contact with people across the nation. One of the premier quilters in the United States, Snyder came from a ranch so far from "civilization" that she flew home from numerous quilt shows before a highway was finished past their ranch in the early 1950s. Approximately twenty years earlier, the Lincoln Highway, an all-weather road crossing the country, had been completed in 1934 in Lincoln County, Nebraska, just south of McPherson County where the Snyders resided. In spite of transportation problems in the late 1920s and early 1930s, her daughter, Nellie Snyder Yost, remembered how Grace had begun buying "materials just for her quilts, searching through a dozen stores, and eventually through the stores of that many states, just to find the exact shade of a color she needed" for her finest quilts.

In her autobiography, Snyder names only a few of the show quilts she pieced from 1927-1932 in Oregon, but she mentions a quilt club she attended with her sister-in-law while she lived there. And even when she stayed home on the ranch, Snyder received

Snyder searched twelve states for the right color fabric for Sitting Bull's face in her <u>Covered Wagon States</u> quilt. On the right, personalized <u>Covered Wagon States</u> block includes her husband's nickname.   Photos by Carol Bosshardt

the latest in quilting designs from such newspapers as the <u>Kansas City Star</u>, which was known for its weekly quilt patterns.

Unlike Suhr, who probably copied her mother's quilt exactly, Snyder developed many of her own patterns. Her individual variations on the <u>Omaha World Herald's</u> "Covered Wagons States" quilt pattern translated an embroidery design into applique. And her most famous work, <u>Flower Basket Petit Point</u>, adapted a petit point design from a give-away dish to a fine patchwork design block. Then Snyder developed her own intricate sashing in lavender and green to set off the basket blocks. Finally, she took the large rose from the basket bouquet and pieced an intricate border of roses and buds reminiscent of wild roses which grew on a hill near her ranch home.

Only after she began winning awards for the quilt did Snyder wonder about copyright infringement in her adaptation. Fortunately, the Salem China Company was so pleased with her work that the president gave Snyder an entire set of the Petit Point Basket dishes, and she eventually corresponded with the German artist who developed the original petit point design. Although Snyder's quilts were known for their original elements, few people until recently knew the <u>Kansas City Star</u> printed Snyder's "Return of the Swallow" and "Semi-Circle Saw" patterns in 1946.

Quilt Guilds

Like Snyder, Louise Howey, Ernest Haight, and Mary Ghormley also participated in local, state, and national quilt idea exchanges. Howey participated in a Round Robin of quilters from Canada and the United States during the 1930s and 1940s. Haight earned many ribbons at the county and state level and wrote an early book on machine piecing and quilting techniques, which he sold locally and at national quilt shows, where he also exhibited quilts. Ghormley, Howey, and other Lincoln Quilt Guild members corresponded and visited with Snyder and Haight regularly, forming a leadership bridge between the early quilters and current quilt leadership.

In addition to informal idea sharing, the current Lincoln Quilt Guild and others across the state developed a network that leads the nation in quilt scholarship. According to <u>Nebraska Quilts and Quiltmakers</u>, the Lincoln Quilter's Guild began a special survey of Nebraska quilts in January 1985 to identify quilts that represented the "ethnic, geographic, cultural, and economic variety of Nebraska." The original Nebraska Quilt Preservation project committee surveyed approximately five thousand quilts at twenty-eight locations across the state from March 13, 1987, to May 20, 1989, after setting up a research plan and training volunteers in fiber and

Bertie Elfeldt and Billie Thornburg in front of their mother's <u>Applique Grapes</u> quilt   Photo by Carol Bosshardt

Central medallion design from <u>Mosaic</u>, one of the top one hundred quilts of the twentieth century   Photo by Carol Bosshardt

design analysis as well as survey techniques. Nebraska Quilts and Quiltmakers presents the results of this project in award-winning fashion.

National Achievements

The Nebraska State Quilt Guild (NSQG) inducted Hollis, Snyder, and Haight into the Nebraska State Quilter's Hall of Fame in 1984, four years after the National Quilter's Hall of Fame inducted Snyder in their second set of awards, and two years before the State Guild began holding an annual conference in 1986. In the last decade, the Quilt Preservation Project moved from the providence of the Lincoln Quilt Guild to the State Guild, and five years years ago, NSQG commissioned Sandy Fox to travel to every large and small museum identified in Nebraska and document each quilt or piece of a quilt in the museum collections. The State Guild also provided acid-free tissue paper and boxes for the museums to store their fabric treasures when they are not on display and has trained museum workers in quilt care.

Both before and after its development, members of the Nebraska State Quilt Guild earned national recognition in a variety of ways. In 1990, Jan Stehlik gave one of eight presentations at the American Quilt Study Group's annual AQGS conference, and, in 1992, Kari Ronning discussed "Quilting in Webster County, Nebraska" at the AQSG conference. Patricia Crews discussed a variety of aspects of Nebraska quilt research when she and several different partners appeared on the AQSG programs in 1988, 1989, and 1993. Crews's work with Sara Dillow, 1997 AQSG President from Fremont, Nebraska, and others helped convince Ardis and Robert James to give their 950 piece quilt collection to the University of Nebraska-Lincoln as the foundation for the International Quilt Study Center.

Although few groups hold regular, traditional quilting bees, a variety of individuals and church groups still meet to piece or quilt patchwork coverlets. More often, individuals take classes at fabric stores, through community college programs, and in quilt guilds. Many towns have one or more quilt guilds, and the 1998-1999

NSQG Membership Roster includes forty-three local guilds as well as more than six hundred individual members. Today Nebraskans like Brenda Groelz, Sharon Rexroad, Joan Waldman and Paulette Peters publish pattern books and teach their special techniques at quilt programs locally and across the nation. Quilters like Molly Anderson, whose hexagon watercolor quilts opened in a single-artist exhibit at the Museum of Nebraska Art on January 16, 1999, compete nationally as Snyder did half a century ago. Certainly Snyder would be pleased to see how quilting, an art which appeared to be dying in the 1950s and 1960s, has not only regained popularity, but also ascended to fine arts recognition. She would be honored to learn her leadership is still recognized seventeen years after her death. Flower Basket Petit Point was recognized in 1999 as one of the top ten quilts from the twentieth century, and Mosaic was also included in the top one hundred quilts of the century. Truly, Snyder and her sister Nebraska quilters have provided a mosaic of leadership in the twentieth century.

Selected **References**

Crews, P. C. and R. C. Naugle. 1991. Nebraska quilts and quiltmakers. Lincoln: University of Nebraska Press.

Haight, E. B. 1974. Proctical machine–quilting for the homemaker. David City: Nebraska. Self-published.

Snyder, G. 1963. No time on my hands. As told to Nellie Snyder Yost. Lincoln: University of Nebraska Press. 1986.

Waldman, J. Uncoverings. An annual publication with research papers of the American Quilt Study group. San Francisco, California: AQSG.

Yost, N.S. "Quilt story." Hobbies. October 1953: 43, 60-61.

art culture

MONA: THE SCULPTURE GARDEN

Sam Umland, Professor of English

The Museum of Nebraska Art—its actual physical existence, its walls, and its roof—is an example of the power of the indomitable human spirit. The sheer marvel of its physical presence demands that it be seen and understood as much more than a mere "regional" museum. Glimpses of beauty are rare and are often discovered in the most unexpected of places. Those who, for the first time, visit the Museum of Nebraska Art have found it nothing less than astonishing, not only because of the impressive art in its permanent collection, but also because it is a testimonial to the animating power of the aesthetic imagination in all human beings, regardless of their geographic location.

Nebraskans by nature are not creatures who boast about themselves. They would rather reveal themselves through actions and deeds. The Museum of Nebraska Art stands as a quiet, elegant testimonial to this quality of their character. Within the Museum's galleries can be found the many works that comprise the "Nebraska Art Collection," the official collection of the State of Nebraska.

The Nebraska Art Collection is a dynamic mix of artists, past and present, including works by artists of international reputation, such as Robert Henri and Sheila Hicks, and of national reputation, such as Lawton

Parker, Kent Bellows, and Keith Jacobshagen. Works by these artists reside with powerful regionalists such as Thomas Hart Benton, Aaron Pyle, and Alice Cleaver and famed Nebraska-born illustrators such as Grant Reynard and John Falter.

The Museum of Nebraska Art also plays a central role in the community: it is frequently the site of workshops for both children and adults, art education outreach programs, lectures, readings, and concerts. Within its beauteous light-filled spaces, the arts—and the human spirit that animates them—are celebrated throughout the year.

Light is

the only

authentic.

DON**WELCH**

Garden sculpture of Cliff Hillegass   by George Lundeen

"Picnic in the Park" Terrence Duran

the kearney goodwill store

by sam umland

No ideas but in things.
William Carlos Williams

Here you will find the fragments of lives past,
Of lives undone and lives that might have been.
Here you will find remnants of many lives
Scattered piecemeal on shelves, in rows and bins.

Here you may find a western by Will Cook,
Within the tattered pages, flecks of ash,
A Zig-Zag paper used to mark the place
Still folded within, now yellowed with age.

Here you may see what becomes of fashion,
Disco records, bell-bottoms, platform shoes,
8-tracks, 45s, unwanted sweat shirts
Emblazoned with bowl games once lost, once won.

You apprehend what becomes of our life,
The bed in which we lay wrapped in childhood
Dreams now collapsed to footboard and headboard,
The dresser emptied of outdated clothes,

Desires we once had, that set of dishes
Still boxed and priced, the rose kitchen curtains,
The vase, those shoes, the record, that picture—
Here become mere things, motionless and cold.

ECONOMICS
POLITICS SOCIETY

AN ECONOMIC PROFILE OF
THE CENTRAL NEBRASKA PRAIRIE

Allan Jenkins, Associate Professor of Economics
Mary Rittenhouse, Lecturer, Department of Economics

The current economic circumstances of the Central Nebraska prairie region are shaped by a variety of geographic, demographic, political, and historical/cultural influences. Early settlement patterns were influenced by public policies like the Homestead Act, aggressive recruitment of settlers by the railroads, and the inherent differences in local agricultural productivity based upon differences in soil, rainfall, and climate. Growing grain, particularly corn, provided the economic foundation for the region. While agricultural production is still an important component of the regional economy, there is an increasing amount of manufacturing and service activity. Technological change has dramatically increased output per farmer, which, in turn, means that fewer farmers are needed. Small towns, which traditionally serviced the surrounding farm population, now must diversify to survive.

Cultural Influence

The Great Platte River Road, running east to west through the region, carried hundreds of thousands of settlers through Nebraska Territory beginning in the 1840s. However, Nebraska Territory was not open to white settlement until passage of the Kansas-Nebraska Act of 1854. Once the territory was opened, settlers rushed to Nebraska, drawn by the economic opportunities presented by a rich agricultural area. The settlers were mostly farmers, but also included some who viewed the Plains as the foundation of their personal fortunes. Speculators, including James N. Paul, John J. Cozad, and Olaf Bergstrom, came to develop towns that each envisioned would someday be the "Gateway to the West." Also among these first settlers of Nebraska were those who saw the new territory as a springboard for political advancement. Thomas B. Cumming was only twenty-five years old when he accepted President Pierce's appointment in 1854 to become acting Territorial Governor.

It was the second wave of migration beginning in the 1870s that gave central Nebraska its dominant cultural heritage. The Federal government, the Union Pacific Railroad, and the Burlington Northern Railroad sponsored a massive advertising campaign in Europe and the eastern United States which enticed thousands of Europeans to migrate to the region. Settlers came because advertisements promised cheap land, fertile soil, and ample water. Railroads determined the location and early development of towns. The townsite was often on land selected by the railroad and sold to settlers and speculators. The Union Pacific guided development in the Platte River Valley and the Burlington Northern in the Republican River Valley.

By 1895, the population of Nebraska was

First train at Broken Bow, Nebraska, 1886   Butcher Collection

452,402, with approximately 26 percent of the population born in a foreign country. Germans, Irish, English, Czechs, and Swedes arrived in large numbers. The settlement pattern, largely determined by the railroads, encouraged ethnic groups to live in segregated communities. For example, Gothenburg, in Dawson County, was founded in 1882 by a Union Pacific Railroad employee from Sweden named Olaf Bergstrom. According to the story passed down through the community since its founding, Bergstrom enticed fellow Swedes to settle in Gothenburg with the promise that this new town was going to be totally Swedish, and the new residents would not need to learn to speak English.

One hundred years later, the majority of the population in the region still list German as their ancestry. Using six counties spread across the region, Figure 1 illustrates the typical ancestral distribution within several representative counties.

Geographic Influences

A major geographic influence on regional development is the inherent fertility of prairie soil. While early European and American explorers who followed the Platte River thought the treeless region was uninhabitable, the area is actually a highly productive agricultural area. Early attempts at farming in the eastern tallgrass prairie proved difficult until

John Deere's steel plow replaced cast-iron plows in 1837. By the 1850s, when farmers began to migrate to south central Nebraska, they had the technology necessary to farm the prairies.

A second major geographic influence is the weather. Local weather patterns are shaped by the continental influence, which means that the area has hot summers, cold winters, and considerable variation in annual rainfall. Average growing seasons range from 160 days in the eastern part of the study area to 140 days in the west. In general, rainfall decreases as one moves west through the region. Madison County, on the eastern edge of the study area, averages twenty-seven inches of annual precipitation. Chase County, on the western edge, receives an average of eighteen inches of precipitation per year. Because there is considerable yearly variation, the transition zone of 18-22 inches of annual precipitation, which marks the boundary between subhumid and semiarid land, shifts across the region from year to year.

The Great Plains environment is a third major geographic influence. With fertile soils but marginal rainfall, farms had to be larger than those in the eastern Corn Belt. The average size of farms in Nebraska has increased significantly since the 1880s. The original 160 acre farms established by the Homestead Act were not sustainable. By 1900, the average Nebraska farm had

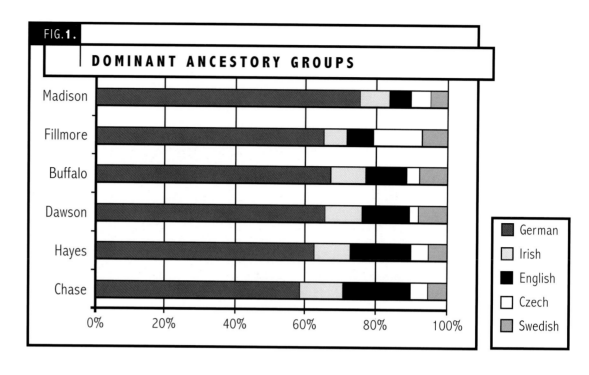

FIG.1.

DOMINANT ANCESTORY GROUPS

German
Irish
English
Czech
Swedish

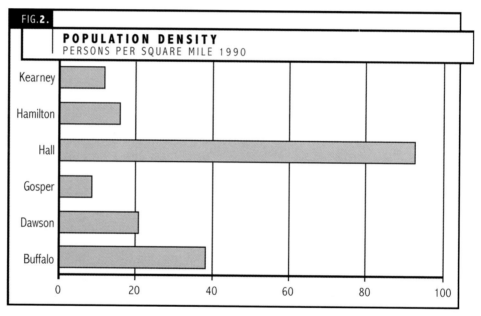

FIG.2.

POPULATION DENSITY
PERSONS PER SQUARE MILE 1990

increased to 246 acres, by 1935, 349 acres, and by 1993, to 846 acres. Larger farms mean lower population densities, more isolation, and more dependence upon the transportation network. With low population densities, the provision of services is expensive on a per capita basis.

A fourth important geographical influence on local economic development is that the region is bisected by a major east-west transportation route. As the early Spanish, French, and Anglo-American explorers passed through the region, they quickly identified the broad, gently-upsloping Platte Valley as the best overland passage to the Rocky Mountains. The Sublette party proved that this route was suitable for wagon traffic, taking ten wagons along the Platte River to the Rockies in 1830 on a fur trading expedition. Between 1841 and 1870, an estimated 360,000 settlers traveled the Great Platte River Road–the combination of the Oregon, Mormon, and California Trails.

Early regional economic development began as entrepreneurs met the needs of these travelers through road ranches, trading

Picking corn with a horse and wagon   Butcher Collection

stores, and blacksmith shops. Road ranches raised horses, mules, and oxen for sale to pioneers whose stock had perished, or would trade fresh livestock for animals exhausted by their journey from St. Joseph or other gateway cities. However, this trail-oriented economic activity was short-lived because the first transcontinental railroad was completed in 1869. Thereafter, most migrants to the West rode the train instead of walking the trails. The railroad defined settlement patterns and presented new economic opportunities. Small towns sprouted along railroad spurs, serving as the shipping points for cattle and agricultural products.

Demographics

Central Nebraska currently has a population of approximately 450,000 people. The region's total population decreased between 1930 and 1990. During the same time period, the population of the State of Nebraska increased by more than 250,000. The general population trends in the region reflect the impact of the economic difficulties precipitated by agricultural problems in the 1930s and 1980s. Starting with 516,280 people in 1930, population decreased by 64,552 over the next sixty years. The 1990 regional population of 451,728 represents a decrease of approximately 12 percent between 1930 and 1990. During this same period, the population of the entire state of Nebraska

increased by fifteen percent while the population of the United States increased by more than one hundred percent. While agriculture continues to provide a considerable portion of regional output and income, central Nebraska is experiencing a continuing loss of farm population. As farming becomes increasingly mechanized, this trend will likely continue.

A significant demographic characteristic of the region is the considerable variation in county population density. Within the study area, only Hall County has a population density greater than the national figure of 73.6 persons per square mile. Generally, population densities decrease as one moves east to west through the study area. Most of the counties in the region have population densities lower than the overall density in the state of Nebraska, which was 21.1 persons per square mile (Fig.2). Hayes County had only 1.7 persons per square mile in 1990.

Demographers often use the dependency ratio as a significant characteristic to describe a particular population. The dependency ratio is the number of persons eighteen years or younger combined with the number of persons sixty-five years or older. A high dependency ratio is typically associated with low per capita incomes because it indicates there is a relatively small number of workers carrying those not in the labor force. The area counties tend to have higher dependency

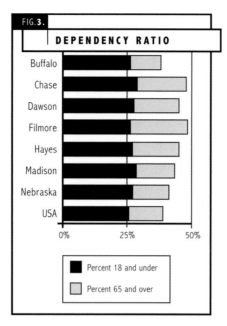

FIG. 3.

DEPENDENCY RATIO

- Buffalo
- Chase
- Dawson
- Filmore
- Hayes
- Madison
- Nebraska
- USA

0%   25%   50%

■ Percent 18 and under

▢ Percent 65 and over

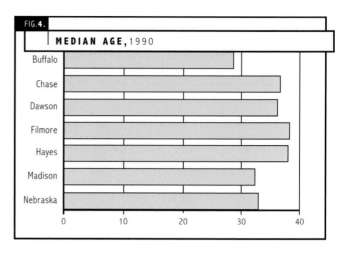

FIG. 4.

MEDIAN AGE, 1990

- Buffalo
- Chase
- Dawson
- Filmore
- Hayes
- Madison
- Nebraska

0   10   20   30   40

ratios than the entire state or the national figures (Fig. 3).

An examination of median age also reveals a population which is generally older than the national population. The low median age in Buffalo County reflects the impact of a sizable university student population (Fig. 4).

Current Economic Performance

One significant indicator of economic conditions is per capita income. In comparing Nebraska with the Great Plains Region and the entire United States, the state per capita income generally approximates that of the region but falls below the national figure. Per capita incomes in the region tend to fall below the state figure (Fig. 5).

Within south central Nebraska, per capita income is generally rising over time. The graph on the following page uses three counties to illustrate the trend occurring across the region. From this graph, one can see the variation in yearly income in the agriculturally dependent counties (Fig. 6).

Unemployment rates provide a second important economic indicator. Within the study area, unemployment rates are typically far below the national average. While the nation was edging toward double digit unemployment rates in early 1982, the local numbers were clustered around five percent. Hayes and Chase counties had rates of three percent and two percent respectively. Occasionally, a major plant closing will create a short-term spike in local unemploy-

ment, as happened in Dawson County in 1985. In the 1990s, the unemployment rate in the region has typically been less than half of the national rate.

Economic Diversification

Responding to the fluctuations in agriculture and the decreasing number of farmers, communities have diversified into manufacturing. Many of the manufacturing facilities, particularly in smaller communities, process agricultural goods. For example, the small town of Gibbon, located in Buffalo County, had 1,525 residents in 1990. Its major employers are Gibbon Packing Company, a meat processing plant with 360 workers, and Growers Cooperative, a turkey processing plant which employs 220 people. Major food-processing plants in the region include Iowa Beef Packers in Lexington (2,300 workers); Monfort, Inc. in Grand Island (2,100 workers); Ore-Ida Foods, Inc. in Grand Island (600 workers); and Armour Food Company in Hastings (280 workers.)

Some of the small communities have a surprisingly diverse manufacturing base. For example, Geneva, in Fillmore County, is home to a variety of manufacturers producing goods for the local, regional, national, and even international markets. As illustrated by the list of businesses in Figure 7, relatively small communities often have a surprisingly diversified employment base.

Agriculture

Regional economic performance is shaped by a heavy reliance on agricultural production and processing. While nationally farm employment is less than two percent of total

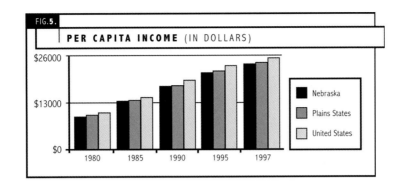

FIG.**5.**

PER CAPITA INCOME (IN DOLLARS)

Legend: Nebraska, Plains States, United States

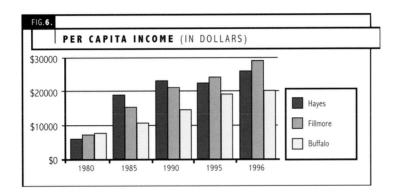

FIG.**6.**

PER CAPITA INCOME (IN DOLLARS)

Legend: Hayes, Fillmore, Buffalo

FIG.**7.**

GENEVA MANUFACTURING ENTERPRISES

COMPANY	PRODUCT	NUMBER OF EMPLOYEES
Aero Mfg Co.	Toy Windmills	4
Andrews Electric Co.	Electrical Controls	9
Doug's Garage & Machine	Irrigation Engine Trailers	5
Geneva Milling Co. Inc.	Livestock Feed	6
Geneva Tomato	Tomato Growers	5
Geneva Welding & Supply Inc.	Steel & Aluminum Products	10
Ipsco Steel Inc.	Steel Pipe	19
Lauber Seed Farms	Seed Production	17
M.C. Industries	Screenprinted Textiles	43
Midwest Steel Inc.	Sheet Metal Fabricators	3
Nebraska Signal Inc.	Weekly Newspaper & Commercial Offset Printing	8
Overland Ready Mix	Ready-Mix Concrete	5

FIG.**8.**

FARM EMPLOYMENT
AS PERCENTAGE OF TOTAL EMPLOYMENT, 1992

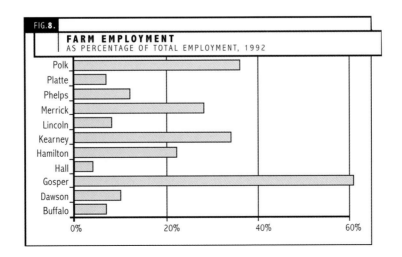

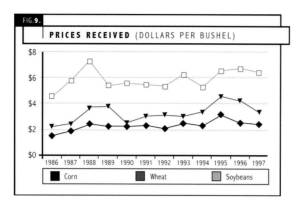

FIG.9.

PRICES RECEIVED (DOLLARS PER BUSHEL)

Legend: ■ Corn ■ Wheat □ Soybeans

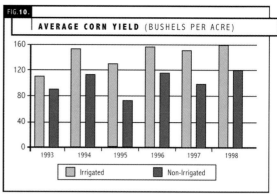

FIG.10.

AVERAGE CORN YIELD (BUSHELS PER ACRE)

Legend: Irrigated Non-Irrigated

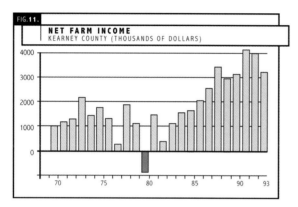

FIG.11.

NET FARM INCOME
KEARNEY COUNTY (THOUSANDS OF DOLLARS)

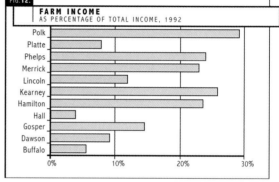

FIG.12.

FARM INCOME
AS PERCENTAGE OF TOTAL INCOME, 1992

Polk, Platte, Phelps, Merrick, Lincoln, Kearney, Hamilton, Hall, Gosper, Dawson, Buffalo

employment, within the study area it is approximately ten percent of total employment. Gosper County is particularly ag-dependent, with sixty percent of employment in the farm sector (Fig 8).

Regions with agriculture as the foundation of local economic activity are subject to a "boom and bust" cycle arising from year-to-year fluctuations in prices, yields, and farm incomes. Because the region produces vast quantities of output, slight changes in the market price of corn, wheat, and soybeans have tremendous impact on agricultural income and the total level of local economic activity. Given the variability of prices, which individual farmers cannot influence or control, it is not surprising that there is considerable variation in farm income (Figs. 9 and 10).

One sees the impact of these fluctuations when examining net farm income over an extended period. (Net farm income is total farm income minus production expenses.) The graphs above use Kearney County in the central portion of the study area as an example of the year-to-year variation (Figs. 11 and 12).

The central Nebraska prairie is a productive agricultural area, but is heavily dependent upon irrigation. Nationally, 5.2 percent of all land in farms is irrigated. In Nebraska, 14.2 percent of all land in farms is irrigated. Obviously, some farm acres are not suitable for cultivation because of limitations of terrain or soil. The importance of irrigation in the study area is illustrated by Figure 13 which compares irrigated acres to all harvested cropland. In the northeastern portion of the study area, approximately one-third of all cropland is irrigated. The importance of irrigation increases as one moves south and west through the region. Hayes County has less irrigation because a significant number of acres of cropland are devoted to winter wheat production, which is not irrigated.

Corn was the dominant crop in the region by the end of the nineteenth century. Sorghum became an important crop in the drought years of the 1930s because it uses less water than corn. In the region, most sorghum is grown in the counties south of the Platte River. Winter wheat is an significant crop in several counties, particularly in the southwestern portion of the study area. Soybeans are an important crop in the eastern third of Nebraska (Fig. 14).

Another general agricultural characteristic of the region is that farm size tends to

a**prairie**mosaic

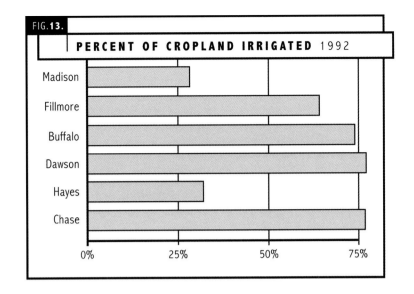

FIG.13.

PERCENT OF CROPLAND IRRIGATED 1992

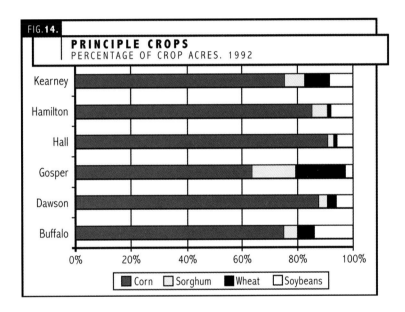

FIG.14.

PRINCIPLE CROPS
PERCENTAGE OF CROP ACRES. 1992

■ Corn   □ Sorghum   ■ Wheat   □ Soybeans

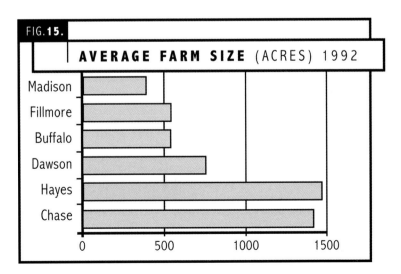

FIG.15.

AVERAGE FARM SIZE (ACRES) 1992

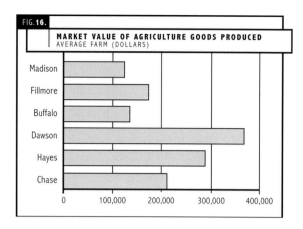

FIG. 16.

MARKET VALUE OF AGRICULTURE GOODS PRODUCED
AVERAGE FARM (DOLLARS)

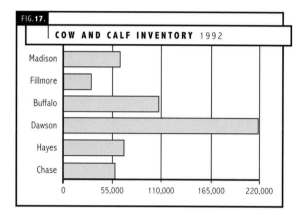

FIG. 17.

COW AND CALF INVENTORY 1992

increase from east to west. By the time one reaches the western edge of the study area, nearly one-half of all farms are one thousand acres or larger (Fig. 15).

In addition to the size of a farm, another important indicator of agricultural structure is the market value of the goods produced during a year. As the above graph illustrates, an average farm (500 acres) in Fillmore County produces nearly as much output measured by market value as an average farm (1,400 acres) in Chase County. This reflects the more favorable soil and climate resources in the eastern part of the study area (Fig. 16).

In addition to grain production, the region also produces significant amounts of livestock. Also shown above, the cattle industry is prominent in the central counties of central Nebraska (Fig. 17).

Travel and Tourism

Tourism is Nebraska's third leading earner of revenue from outside the state with expenditures totaling over $2.4 billion in 1997. This figure includes spending by non-residents as well as by residents on trips to places one hundred miles or more from home. The average nonresident traveling party visiting Nebraska by highway during the summer consists of 2.5 persons who stay 2.2 nights and spend $171. The majority of summer visitors to Nebraska live in Colorado, Iowa, Illinois, California, or Minnesota. Foreign visitors make up less than one percent of all tourists, with Canadians accounting for three of every four foreign visits.

The travel industry employs approximately 36,000 workers in Nebraska. The Department of Economic Development calculates that the Nebraska tourism "multiplier" is 2.7. This means that each dollar a visitor spends in the state is typically respent to produce an additional $1.70 in business and income, creating an overall impact of $2.70.

There is a growing awareness in the region of the potential benefits created by nature-based tourism, particularly the opportunities presented by the springtime migration of sandhill cranes. Each spring, approximately four hundred thousand cranes congregate in the Big Bend region of the Platte River in March and April. Surveys indicate that tourists coming to see the cranes now have a total economic impact of $21.8 million to $48.5 million annually. Significant Nebraska attractions within the study area are shown below (Fig. 18).

A new, potentially significant tourist attraction is now under construction near Kearney in Buffalo County. The Great Platte River Road Memorial, sponsored by a non-profit

FIG. 18.

SIGNIFICANT NEBRASKA ATTRACTIONS

Attraction	1997 Attendance
Ashfall Fossil Beds State Historical Park	32,057
Buffalo Bill Ranch State Historical Park	28,459
Harold Warp's Pioneer Village	90,087
Hastings Museum & Lied IMAX Theater	168,201
Plainsman Museum	13,712
Stuhr Museum of the Prairie Pioneer	64,760

Further conditioning life in Nebraska is the fact that the state's agriculture over the years has been subject to violent fluctuations, resulting from both man-made and natural causes, with the result that at no time, save for the past fifteen years, has the state's basic industry enjoyed uninterrupted prosperity for as much as a decade. This, of course, has had its effect upon the support Nebraskans could give schools, churches, and other cultural agencies, and upon the energy they could devote to pursuits not directly related to making a living.

foundation, will include an arch stretching over Interstate 80. Sponsors predict that the sixty-million dollar project will attract more than one million visitors per year.

Economic Future

Predictions concerning future economic circumstances are always risky. The Bureau of Business Research at the University of Nebraska-Lincoln estimates that non-farm employment in the entire state will grow 1.6 percent in 1997, with personal income growing 6.1 percent. The Bureau predicts that Nebraska will continue its current pattern of steady growth in the near future. Individual counties will likely experience considerable variation in economic growth rates. One reason for the variance stems from large differences in population density. In recent years, the fastest growing sector of the economy, both nationally and at the state level, is the service sector. However, low population density limits service opportunities. Not surprisingly, in Nebraska more than two out of every three service jobs are in Douglas County (Omaha) or Lancaster County (Lincoln). The more rural counties have limited potential in this sector.

In the long term, regional economic prospects are greatly influenced by national agricultural policy. A cornerstone of the latest Farm Bill is a year-by-year decrease in agricultural subsidies. These subsidies now provide a substantial cushion for local producers. For example, in 1992 Chase County farmers received $5,269,000 in government payments. The average farm in the county received $19,513 in government payments that year. While payment amounts vary as yields and market prices fluctuate, the long-term impact of a substantial decrease is an area of considerable concern.

Economic growth also requires a well-educated workforce. A variety of educational opportunities are available today, reflecting the value that early settlers placed on access to education. In 1855, the first territorial legislature enacted the Free Public School Act, which provided for free education. Today, education still plays an important economic role in the region, home to the University of Nebraska at Kearney, Hastings

Steam Plow at Newark

College, and community colleges in Hastings, Grand Island, Norfolk, Columbus, North Platte, and McCook. The University of Nebraska has a special agricultural campus located at Curtis.

The economic challenges facing central Nebraska in the 21st century are as varied as the influences that now shape the region. Agriculture will continue to provide the economic base for the region. The number of farmers will continue to decline, which will impact the small ag service-providing communities. To prosper, communities must continually adapt to changing circumstances, identifying new opportunities in tourism, information-based economic activities, and diversified manufacturing.

At this fault the ways of life and living changed. Practically every institution that was carried across it was either broken and remade or else greatly altered. . . .When people first crossed this line they did not immediately realize the imperceptible change that had taken place in their environment, nor, more is the tragedy, did they foresee the full consequences which that change was to bring in their own characters and in their modes of life.

Selected**References**

Boohar, J. A. and Walczyk, V.C. 1998. Water resources data: Nebraska water year. 1997. United States Geological Survey Report Ne-97-1. Washington D. C.: United States Department of Interior.

Central Nebraska Public Power and Irrigation District. 1994. Holdrege, Nebraska: A journey through the Central District.

Central Nebraska Public Power and Irrigation District. 1995. Reservoir storage in the Platte basin. (map) Holdrege, Nebraska: Central Nebraska Public Power and Irrigation District.

Farrar, J. 1991. "The impact of crane watching." Nebraskaland Magazine. 69 (2): 8-23.

Nebraskaland Magazine. 1997. Spring migration guide. Lincoln, Nebraska: Nebraska Game and Parks Commission,

Nebraska Public Power District. 1996. Answers about: Relicensing NPPD's Sutherland project and balancing the competing interests for Platte River water. Brochure. Nebraska Public Power District.

Olson, J. 1966. History of Nebraska. Lincoln: University of Nebraska Press.

Stone, M. 1993. Climate the Platte River: An atlas of the Big Bend Region. A. Jenkins, and S.K. George, eds. University of Nebraska – Kearney, p. 13-17.

Webb, W. 1931. The Great Plains. Boston: Ginn and Company.

Useful Internet Sites

Nebraska Agricultural Statistics Service. 1998. County Profiles. Nebraska Department of Agriculture. http://www.agr.state.ne.us.

Nebraska Department of Economic Development: http://www.ded.state.ne.us/

University of Nebraska at Kearney Platte-related website: http://platteriver.unk.edu/

For Census, Agricultural Census, and Regional Economic Information: Oregon State Government Information Sharing Project: http://govinfo.kerr.orst.edu/

OPEN RANGE RANCHING

Gordon J. Blake, Professor Emeritus of Economics

The first ranching operations in the mixed-grass prairie of central Nebraska occurred in the Platte Valley along the Oregon Trail. These ranches, referred to as road ranches, specialized in trading livestock with travelers and freighters along the trail. They would sell or trade animals in good condition for those of travelers and freighters that had been weakened by the rigors of the trail. The weakened horses and oxen were then pastured on native grass until the animals had recovered their health and strength, and they would be sold to other travelers or freighters, usually the next year. The road ranches lost most of their business in 1867 as the Union Pacific was constructed along the Platte.

In the 1860s, two important new markets were being created for beef. One new market was to supply beef for the military operating in the area; the other was to provide beef to the Board of Indian Commissioners for distribution on Indian Reservations. The purchases of this Board were substantial, although not all of the cattle came from the central Nebraska mixed-grass prairie. The Annual Reports of the Board of Indian Commissioners record the purchases from 1870-1880. Starting with a purchase of a little over 12.5 million pounds in 1870, total purchases increased rapidly, peaking at nearly 43 million pounds in 1879 (Fig. 1). The Commission's reports do not record the

prices paid during all the years listed. The reports indicate that the price was $2.60 per hundred pounds in 1871, about $49.88 in 1999 dollars. Therefore, the Commissioners purchased $713,485 of beef in 1871, about $13,690,349 in 1999 dollars. Since there were a number of ways in which contractors could cheat the government Indian Agents, or simply bribe them, the Indians did not receive all of the beef or the quality of the beef specified in the government contracts. But that is another story.

Also, with rapidly growing railroad networks, the area was becoming increasingly open to existing eastern markets. Adding to the eastern demand for western beef was the opening of the Union Stockyards in Chicago in 1865. Thus, there was a rapid increase in demand for beef, both from Indian reservations and from eastern markets. As is normally the case, when demand increases, market prices also increase, providing an incentive for producers to expand their output.

Prior to the Civil War, many longhorn cattle roamed freely in parts of Texas and were the property of anyone who could place a brand on them. Some of these cattle were rounded up and driven to New Orleans and to St. Louis. The Civil War put a damper on the cattle business. Northern markets were off limits, and Texas was cut off from using eastern markets when Union forces gained control of the Mississippi River. In the

FIG. 1.

BEEF PURCHASED FOR INDIANS

(In pounds on the hoof)

Year	Pounds
1870	12,660,790
1871	27,441,750
1872	27,850,000
1873	28,647,000
1874	36,000,000
1876	30,790,173
1877	29,173,000
1878	37,230,000
1879	42,878,000
1880	39,160,900

meantime, the numbers of cattle had grown even larger. After the Civil War, many Confederate veterans returned to their homes in Texas in need of employment. Some of them began to collect the wild longhorns, either independently or in the employ of others. Some of these people would play a role in the development of central Nebraska. The most famous, or infamous, were the Olive Brothers.

Early Ranchers

Everett Dick, in The Long Drive, argues that Texas cattlemen discovered that Nebraska was good cattle country by accident. If market prices were poor in Kansas cattle towns, such as Abilene, they drove their herds slowly northward where they hoped to find a government contractor. If that did not materialize, they shipped their cattle to eastern markets on the Union Pacific Railroad. In the process, they discovered that Nebraska had abundant grass and adequate sources of water. While Texans were important in open range ranching generally, most open range ranchers in Nebraska were not Texans. They were men who had had some acquaintance with the area and realized that it was good cattle country. Businessmen, such as Bill Paxton, John Bratt, and others who had freighted through the area or Edward Creighton, who had built the transcontinental telegraph, purchased cattle

that had been driven from Texas. They placed them on the open range, part of the public domain, land owned by the Federal Government that had not yet been homesteaded or sold. There were no enforced restrictions or charges for the use of unsettled land.

In 1871, the Nebraska State Board of Agriculture reported that cattle raising was quite successful in Nebraska. They noted that it was "very profitable to purchase Texas or Cherokee cattle to graze upon . . . wild grasses for one season before shipment to market." They also noted that "good pastures and a change to a mild summer temperature causes them to take on fatness." The board believed that "grazing must eventually be a great interest in Nebraska." Since ranchers were operating on the open range, frequently in areas where counties had not yet been organized, it is difficult to know who the first ranchers were or where they were located.

Three early ranchers were Captain Streeter, M.H. Brown, and John Bratt. Captain Streeter placed longhorn cattle on land south of Broken Bow along Ash Creek. M.H. Brown had a herd of cattle south of the Platte River near North Platte. John Bratt entered ranching in 1869 with General Coe and Levi Carter under the business name of John Bratt & Co. We know more about John Bratt than most other early ranchers because of his autobiography entitled <u>Trails of Yesterday</u>. The experiences of Bratt and Coe are fairly typical of many early ranchers. In October 1869, their Texas herd of about 2,500 head arrived at Fort Kearny or "Dobytown." About five hundred of the cattle were crippled or otherwise in poor condition. Mr. Bratt and several employees took these cattle, which he called "skins and crips," to a sheltered spot near Fort Kearny on the Platte River where the cattle could recover their health prior to being moved to the ranch. General Coe drove the remainder of their cattle to their ranch west of Fort McPherson.

Prior to 1875, fairly large herds of buffalo still roamed the Republican River Valley, attracting a number of Indian hunting parties. Because of this, the herds of cattle being brought from Texas were generally driven to Schuyler or to Kearney. Many acres of land were available in the vicinity of Fort Kearny to hold cattle until they were delivered to ranchers or shipped by rail. By 1875, the Republican River Valley had been cleared of Indian activity and buffalo, so the center of activity moved westward to Ogallala.

Bratt tells an interesting story of having to share the sheltered area with a band of Pawnee Indians. Bratt purchased five hundred tons of hay on Denman Island, a few miles south of Wood River, from James Jackson, who owned a store in Wood River. He then found an "ideal place–heavy timber, lots of brush and a nice flowing spring–on the north bank of the Platte River" where he could safely winter his "skins and crips." After moving his cattle to that location, he went to Grand Island to preempt the land, having discovered that it was vacant government land.

Upon Bratt's return, he was surprised to find his "cattle horses and men surrounded by about seven hundred Pawnee Indians." The Indians told him that he had to move his cattle immediately, since this had been their winter camp for many years. The chief gave him only until the next morning to move his cattle, even though he tried to explain that he would move in the spring when the grass was green. In an effort to win the Indians over, he secured a wagon-load of flour, sugar, coffee, beans, syrup, crackers, soda, and other provisions from the store at

Wood River. He then killed the two fattest cows in his herd and gave a big feast, after which the Indians said that he had a good heart, but he still had to go.

The next morning, Bratt moved his cattle to the open prairie north of the Pawnee camp and wired a bank in Omaha to send him "seven hundred ten-cent shin plasters," which arrived the next day, "all new, crisp and attractive looking." He then asked the Indians to line up, and, as they filed by, he gave them each, including the babies, "one little ten-cent greenback." This so pleased the Indians that after another feast, they gave him permission to stay, on the condition that he erect a "building large enough to accommodate the squaws, papooses and old warriors in case of a Sioux or Cheyenne attack."

Bratt agreed, telling them that in case of attack, he would help fight their enemies. One warrior was so pleased with Bratt's actions that he expressed a willingness to give Bratt his beautiful, sixteen year old sister for a wife, an offer Bratt courteously declined.

Bratt also encountered a problem that was to become all too common for early ranchers. He caught some "thieving white men" driving some of his cattle "to an island in the Platte River, where they butchered them, took the meat to Grand Island and sold it." About May 10, 1870, John Bratt drove the surviving cattle to the ranch.

Open Range Profits
Open range ranching was proving to be a very profitable and rapidly growing business. Ranchers' only expenditures were for cattle and wages for a few cowboys, from $25 to $45 per month, approximately $403 to $879 in 1999 dollars. Yearlings could be purchased for approximately $5 to $6 per head, about $81 to $97 in 1999 dollars, and after being held on the range from eighteen months to two years, they could be sold from $25 to $45, $407 to $733 in 1999 dollars. The ranchers, incurred little or no real estate expenses or taxes. In 1870, a half million dollars directly related to the sale and purchase of cattle passed through the First National Bank of Omaha.

The Office of the United States Commissioner of Agriculture published the average prices of oxen and other cattle

AFTER HAYING

there is a moment

when the land draws the sky

across its pelvis,

blue coming

softly down, marrying

the brown,

filling the windbreaks

with the shadows

of soft songs.

DON**WELCH**

Residence of Mr. Meisner, a "Millionaire Stockman" in Shelton, Nebraska   Butcher Collection

in Nebraska yearly. Prices fluctuated from year to year with prices from 1869 through 1871 being quite high (Fig. 2). After that, prices gradually decreased, partly due to increased numbers of cattle being brought to market, and, also, due to general deflationary conditions in the economy.

Many ranchers earned substantial profits even in those years when prices were lower than the peak years. Such large profits attracted many to the business, including Frank North and William Cody. According to North, "Buffalo Bill told him in 1877, 'Let us go into the cattle business together ... everybody who is engaged in stock raising ... is making money.'" Eventually, the high profits attracted investors from England and Scotland, but that took place farther west than central Nebraska.

No accurate figures exist as to the number of cattle placed on the range in the years of open range ranching. Personnel from the Office of the United States Commissioner of Agriculture frequently complained of the difficulty of making any accurate estimate of cattle numbers on the range. Since most of the open range was located in areas where counties had not yet been organized, no

taxing authority was interested in determining numbers. Even in those areas which fell into the jurisdiction of organized counties, the practice of under-reporting cattle numbers for tax purposes was widespread and seldom penalized.

Cattle Rustling

By the late 1870s, the ranges of the cattlemen on the mixed-grass prairie area of central Nebraska were being encroached upon by settlers who were homesteading or buying the land. While some friction existed between these groups, many individual acts of kindness also occurred between them. However, explosive friction did develop when some of the settlers, who were outright rustlers, stole and sold large numbers of cattle using falsified bills of sale. A more common annoyance were settlers who killed ranchers' cattle and sold the meat in Kearney or Grand Island. The settlers referred to such beef as "slow elk." The problem was compounded when, in August of 1878, much of Custer County range was burned by a prairie fire. Ranchers who had been grazing stock in that area were forced to move their herds eastward, which brought

N.C. Dunlap, foreman of the Watson Ranch, Buffalo County, 1888

Butcher Collection

Cattle Ranch in Cherry county, 1900

Butcher Collection

FIG.2.

AVERAGE PRICES OF CATTLE AND OXEN IN NEBRASKA

		In 1999 Dollars (Approximate)
1869	$29.84	$485
1870	29.77	485
1871	29.95	488
1872	24.38	397
1873	25.14	410
1874	23.62	384
1875	22.85	372
1876	20.08	327
1877	21.30	346
1878	19.45	318
1879	21.52	351
1880	21.40	349

Source: Annual Reports of the United States Commissioner of Agriculture 1873–1880.

them into closer contact with new settlers, increasing their losses. This was especially true of the Olive Ranch.

As settlement increased rapidly in the 1880s, some cattlemen left the range, such as the Olive brothers. Other ranchers remained, but more and more of their range was claimed by settlers, and large scale open range ranching gradually decreased. Some of the ranchers acquired title to more land and continued to operate ranches on deeded land. Most who stayed did so with improved herds and mixed farming and ranching operations. As a result, by the early 1880s, large-scale open range ranching was largely a thing of the past in the mixed-prairie central Nebraska. Today, some existing farm and ranch families can trace their roots back to open range ranching.

Selected**References**

Bratt, J. H. 1921. Trails of yesterday. Lincoln: University Publishing Co.

Dale, E. E. 1960. Range cattle industry. Norman: University of Oklahoma Press.

Dick, E. 1928. Long drive, the origin of the cow country. Topeka: Kansas State Historical Society.

Frink, M. 1956. When grass was king. Boulder: University of Colorado Press.

Yost, N. S. 1966. Call of the range. Denver: Sage Books.

FROM PRAIRIE TO CROPLAND:

IRRIGATION'S IMPACT ON SOUTH CENTRAL NEBRASKA

Deborah E. Bridges, Assistant Professor of Economics
Allan Jenkins, Associate Professor of Economics

Agriculture has traditionally provided the economic foundation for south central Nebraska. The region is blessed with fertile soils, a relatively long growing season, and a rolling topography suitable for cultivation. Rainfall diminishes as one moves east to west through the region, with irrigation required for successful crop production in the western two-thirds of the study area. Irrigation is provided by the surface waters of the Platte, Republican, and Loup Rivers and by groundwater from the Ogallala Aquifer. Surface water provided the majority of irrigation water until pump technological advances in the 1940s and 1950s made groundwater use feasible. Since then, groundwater use to meet irrigation demands have more than tripled and now provides seventy percent of the water utilized for irrigation in Nebraska. The agricultural production system now in place in south central Nebraska is one of the most productive in the world.

The First Farmers

As the Pawnee moved northward during their great expansion of the thirteenth and fourteenth century, they refined techniques of cultivation, particularly of corn. By the time they settled along the Loup River in Nebraska, they grew ten varieties of corn, seven types of pumpkins and squashes, and eight kinds of beans. Women did most of the field work, tending plots from one half acre

to one and a half acres. Farming was generally confined to the bottomland of creeks and rivers where the soil could be turned with a hoe made from the shoulderblade of a buffalo. The plots were planted in a patchwork manner, alternating pumpkins and squashes between the various corn and bean varieties to separate and preserve the individual breeds. The Pawnee had no plow capable of turning the thick prairie sod and did not use irrigation, so food plots were small, and harvests were influenced by the amount of rainfall during the growing season. In addition to providing nourishment, corn was an important component of Pawnee religious ceremonies. The Lakota, Cheyenne, and other Native American tribes who used the western reaches of the study area did not practice horticulture.

The Great American Desert

After the Louisiana Purchase of 1803, the United States began sending scientific expeditions onto the Great Plains. Major Stephen Long's 1819-20 expedition was particularly influential in shaping the public perception of south central Nebraska. Major Long followed the Platte River to the confluence of the North Platte and the South Platte, then traveled along the South Platte into the Rocky Mountains. Journal entries about present day Dawson County described the region as a place of "irreclaimable

Fertile prairie soil under cultivation   by Allan Jenkins

sterility." Dr. Edwin James, the expedition's geologist and botanist, wrote, "The traveler who shall at any time have traversed its desolate sands, will, we think, join us in the wish that this region may forever remain the unmolested haunt of the native hunter, the bison, and the jackal." The expedition map labeled western Nebraska, western Kansas, eastern Colorado, and western Wyoming as the "Great American Desert."

For forty years following Long's journey, interest in the region was largely confined to finding the fastest route to get through it. The Great Platte River Road, the combination of the Oregon, Mormon, and California trails, carried 360,000 travelers through south central Nebraska between 1849-70. These migrants were uninterested in settling in an area still perceived as unsuitable for agriculture, and, furthermore, permanent settlement in the area was prohibited before the Kansas-Nebraska Act of 1854. After the opening of Nebraska Territory, early settlers along the west bank of the Missouri River found the land productive, and the eastern boundary of the Great American Desert was pushed steadily westward. By 1883, the Plum Creek Pioneer (published in Dawson County) boasted, "As the sturdy farmer takes possession of and cultivates the soil the Great American Desert moves still farther west, and soon we may look for it to entirely disappear, and its place—as has already occurred for

hundreds of miles—find the most fertile and productive grain fields in the country."

From Prairie to Cropland

Settlement of the region was shaped by government policy, the improvement of the steel plow, access to the railroad, and, later, by the development of irrigation. The Homestead Act (1862) gave 160 acres of land to anyone who would live on a farming claim for five years. The lure of free land brought thousands of people to south central Nebraska. The free land policy was later altered by the Kinkaid Act (1904), which allowed settlers to take 640 acres in western Nebraska. This change reflected the realization that 160 acres were insufficient to maintain a family in the drier climate of western Nebraska. The problem of turning the virgin prairie sod was solved with the development of the "rod" or "grasshopper" plow, which had an upright cutter to slice through the sod. The Union Pacific, Burlington and Missouri River (today's Burlington Northern) and other railroads pushed across Nebraska in the 1860s and 1870s.

While the area saw substantial growth beginning in the 1860s, there was still considerable concern about water. For many early travelers through the region, the treeless nature of the plains indicated a shortage of water for agriculture. Farmers were hesitant

Early Irrigation ditch east of Cozad, Nebraska

Butcher Collection

1878

With a logic that cannot rest we are forced to this conclusion, that the agencies of civilization now in action are such as will secure a complete victory over the wilderness and waste places of western territory. The plow will go forward.

CHARLES**WILBER**

to move into a region with insufficient water. Their worries were addressed through the cultivation of an idea that conversion of the prairie to cropland would increase yearly precipitation. Charles Dana Wilber, Superintendent of the Department of Geology and Mineralogy, Nebraska Academy of Sciences, and Samuel Aughey, a professor of Natural Sciences at the University of Nebraska, popularized the notion that "rain follows the plow." Wilber and Aughey theorized that native prairie sod was so thick that it prevented rainfall from seeping into the ground. Once the sod was broken, the newly-exposed underlying soil would act like a giant sponge. The captured moisture would gradually return to the atmosphere promoting cloud formation and a new round of precipitation. Over time, the plowed land would create its own micro-hydrological cycle.

The years immediately following the Homestead Act were unusually wet, which seemed to vindicate Wilber and Aughey. Reality returned when the wet cycle ended, and severe droughts in 1874, 1880, and 1890-95 destroyed the theory and drove thousands of settlers from the region. Responding to the stress, in 1894 the editor of the York Times cautioned people not to commit suicide, writing, "If you call this dry what do you think of the home of Col. Satan? It has not rained there since the flood

and the weather has been as hot as yesterday nearly all the time. The man who commits suicide in this country does not gain anything in the way of climate." With drought conditions prevalent in the late 1800s, irrigation was seen as a means to conquer the Great American Desert.

Early Irrigation

While railroad advertisements and community boosters had pronounced that there was sufficient rainfall for crops, the more pragmatic farmers west of the 98th meridian recognized the need for irrigation very quickly. However, proponents of irrigation faced a difficult task. Irrigation was very labor intensive and limited by the technology then available. This, combined with the general lack of knowledge of how to farm with supplemental moisture, hindered the widespread acceptance of irrigation.

Surface water irrigation depends on gravity to move the water from one point to another in a field. Water diverted from streams and rivers flowed from diversion structures to canal systems that went to on-farm irrigation ditches. Irrigation was possible as long as the water could flow from the diversion structures of the canal and from the canal to the highest point in the field by gravity. If not, some type of pump would be required to lift the water. To deliver the water from the high end of the field to the rest of it required releasing the water from the ditch by hand, cutting the irrigation ditch at regular intervals with a spade. Irrigation projects initiated during the 1870s included one near North Platte, where a group of individuals used river water to irrigate cropland; near Fort Sidney, where diverted water was used to water gardens, trees, and lawns; and west of Fort Sidney, where hay meadows were irrigated.

Throughout Nebraska, greater attention was being paid to irrigation during the 1890s. Drought conditions brought about heavy crop losses in 1890, 1893, and 1894, driving home the point that irrigation was essential for successful agricultural development, especially in the more arid western half of the state. Although the need for irrigation was recognized, financing the building of canals to move the water from the river to the cropland was hampered as interest in irrigation varied with precipitation levels. Interest in irrigation increased in dry years, but, in these years, farmers had little or no extra money. In years of adequate precipitation, farmers viewed irrigation as something not needed. Thus, the early proponents of irrigation found it difficult to find the financial backing for their irrigation development, and many went broke trying to show that irrigation was feasible. For example, the first irrigation project in Dawson County, began in 1890, failed. The project, funded by non-Nebraskans, met opposition and indifference by farmers early on, and, after a year, the financial backers pulled out.

Despite the recognition that irrigation could provide insurance against crop failures during dry years, acceptance was slow in coming for several reasons. Although gravity flow irrigation systems supplied water to the farms, releasing that water from on-farm irrigation ditches was labor intensive and required long hours of backbreaking work. Water flow from ditch cut to ditch cut was highly variable, causing soil erosion problems and difficulty in achieving uniform water distribution in the field. Achieving greater uniformity meant that the irrigator had to be present, both day and night. Farmers also lacked the experience and knowledge of how to farm with supplemental moisture.

Successful crop production depends not only on the timing of moisture but also the application level. Many farmers, lacking this knowledge and experience, could not see past the hard work associated with irrigation.

Early irrigators relied on waters in streams and rivers for irrigation. This dependence on surface water meant that water had to be flowing in the river or stream at the time it was needed. This was not a problem in years of adequate rainfall when rivers ran during the peak irrigation season. However, in dry years, the rivers all but disappeared, so when irrigation water was needed the most, it was not available. The reliance on surface water for irrigation also meant that only land adjacent to or close to the water source was accessible for irrigation. Thus, the frustration of both farmers and developers grew as each recognized the potential of irrigation but were unable to take full advantage of the possibilities.

As farmers gained an understanding of the practicality and the necessity for irrigation, they began to look to scientists, engineers, and water specialists for information about using and managing water. Irrigation studies had shown that surface water alone was insufficient to irrigate all the potentially tillable lands in Nebraska. During the 1880s and 1890s, careful study of Nebraska's water brought new knowledge about the supply of water lying beneath the plains. With this knowledge, farmers recognized the potential of bringing irrigation to lands lying outside the easily irrigated river valleys, but they still lacked the appropriate technology.

Initially, many felt that artesian wells would provide the answer. An artesian well occurs where the water rises higher than the top of the aquifer because it is held under pressure by fine grained sediments. Water from artesian wells commonly flows at the surface. Proponents of artesian wells reasoned that they could tap into the underground water supply and this water, which was under pressure, would rise to the surface unaided by mechanical assistance. Thus, artesian wells were seen as a way to expand agricultural production to lands beyond the reach of diverted surface water.

In 1890, Congress appropriated funds and appointed Richard J. Hinton to conduct

Hart and Company well diggers at Cliff Table, Nebraska, 1890

Butcher Collection

an investigation on the feasibility of using artesian wells for irrigation. This study is one of the first systematic investigations of the nature and extent of groundwater. In the study's conclusions, Hinton indicated that although a considerable supply of water existed underground, the technology did not yet exist that could raise the water. Hinton concluded that artesian wells could never raise adequate water to meet irrigation needs.

Windmills represented another early effort to tap into groundwater supplies. Windmills were seen as an answer to providing water in arid areas by using wind to pump the groundwater to the surface. In 1897, a University of Nebraska professor named Erwin Hinckley Barbour, an early supporter of windmills, conducted a field investigation of windmill usage in the Platte Valley. Barbour, one of the first to recognize that groundwater supplies were not limitless, had high expectations about an increase in the use of windmills. However, he was also realistic and cautioned farmers that windmills in use then had technical limits and were inefficient at pumping water from depths greater than seventy-five feet, limiting their irrigation potential. Barbour also recognized the importance of using groundwater to the future of irrigation in Nebraska and encouraged further studies that would lead to improved windmills and pumps. As recognition of the importance of irrigation

for agricultural production grew, so did concern over ownership of the water.

Water Rights

As irrigation technology and techniques developed, it became obvious that the legislature would have to define water rights before large scale projects were built. Water law developed piecemeal as the Legislature responded to new issues. Creating appropriate water law was complicated by Nebraska's geographic characteristics and settlement patterns. The first settlers established themselves along the eastern borders of Nebraska, where water was relatively abundant. These farmers followed the doctrine of riparian rights, which was the standard view of water in the eastern part of the United States. Under riparian rights, a landowner whose property borders a river or stream may claim use of the water for reasonable purposes.

As settlement proceeded west, farmers moved into the semiarid portions of the state. Once irrigation began, the economic importance of access to water led to legislation in 1895 which authorized the doctrine of prior appropriation. Prior appropriation is often described as "first in time, first in right." Water users are given a permit to withdraw a specific quantity of water from a river or stream. Priority is based upon the date of the permit. During dry periods, after senior users take their allotment, there may be insufficient water remaining for junior users. While the 1895 water legislation established prior appropriation, court decisions in the state held that riparian rights were not abolished. Nebraska has the unusual distinction of having dual systems of surface water law, recognizing both riparian rights and prior appropriation. Importantly, all flowing water is considered the property of the state, not the property of the landowner.

Although surface water and groundwater are inherently interrelated in the hydrology cycle, Nebraska law has historically treated each separately. Over time, the Legislature and courts developed specific statutes and different case law for both kinds of water. Unlike surface water, groundwater has received little regulatory attention from the state. Nebraska adopted a modified "American Rule," which recognized that the property owner has the right to use groundwater for beneficial purposes. The landowner has the right to use the groundwater but is not the owner of the resource. The locally-controlled Natural Resource Districts (NRDs) are the primary groundwater regulatory institutions. In April 1996, Nebraska enacted a new "conjunctive use" law, which recognizes that underground water and the flows in nearby rivers are intrinsically connected. Thus, for the first time in state law, the potential impact of groundwater irrigation on river flows was considered. Legislative actions came in response to increasing rates of irrigation development, both surface and groundwater.

Groundwater Development

In 1900, realizing that the supply of water in streams and rivers was limited, irrigators were thinking about how to access the supply of water underground. Artesian wells had proved unworkable for irrigation, and windmills were unsuited for large scale irrigation. Talk began about using steam or gasoline-powered engines to access supplies of underground water. However, exploitation of groundwater as a source of irrigation did not really take place until technology caught up with the needs of irrigators in the 1940s and 1950s.

In the early 1900s, the internal combustion engine revolutionized machinery but provided for only shallow lifts of groundwater, given the centrifugal pumps then available. In the 1930s, deeper wells and heavier lifts were made possible through the application of the turbine engine to irrigation. Also during this period, costs of drilling and installation were reduced with the adoption of new drilling techniques. Development of more efficient power units (used to power the pumps) also contributed to the increased use of irrigation. Western Land Roller, a Nebraska-based company, was one of the first to bring drilling equipment to the area and developed a turbine engine, similar to the ones produced today, for use in irrigation wells.

Technological developments from 1930 to 1950 brought irrigation potential to millions of acres. However, the adoption of this technology was gradual, as irrigation systems, especially groundwater pumping, were viewed with varying degrees of skepticism by farmers and their bankers. Drought conditions in the 1950s prompted many to overcome their reluctance and brought rapid development. Prior to 1950, the average number of new wells installed annually statewide was less than five hundred. The adoption of new well drilling techniques, innovations in pump technology, and drought conditions during 1953-57 encouraged rapid expansion, with the number of new wells increasing from less than one thousand in 1953 to over 4,500 in 1956. New well drilling between 1957 and 1964 declined and remained fairly low, with around five hundred new wells being drilled each year. However, groundwater development increased from 1964 to the early 1980s with rapid expansion during the years 1972-77.

New well drilling reached a peak in 1976, with over 5,500 wells installed. In the 1980s, as the agricultural recession took hold, groundwater development slowed dramatically from 2,200 annually in 1982 to 700 in 1983, reaching a 50-year low of about 200 in 1987. In the late 1980s, a recovery of sorts began as development of groundwater increased. For example, the number of new wells (702) drilled in 1989 almost equals the number of wells drilled during 1986, 1987, and 1988 combined. Since 1990, new well installations averaged

500 per year, bringing the total of wells in the state to 81,112 by January 1, 2000.

Groundwater irrigation had several advantages over surface water irrigation. Groundwater was available on demand, whereas surface water relied on water being in the stream or river at the right time and all season-long, whether it was needed or not. Pump irrigation was more efficient than surface water irrigation because there was less evaporation and seepage, allowing for the conservation of water. Although pump irrigation allowed more acreage to be irrigated, it still relied on gravity to move water from one point to another in the field. Irrigation was still very labor intensive, which limited the number of irrigated acres a single farmer could manage, and the need to use gravity to move water also limited the acreage irrigated. The next major improvement in irrigation technology, the center pivot, overcame these constraints.

Center Pivot Irrigation Systems

In 1953, Frank Zybach of Colorado joined with A.E. Trowbridge of Columbus, Nebraska, and began producing center pivot irrigation systems (automated, self-propelled sprinkler systems). In 1954, Zybach and Trowbridge sold the manufacturing and sales rights to Valmont Industries, now the oldest and largest producer of center pivot irrigation systems. Of the seven United States firms making and selling center pivots, five are in Nebraska. These five companies provide the majority of the systems and support services in both the United States and abroad.

Center pivot irrigation systems brought irrigation potential to millions of acres unsuited to gravity flow. Adoption of center pivots were enhanced by economic forces and geographic reality. High grain prices in the early 1970s due to Soviet Union purchases of United States grains encouraged increased crop production. High grain prices provided both the incentive and the financial means to adopt the new center pivot technology. In 1972, there were 2,735 systems in Nebraska; by 1975, the number had risen to 8,517, and as of 1988, the last year statistics were available, there were 26,741 center pivot systems in the state. The acceptance of center

pivot irrigation is due to its beneficial characteristics. Center pivot systems are less labor intensive, allowing a single operator to oversee more acres. For example, a single person working to the point of exhaustion could oversee at most about four hundred acres of gravity flow irrigated crops during a single irrigation season. However, that same person, utilizing center pivot irrigation, could oversee eight hundred acres or more. Center pivot technology offers another advantage in that it is more sparing in the use of water and provides a way to apply chemicals through the sprinkler nozzles themselves.

The abundance of groundwater in Nebraska was an important factor in irrigation development and in making the state a leading agricultural producer. In 1960, Nebraska had two million irrigated acres. Today, there are 8.4 million acres. While the economic benefits of conversion to irrigation are immediately evident, the transformation of Nebraska agriculture also has a downside.

Monoculture Agriculture

Farmers use irrigation because it pays. Irrigation increases the productive capability of cropland, with yields on irrigated land far surpassing dryland yields, even in years of normal precipitation. For example, during 1973-75, dryland corn averaged fifty-one bushels per acre, and, during 1990-92, dryland yields for corn were ninety-four bushels per acre. During this same period, irrigated yields for corn were 110 and 147 bushels per acre for 1973-75 and 1990-92, respectively. Irrigation also allows for more reliable production, enables farmers to switch to higher valued crops, namely corn and soybeans, and increases land values. Although Nebraska farm land is fertile and capable of producing a variety of crops, such as sugar beets, dry edible beans, sorghum, wheat, and alfalfa, irrigation has turned Nebraska farmers into corn growers. Of the principal field crops, corn is the most responsive to well-timed applications of water and fertilizer. Thus, as the number of irrigated acres in Nebraska increases, so does the number of acres planted to corn. Nebraska now ranks third in the nation for corn production, behind Iowa and Illinois. However, this corn production has come at the exclusion of producing other

1976

Center-pivot irrigation (is) perhaps is the most significant mechanical innovation since the replacement of draft animals by the tractor.

WILLIAM**SPLINTER**

Center pivot irrigation

crops, resulting in a trend towards monoculture agriculture. Some irrigated fields in Nebraska have produced nothing but corn for the last thirty years.

Producing a single crop, such as corn, makes Nebraska farmers vulnerable to price shocks. Total farm income is significantly impacted by the price of one commodity, thus exposing farmers to greater income risk. For example, when the price of corn declines dramatically, as it did in the summers of 1998 and 1999 (less than $2.00 per bushel), the resultant decline in farm income often brings up the question of whether individual producers can survive. The trend towards monoculturism has also resulted in increased pest problems. Growing the same crop year after year encourages large populations of corn rootworms, corn borers, red spider mites, and other crop pests. Furthermore, continued widespread use of single-spectrum insecticides have resulted in insect populations that are increasingly resistant to the chemicals. Although irrigation increases yield potential, to obtain and maintain these higher yields requires proportionally larger application levels of agricultural chemicals. As more and more acres are planted to corn year after year, this increased use of chemicals and fertilizers to maintain productivity and alleviate pest damage means more agricultural runoff and nonpoint pollution. The lack of crop rotations also creates the potential for increased soil loss through wind erosion.

Groundwater Levels

The extensive supplies of groundwater under Nebraska, estimated at 1.87 billion acre-feet or enough water to cover the entire state with thirty-eight feet of water, have enabled the state to become an agricultural powerhouse. Over time, groundwater levels change as a result of the imbalance between discharge and recharge. Discharge from the aquifer occurs naturally, through the processes of evapotranspiration or seepage, and by human activities, such as pumping for irrigation. Recharge occurs primarily through precipitation, although other sources include seepage from streams, canals, and reservoirs, as well as return flows from irrigation. Both precipitation amounts and irrigation development have impacted groundwater levels. In years of below normal precipitation or when drought conditions exist, the need for supplemental moisture increases. Under these conditions, groundwater levels are expected to decline as the rate of discharge exceeds recharge. On the other hand, during years with normal or above normal precipitation, water levels are expected to rise as the rate of recharge (precipitation) exceeds discharge (decreased pumping).

As pump irrigation expands, people are increasingly concerned about the overall supply and condition of Nebraska's ground water resources. Portions of the high plains, particularly the Texas panhandle and south-western Kansas, face growing concerns over rapidly declining groundwater levels. Prior to 1980, declines of more than one hundred feet were observed, and, more recently (1980-1995), declines of more than forty feet have been observed in Texas and Kansas. Fortunately, water levels under Nebraska have remained fairly stable during this period, with the exception of the extreme southwest, where levels have declined by twenty feet or less. In some areas of Nebraska, especially just south of the Platte river from Gosper County to the east, groundwater levels are rising. While one might conclude that rising water levels are desirable, this is not necessarily the case. Rising water tables can change the productivity of land, turning tillable acreage into marshy areas.

Instream Flows

The Nebraska Constitution and various statutes specifically recognize that the state's water resources may be used for domestic, agricultural, manufacturing, and hydro-electric power purposes. State law gives domestic use first priority, followed by agricultural use, then manufacturing use. While Nebraska law does not give a specific priority to recreational, environmental, or scenic use, as a general rule, the Nebraska Supreme court has shown concern for water management and has favored those uses which benefit the public. This approach is consistent with state law, which holds that the water belongs to the public, not to the individual landowners, and that the resource is dedicated to the use of the people of the state.

The need to meet the habitat requirements of endangered species, such as the whooping crane and piping plover, has impacted Nebraska's water policy. Legislation enacted in 1984 allows the state Game and Parks Commission or a Natural Resource District (NRD) to apply for an instream flow to meet recreational or wildlife habitat needs. Central Platte NRD was granted a five hundred cubic feet per second instream flow right for fish and wildlife habitat on the Platte River in 1992. When the Game and Parks Commission submitted an instream

flow application for the Platte in 1993, a group of irrigators, power districts, and other water users filed a vigorous objection. In response, Game and Parks reduced its flow request in 1996. When the Department of Water Resources finally granted the flow rights in 1998, it granted less water than Game and Parks had requested.

The Three-State Plan

In 1997, Nebraska signed a Memorandum of Agreement to work jointly with Colorado, Wyoming, and the Department of the Interior on flows to meet the Endangered Species Act requirements for the Central Platte River. The United States Fish and Wildlife Service has identified flow levels believed necessary to provide adequate habitat for endangered species. Existing flows in the Platte River fall short of these targets. The three states agreed to work together for three years to review the flow targets, to develop a basin-wide plan to find additional water, and to take mitigating action to increase habitat. At the end of the three years, the states will decide whether to continue to cooperate or proceed independently.

In 1998, hydroelectric projects operated by Central Public Power and Irrigation District and Nebraska Public Power District were granted new forty-year Federal Energy Regulatory Commission operating licenses. The relicensing process had taken fourteen years and cost the Districts approximately $35 million in legal fees, scientific studies, and habitat improvement. A key component of the agreement was the creation of an "environmental account" of up to 100,000 acre feet of water in Lake McConaughy, controlled by the United States Fish and Wildlife Service. (An acre foot is the amount of water needed to cover an acre with one foot of water.) The Service would use this water to supplement existing flows during critical periods of the year.

Regulating Water Quality

In general, the major water issue in south central Nebraska is the quantity available. However, concerns about water quality, related chiefly to the impact of agricultural chemicals, do exist. Regulation of agricultural chemical application to cropland in Nebraska is the responsibility of Natural Resource Districts (NRDs), established by the Legislature in 1972. The state is divided into twenty-three Natural Resource Districts. The eastern section of the study area includes portions of the Upper Elkhorn, Lower Elkhorn, Lower Platte, Upper Big Blue, and Little Blue NRDs. The central section includes the Lower Loup, Central Platte, and Tri-Basin NRDs. The western reach of the study area includes the Twin Platte, Upper Republican, and Middle Republican NRDs.

In 1984, the Legislature required that all NRDs create groundwater management plans, with the first of these plans initiated by Central Platte NRD in 1988. Each district is divided into zones based upon the existing level of nitrogen in the groundwater. Phase III zones are those which have the highest levels of nitrates in the groundwater. In these areas, the NRD maintains stringent controls on the application of fertilizer. For example, farmers in Phase III areas cannot apply nitrogen in the fall, regardless of soil type. Irrigators are required to keep track of water pumped, and farmers must determine the nitrogen in both their irrigation water and soil. At the end of each crop year, farmers submit an annual report to the district, including soil and water sample results, crop yields, and nitrogen application information.

Looking to the Future

Irrigation continues to evolve as new technology and techniques are developed. Farmers and university researchers continue to experiment with a variety of new systems aimed at increasing irrigation efficiency and improving water conservation. For example, the new surge irrigation technique, in which a surge of water floods across a "perfectly" level field, uses less water than traditional irrigation. Drip irrigation utilizes a buried line and drip nozzles under low pressure to deliver supplemental moisture directly to the plant's root zone, thus reducing moisture loss

*Walking beside Calamus Reservoir
in September, orange and black
butterflies hovering above the sandy beach,
we feel the great lightness
of their wings stirring the air,
deftly as the fans
Willa Cather's neighbors used
on their front porches,
dreaming of dusty roads
west and out of town.*

through evaporation. Irrigators are beginning to use high tech equipment to monitor soil moisture content and deliver precision applications of water and chemicals. Certainly, new challenges will emerge: increased competition for scarce water, concerns about agricultural chemicals, and changes in groundwater levels. In addition, the economic uncertainty of the immediate future poses a significant financial challenge to local farmers. Notwithstanding these issues, where the early explorers saw the Great American Desert, today one sees an extraordinarily productive agricultural region.

Selected**References**

Buettner, J. 1994. A journey throught the central district. Holdrege, Nebraska: The Central Nebraska Public Power and Irrigation District.

Flowerday, C.A., ed. 1993. Flat water: A history of Nebraska and its water. Institute of Agriculture and Natural Resources: Resource Report No. 12. University of Nebraska-Lincoln.

Jenkins, A., and S.K. George, eds. 1993. The Platte river: An atlas of the big bend region. Kearney, Nebraska: University of Nebraska at Kearney.

Locklear J. 1999. Journeys of inquiry. Nebraskaland 77 (6): 20-29.

United States Geological Survey. 1997. Water-level changes in the high plains aquifer, 1980 to 1995. Fact Sheet FS-068-97 (July). Lincoln, Nebraska.

THE BUFFALO COMMONS:

A PROPOSAL FOR THE HIGH PLAINS

Ron Konecny, Associate Professor of Management and Marketing

Frank J. Popper and Deborah Epstein Popper, professors at Rutgers State University of New Jersey, grabbed national headlines in the late 1980s when they proposed a radical conversion of the High Plains back to a natural habitat. The Poppers argued that the current land use was only sustained by massive government subsidies, favorable loans, and export-oriented foreign policy. Rather than indefinitely continue this support, the Poppers proposed that government begin a gradual buy-back of agricultural lands. Eventually, the goal of the proposal is to tear down the fences, replant native vegetation, and restock the area with bison and other native species. Collectively, these changes would create a region which the Poppers named "The Buffalo Commons."

Geographically, the region targeted for conversion is the High Plains–stretching from west central Texas to North Dakota and bounded on the east by the 98th meridian and on the west by the foothills of the Rocky Mountains. This region is marked by rainfall of less than twenty inches per year, has America's hottest summers and coldest winters, and the nation's largest daily and weekly temperature swings. Occupying twenty percent of the contiguous United States land area, the High Plains only holds two percent of the national population.

Nineteenth Century Policy

Public policy in the mid 1800s encouraged settlement of the plains region. Railroads extended their lines through fertile river bottoms, receiving prime sections of land from the federal government. Settlements along the rail lines developed at the train water stops, where steam engines stopped to refill with water and fuel. The railroads advertised aggressively, bringing trainloads of immigrants onto the plains. In 1862, the Homestead Act gave 160 acres to anyone willing to settle on farm land in this region. Through these actions, thousands of families were drawn onto the plains.

However, immediately following the initial settlement push, geographic reality and economic forces started the process of depopulation. Droughts, locusts, prairie fires, isolation, and lack of economic opportunity forced many to move elsewhere. While gateway cities such as Omaha, Kansas City, and Denver grew on the edge of the High Plains, cities within the region remained small, local service centers. Even today, cities within the region are sparsely populated and widely scattered. Excluding Texas, only six cities have populations greater than forty thousand: Lawton, Oklahoma; Billings, Montana; Grand Island, Nebraska;

Abandoned house northwest of Red Cloud, Nebraska

by Susanne George-Bloomfield

EXCERPT FROM
WASHINGTON POST

by FRANK&DEBORAH**POPPER**

8/6/89

They are America's steppes, extending over much of 10 states— endlessly windswept, nearly treeless, semiarid, austerely beautiful, historically untenable, increasingly employ and now facing ecological devastation.

Bismarck, North Dakota; Rapid City, South Dakota; and Cheyenne, Wyoming.

Depopulation

According to the Poppers, the process of depopulation will continue over the next twenty to thirty years. The day of reckoning has been postponed through technological innovation–better hybrids, improved irrigation, and more sophisticated farm equipment. From the Poppers' perspective, these innovations do not change the fact that the region can not sustain itself without government subsidies.

Not surprisingly, many current inhabitants of the High Plains disagree with the Poppers' assessment of their immediate future. The long term sustainability of the High Plains is subject to a variety of influences. The economic foundation of the area has traditionally been the production of food grains, feed grains, and livestock. Can the region continue to successfully compete internationally in the production of agricultural

goods? The long term outlook depends on how the region responds to changing circumstances–as competition for scarce water increases, as concerns about chemical intensive farming grow, as environmental concerns increase, and as energy costs continue to rise.

THE POPPERS: THE 'BUFFALO COMMONS' CONTROVERSY

Afterall, They're Easterners

John Anderson, Associate Professor of Political Science

In democracies, the role experts play has persistently been the source of a perplexing question. How do we balance expertise with the public's sovereign ability to decide public policy? As early in history as the time of the Greek city-states, problems with experts occurred. Plato, the great Greek philosopher from that time, expressed a deeply held concern that democracies easily become mobocracies under the influence of demagogues. Demagogues are little more than experts who use forms of rhetoric. These expert/rhetors were known as sophists, and Plato was sure they would only bring the worst in people into public life. The great philosopher believed the rhetorical experts of his time merely used the "moods and anger" they studied to "reduce (understanding). . . to a system, and set up a school." Once the school was established, the experts could use their system to make a living at the expense of the public.

More recently, it has been suggested that the role of the scientific expert ought to be carefully scrutinized because scientific values and public interests easily conflict. On the other hand, there is some reason to believe that expert analysis can be used to enliven debate. The expert may help people better understand the facts and values at issue in important public matters. In Nebraska, experts have attempted to take effective roles in every imaginable arena of public policy,

including, but not limited to, debates concerning river flows, prison construction, tourism, state budgets, and land-use. Almost a decade ago, a peculiar pair of experts entered our public debate about economic development on the Great Plains, making over fifty trips in an attempt to inform and persuade residents, including Nebraskans. The experts were Frank Popper of Rutgers University in New Jersey and his wife, Deborah, a geographer currently employed at the City University of New York.

The Buffalo Commons

The Poppers, as they are now known in this region, employed their expertise to suggest the Great Plains might be best used as a "Buffalo Commons." The Buffalo Commons was a vision of a largely depopulated prairie filled with buffalo. This term, Buffalo Commons, was often noted and remembered by citizens west of the 98th Meridian (an imaginary north-south line running roughly through Aurora, Nebraska) in less than positive terms. Plains residents did not like what the Poppers proposed because it challenged their existence there. For the most part, the Poppers believed that this region, as a place populated primarily by people in small towns and villages, was not viable without the support of governmental programs like those run by the United States Department of Agriculture. As natural

George Burns and his three motherless children by their destroyed sod house, 1887   Butcher Collection

droughts and changing world economies impacted the region, it was slowly being depopulated–so much so that the best public policy option would allow the region to slowly become a vast, new, wild space occupied by buffalo. Of course, the residents of small towns, such as Broken Bow, did not like to hear that their life would be taken from them nor did they find it palatable to hear that their lives had been propped-up by governmental programs.

It certainly is not surprising that the Poppers became notorious among plains residents, a fact even the Rutgers professors have noted. While many of the judgments that added to the Popper's notoriety might have been influenced by residents' self interest in maintaining their economic standing, a clear question remains. Were the Poppers effective stewards of their role as experts informing public debate? Or, were they manipulating the public? Or, did the Poppers' work serve to further public discourse about the political and economic future of the plains. We can begin to answer these questions by examining how Nebraskans reacted to the Poppers as experts.

Small Town Reactions

A review of many small town newspapers indicates that Nebraskans had several real problems with the two experts. Editorials and syndicated columns tended to echo a sentiment common to citizens of small western states. Can outsiders be trusted? Shouldn't we question the heritage and knowledge of Frank and Deborah Popper? They were, afterall, "Easterners."

One element of our predecessors' frontier mentality included a consistent suggestion that "Easterners" were not knowledgeable about the West or Midwest. Nebraska spokesperson, Roger Welsch, exhibited this reticence to listen to outsiders, especially the Poppers as quintessential easterners, when he wrote that they were "crackpots from Rutgers University." Welsch suggested that concerned Nebraskans should ignore the Poppers' advice because they were "1) from New Jersey and 2) specialists in URBAN studies." In another article, a Wyoming state government official put Western disdain in more apt terms: "perhaps people in the Plains don't see much wisdom coming from Easterners who have screwed up their states so much . . ." These two experts, Frank and Deborah Popper, certainly faced a difficult task in surmounting ill feelings about the East and outside experts, if they were to influence public sentiment on the Great Plains of this country.

Another element of disdain for experts can be found in the newspapers of towns on Nebraska's western plains. Community boosterism always held that hard work would solve problems, and outside experts never have dirtied their hands with that kind of effort. As one resident of Custer County, Nebraska, put it: "some of us have decided to stay. This is our way of life. And it's worth a fight." Or, as Baxter Black wrote in his syndicated column, the Poppers don't understand because they have asked the wrong question. The right question, according to Black and many who live on the plains, should be "why are so many" here. Of course, the answer would be that people stayed because they were willing to work to live on the Great Plains, where existence has always required physical exertion, a fact of life urban or suburban dwellers might not easily recognize.

Perhaps, the most damning critique was one that raised an important theoretical question. From Marx to Aristotle, thinkers have wondered about the past and its relationship to the future. Could the past predict the future, as though some causal chain informed the future? Were the past one hundred years on the plains of North America sufficient to predict its future? Or, can we assume the general history of the Great Plains could be used to predict specific outcomes in specific communities?

Simply put, the Poppers had used economic, geographic, and demographic statistics from the past one hundred years to argue for their preferred option, a Buffalo Commons. Some residents realized questions existed about using past trends to generalize, and they raised them. North Dakota's Director of Economic Development, William Patrie, stated in 1988 in the <u>Chicago Tribune</u>: "He [Frank Popper] is assuming the future will be like the past. Well, we've seen the past and know it doesn't work." In particular, residents suggested that certain pockets of rural life, such as the Red River Valley in North Dakota as well as the beautiful grasslands of the Sand Hills in Nebraska, have proven to be productive. These regions can not be labeled as unproductive, nor have they become marginally productive in drought years.

In sum, the initial receptions of Frank and Deborah Popper's expertise were negative in character but well known, nonetheless. Better yet, the reception brought Midwesterners to raise critical questions that would ultimately lead to thinking based upon clearer understandings. Just as suggested by the heralded Socratic method, simply taking on the task of raising a good question furthers understanding. Even if the Poppers did not know it, as experts they informed public policy debate.

Favorable Press

To suggest the Poppers only had success through a backdoor manner would miss some truth. Frank and Deborah Popper received more favorable press from larger, urban newspapers, especially those ringing the region. Large, eastern newspapers like the <u>Washington Post</u> provided the Poppers with a forum for their insights. The "city-folk," as they're often known in rural areas, sought stories that supported a policy moving toward a Buffalo Commons. The <u>Minneapolis Star Tribune</u> found a man who already raised buffalo, Ken Throlson, to suggest there were many good reasons to bring back the buffalo. Throlson simply admitted, "One thing about this big debate about the so-called Buffalo Commons: It sure has got the word in print. It's been great advertising." The same newspaper printed a story that included an apology to Native Americans for disrupting their buffalo culture–apparently the Popper's thinking could be used to help solve more than one dilemma in American thinking!

Yet the paper still didn't miss the tone others had used when it included this quote from a Midwestern rural demographer, Calvin Beale: "It's taken these effete Eastern outsiders to get some serious discussion of what the future will be, could be or should be." The real truth was that the Poppers had been able to generate enough heat to make the conversations about land-use issues on the Great Plains serious. It might not be so accurate to suggest that the discussion was simply the result of the Popper's foray.

Long before the Poppers began telling their jeremiad-like story of the Plains, serious work was being done by residents of the region. In Nebraska, the work was being performed by research scientists, ranchers, and occasional civic boosters. Even while the "Buffalo Commons" debate raged, people worked to address matters related to their difficult economic fortunes.

Importance of Public Debate

In sum, we can objectively say the Poppers

They come riding up the path,
kicking up a trail of dust.
In their tight black racing shorts,
yellow shirts, and white helmets,
they could be a swarm of yellow jackets.
They come buzzing up past the sunflowers,
through short and tall prairie grasses,
past prairie dogs out on the draw.
They slice the air
as they circle the bend
and tear down the hill, hard.

"Give her a good push," one spectator yells.
"Stick close," says another.
"Let her fly, no brakes," calls a third,
cheering on their friends, neighbors, lovers.

The ponderosa pines quiver in the breeze
as the mountain bikers round another bend
and head toward Cottonmill Lake.
Through the thicket of trees
down a snake path they ride,
their muscular calves pushing, pumping,
as their wheels spin, then jump
over an exposed root
cutting across their path.

None of them wants the race to end.
Like the slate-gray sky above
that goes on forever,
they want to keep pedaling,
dividing the air,
sucking it up,
drinking in all the nectar they can
oblivious to the distant sound of a train whistle
and its freight
chugging across the prairies.

did well in bringing their perspective to the public arena in the Midwest. While we can point fingers to many misconceptions or specific inaccuracies related to the "Buffalo Commons" perspective, we can also find much to recommend experts bringing a provocative idea into the forum of public discourse.

For one, people of the Great Plains began to address their economic setting in new ways. As each person approached the idea of the "Buffalo Commons," their thinking was forced to change and move to a more complex understanding of the real world in which they found themselves. John Dewey referred to the reflective process created here as a "double movement." People were placed in a situation where they had to understand their community and livelihood in new terms, and, while doing that, they went from commonsensical facts and ideas as they had known them to using new understandings– being forced to embark on a journey that would make each consider what they knew once again. Frank and Deborah Popper, much to their credit, introduced a new idea, the "Buffalo Commons," and new facts about individual relationships to the geography of the Plains and the role government had played in its development. By working back and forth between those new facts and ideas and their previous ideas and facts, people of the Great Plains have come to slightly different judgments of what it means to live here. We can thank the Poppers for this and recognize that the new words in our lexicon have helped us, even though they have created considerable consternation as well.

We can also learn that experts, like the Poppers, who enter the public forum do us far greater good than we might think. Certainly, the expert who studies the minute details of a scientific idea may do some good by leading to new treatments for cancer, but, the expert who brings big ideas to public debates is also doing some good. These experts simply have to have the courage to lose control of their work. Once the Poppers gave us the "Buffalo Commons" to think about, they also lost control of how the meaning of the idea might develop. It became an object of public debate and turned into an idea with a meaning that differed from what its authors intended. In effect, the Poppers can only follow the new meanings given to the "Buffalo Commons" by the people of the plains as they try to understand the term's meaning within the material existence of their lives.

Selected**References**

Aristotle. 1948. *The politics of Aristotle.* Trans. E. Barker. Oxford: The Clarendon Press.

Dewey, John. 1954. *The public and its problems.* New York: Swallow Press.

Majone, Giandomenico. 1989. *Evidence, argument and persuasion in the policy process.* New Haven, Connecticut: Yale University Press.

Plato. 1941. *The republic of Plato* Trans. F. Cornford. Oxford: Oxford University Press.

Yankelovich, Daniel. 1991. *Coming to public judgment: Making Democracy work in a complex world.* Syracuse, New York: Syracuse University Press.

NEBRASKA FARM WOMEN:

SOCIAL SUPPORT NETWORKS AND PERCEPTIONS OF THE FUTURE

Deb Kershaw, Sociology/Psychology Graduate of UNK

As of 1991, according to the Department of Agriculture, 4,632,000 people lived on farms in the United States. Of those, 2,178,000 were female. Of the 2,848,000 residents listing farming as their occupation, 186,000 women were farm operators and managers, and another 205,000 women were farm workers or in related occupations. The number of female farmers and farm managers doubled in the decade between 1970 and 1980, from five percent of the total number to just under ten percent.

Agriculture in our country has, to varying degrees, been experiencing transitions since its beginnings. A new transition is likely as a result of the most recent farm legislation signed into law by President Clinton in February of 1996. One important tool in the arsenal of the family farm in adapting to these changes is the farm woman. Throughout the history of agriculture in the United States, women have made vital and largely unrecognized contributions to the survival of the family farm. They have been important participants in the production of wealth by engaging in a wide range of activities to benefit the farm and the family.

Because the farm woman is, in general, most likely to be connected with multiple aspects of farm life, including the household and the family, an understanding of the standpoints of these women is an important

endeavor. For all of these reasons, a qualitative study of Nebraska farm women was conducted. Employing a snowball sampling technique and semi-structured interviews, thirty-six women contributed to the results of this study.

The areas of concern to this study were Fillmore County, in south central Nebraska, Greeley County, in the north central part of the state, and Buffalo county, near the center of the state. Twelve of the women included were from the Fillmore county area, eleven were from Greeley county, and thirteen were from Buffalo county.

Demographic information about each woman and her farm was gathered. The overall average of farm acreage for the women interviewed was 625 acres. Although the average-sized farm in the Fillmore County area is just 462 acres, the average of the farms of the women interviewed in the area was 595 acres. The average farm in the Greeley County area is also 462 acres, while the average for those women was 744 acres. A different pattern emerged for the women in Buffalo County. Although the average farm in the county is 495 acres, the average for those women interviewed was just 468 acres. Corn was a vital crop in each of the areas, with additional production of dairy products, beef cattle, soybeans, wheat, milo, and some organic crops, including blue and white corn, sunflowers, and soybeans.

The women ranged in age from 27 to 67 years, with an average of 47 (50 in Fillmore County, 42 in Greeley County, and 47 in Buffalo County). The number of years that the women were engaged in agriculture ranged from 4 to 43, with an average of 20 years as involved adults (28 in Fillmore County, 16 in Greeley County, and 17 in Buffalo County). All but two of the women had raised or were in the process of raising children on the farm. The number of children, for those women who did have children, ranged from 2 to 7, with an average of 3.1.

Farm Women's Contributions

Some studies reveal that the proportion of women's contributions to the farm labor itself is reduced with the mechanization of farming. This may be true of some of the women with whom I visited. Some of them felt that their labor was not needed, and, in each case, they worked off the farm and did not participate extensively in on-farm labor. But these women were in the minority in this study. Most of the women included in this study participated in a wide range of activities to support the family farm.

A review of the literature reveals that the on-farm, unpaid work most likely to be performed by women includes bookkeeping and errand running for the farm. Some women also participate in a wide range of other farm activities, such as field work, live-stock care, transport of crops or livestock, and equipment repair. A 1983 study by Coughenour and Swanson showed that women often participate in more than one half the activities on the farm. The division of labor on the family farm can be seen as a continuum. On one end is the strict gender-based division in which women are exclusively responsible for the work in the home. On the other end, women participate in all aspects of labor on the farm, from cultivating and working with stock to planning and organizing. Women today, as in the past, can be found on every level of this continuum.

In the course of this research, I met women who fit at each level of the continuum. For example, two of the women included in this analysis are the exclusive managers of their farms, participating fully in all aspects of agricultural production, including planning and decision-making. On the other end of the continuum, I met one woman who told me, "All I do is live on the farm, and I want nothing more to do with it than that."

Most of the women interviewed fell between these extremes on the continuum. Most perform such tasks as errand running, livestock care, hauling grain to the elevator during harvest, and moving hay bales and irrigation pipe. One Buffalo County woman, a twenty year veteran of farming, said, "We have over five hundred head of cattle. Last week we ran them through and gave them all their shots and tagged them. It was a long day." In addition, over fifty percent of the women engage in some field work. A Fillmore County woman, now involved in organic farming, told me, "When the girls were big enough to be pretty much on their own, I went out and worked in the field pretty much full-time. I mow hay and work the ground and do some cultivating. I really enjoy being outside, so I don't really mind the work."

1996 Farm Bill

Because many of the women were found to be so heavily involved in farm labor, it was surprising how few actually held an opinion of the 1996 Farm Bill. Nearly half of the women included in this analysis said that they did not know enough about the Bill to form an opinion on it. Of those women who did have an opinion, reactions were mixed. A Fillmore County woman, a dairy and corn farm operator for over twenty years said, "I think it is a lot better than what they had before. I don't think that the really large farms will be able to take as much advantage of this program as they could the old one." A Buffalo County woman living on the homestead that her grandfather had established over a century ago told me, "I think it is designed to continue the push of the small farm right out of existence." Because so few women verbalized a solid opinion of the potential effects of the Farm Bill, their perceptions of the future of the family farm in general, regardless of the bill, may be important.

Future of the Family Farm

Each of the women interviewed expressed, to some degree, a negative perception of the future of the small family farm. Many of the women expressed a fear that in the future, the family farm, and, ultimately, many small towns, would no longer exist. One fourth generation Buffalo County farm woman told me, "It is so sad to think that some day all of our children will be raised in the city. I just hope I don't live to see the chain reaction of the farm and then the small town going down." A young Fillmore County farm woman said, "My feeling is that there will be fewer and fewer family

I just rely on my income and the money that my husband makes in his job to support the family. I quit counting on farm income a long time ago.

farms and more and more corporate farms across the country. It seems like it takes so many acres to produce enough to compete any more. These big companies come in and offer so much money for land, and people just about have to take it. I think that it won't be too much longer and the small family farm will be a thing of the past."

When asked if they believed that their children or grandchildren would have the opportunity to engage in farming in the future, several of the women said that they hoped that it would not be a decision that their children or their children's children would make. One Greeley County woman told me, "Our son is struggling to make enough money on the farm to support his family. He is having to work part-time off the farm just to make it. I think it will only get worse. I'd like to see the place stay in the family, but I wouldn't want to see my grandkids go through the pain and hassle that is part of farming today."

Only nine of the women expressed any confidence that the opportunity would be available for their children or grandchildren to participate in the future. For these women, the average size of their farms was just over 900 acres, including two farms of 2000 acres or larger. One woman, living on a 2200 acre farm in Greeley County said, "I hope that the kids and their kids will want to continue. Part of what we farm has been in the family for over one hundred years. We have enough land now, and we keep buying more as we can, to support at least one of them in the future, I hope. You never really know for sure what is going to happen, though. I do think that they will have the chance, though, if that is what they want to do."

Although most of the women saw some changes coming to their particular farms over the next ten years, all believed that their farms would still exist at the end of that period. This was not true over a fifty year time frame. Only three of the women interviewed expressed any certainty that their farms would still be in existence at the end of that time. One Fillmore County woman whose farm produced organic crops, including blue and white corn, sunflowers, and soybeans, told me, "I do think that this

Mrs. Neidacorn feeding her flock, Buffalo County, 1903   Butcher Collection

farm will still be around. We are only a few years from paying it off and the kind of farming we do can sustain the land."

A more typical response came from a Buffalo County woman with over twenty years on the farm. She told me, "I don't think that there will even be small family farms in fifty years, this one or any others. At the rate that technology is changing today, it is unlikely that the small farmer will be able to compete in the future." A woman now retired from farming in Greeley County said, "I just don't see it happening at all in fifty years. Right now, you drive around in the country and see all these vacant homes. We just keep seeing more and more all the time. In fifty years, there won't even be any empty homes to testify that a family lived there in the past. It's sad because it is a good life. A lot of people seem to move to the city and years later want to come back and farm, but it is usually too late by then. Some big farmer usually owns the land, and the options are really limited for the smaller farmer, already today. They won't be there at all in fifty years."

Support Networks

The negative perceptions expressed by the majority of the women raised another important question. Who are the people that these women can count on for social support, now and in the future? Most of the women with whom I spoke described extensive social support networks made up of both immediate and extended family members, the church, neighbors, and friends.

Most of the farm women talked about ties and mutual support networks with family members. Mentioned most often were their husbands and the children. Many of the women expressed a strong feeling of closeness with their husbands. Over half said that their spouses were their most important source of social support. They discussed shared dreams, values, and a dedication to working for the same future. As with all marriages, many were open about rocky periods in the spousal relationship, but most saw their marriages as partnerships, providing mutual support and care. For instance, one woman told me, "At times, my husband really helps me feel good about myself. Of course, at other times, I would like to choke him. Sounds like a typical marriage, huh?"

A woman who had been running and managing a dairy farm for more than twenty years said, "I had always done a lot of the milking, but I was never really a farmer or

If something needs to be done and my husband needs help, I do pretty much whatever needs to be done. You have to be a team. You know, "United we stand. Divided we fall!"

I look back at my mother and realize how wonderful she was. There were six children and we had several hired men. This woman had a tremendous sense of organization, and she tried to instill some of that in each one of us. She helped me organize my home once a year for the first years we were on the farm. It made life a lot easier to just sort of start from scratch once in a while. And it was wonderful to do the job with her.

a mechanic. As it turned out, when my husband got sick and couldn't do a lot of the work, I could. He only had partial use of his right arm, so he guided me through a lot of things. We did as much as we could that way, and together we kept the farm going." A woman who ranches with her husband on the edge of the Sand Hills of Nebraska said, "My husband was very patient with the children and with me. We never had to fight about what the kids were capable of doing on the ranch, so I was lucky."

Thirty-four of the women had raised or were in the process of raising children on the farm. Many of these women talked about the advantages for the children of being raised on the farm. A woman with three small children told me, "Raising kids on the farm is definitely my first choice. I feel that they are forced into having an imagination and into doing things for themselves and for each other. The experience of having responsibilities as children is good for them, too." A woman who is now retired from farming, but who raised seven children on the farm, said, "I'm sure there is an easier life out there, but when I look back on it and see how good it was for our family to grow up on the farm, and how beautifully they all turned out, I think the tough years were worth it. The kids all got so close to each other and to us on the farm. We are really close yet today. The kids had to play with each other, and they had to make their own entertainment. They shared so much."

When asked about their relationships with their children, many women expressed a joy at the entire family spending time working together and depending on one another. "The kids always helped with chores. We did everything together. We went out in the fields together a lot. We had a cab on the tractor, so the children could come with me when I was cultivating or raking hay. We would sing songs and tell stories. It made the

time pass much more quickly for me, and we all just had fun together," one woman told me. A woman who worked on the farm while her husband worked a regular job for a paycheck said, "Since my husband always worked off the farm to bring in some money, that left me to do most of the farm work. It was hard when all the kids were young, but when the oldest got old enough to take care of the little ones, it sure helped. They just pitched in and took care of their younger brothers and sisters. I am very thankful for those kids. They were just great. They still are!" A woman who works full-time off the farm told me, "The boys spend quite a bit of time during the week with their dad in the field, but the weekends are mine. The garden has always been a family project, a time to spend all together. We all enjoy it." Another woman who was heavily involved in the farm labor said, "The whole family went out to move pipe or haul bales. It was great because we were all together, sharing time and effort."

Parents and In-Laws

Many of the women also depended on their parents and their in-laws for social support. In fact, thirteen of the women were currently living on farms that had previously been the homes of their parents, and another five were living in the previous homes of their in-laws. A total of eighteen women had been raised on the farm themselves. These women were especially likely to stress the importance of parental support to their networks. One woman said, "We did pretty well with my dad. He was generous enough to let us come in here and split the income off the farm for about five years. Then he decided to retire and bought a house in town." One young woman with whom I talked had been managing her father's farm for nearly ten years since he was paralyzed in a farming accident. She told me, "Dad is still the owner, and I am just the manager, the hired 'man.' We still make a lot of the decisions together. Dad takes care of the farm program books, and I take care of the bookwork on the cattle. We both do our share to keep things going." A woman who had been on the same creek-lined farm for forty-one years said, "The only real physical help I had when the kids

William Couhig and wife with her sheep, Dale, Nebraska, 1886

Butcher Collection

Keller family celery field west of Kearney, Nebraska, 1904

Butcher Collection

were little was from my mother-in-law. His parents were wonderful. They had lived here, and when we got married, they bought a house in town and moved, so we could live here. She came out often and helped me so much."

Both parents and in-laws were mentioned as sources of support in other ways as well, from babysitting to helping with such "mundane" tasks as gardening, canning, or butchering chickens. Both were mentioned as strong sources of emotional support and comfort, too. Several women told me that their mothers were part of a small group of people with whom they felt totally comfortable in just being themselves. In addition, several more mentioned their mothers-in-law. Many also mentioned that these women have also been important in helping them feel good about themselves.

Fathers and fathers-in-law were more often mentioned in connection with physical support, often in the form of farm labor, but several talked about receiving emotional support from their fathers as well as their mothers. Other family members mentioned as sources of support were siblings, aunts, uncles, grandparents, and cousins.

Spiritual Support

Another important source of social support mentioned by over half of the women interviewed was the church. A Buffalo County woman who worked full-time off the farm, but was still heavily involved in farm labor, told me, "My spiritual family has been an important source of stability for my biological family." A Greeley County woman said, "I have become much more church-oriented since we started farming twelve years ago. My connections with God and other members of my church have been vital to maintaining my acceptance of the difficulties in farming." A Fillmore County woman who is still, at sixty-seven, heavily involved in the farm and farm work, told me, "I look at the land, and I think, none of this really belongs to us. It was here when we came, and it will be here when we're gone. It belongs to Him, not us. The church helps us remember that."

Neighbors and Friends

Over ninety percent of the women inter-

viewed mentioned a close working relationship with neighbors, with the exchange of labor and other various kinds of help and support. One woman with four small children said, "Because we have neighbors with similar needs, it is easy to trade back and forth. We trade work when one of us needs to be away, and we trade babysitting on a fairly regular basis." A woman from Greeley County, now retired from farming, talked about her days on the farm in the early 1950s. "We all depended on each other. One person can do a lot more now than he could in those days. Years ago, they had threshing crews and crews who sorted cattle, all made up of neighbors. We just couldn't have done it alone in those days." A Fillmore County woman said, "One woman who lives just about half a mile down the road has become my best friend over the years. She got married the year after we did and moved to the farm. We have depended on each other for a lot of things over the years. We traded babysitting, since we both had three little ones about the same age. Over the years, we traded secrets and shared so many of the same experiences. If I need a little boost, I just call her." In addition, two of the women mentioned sharing equipment with neighbors.

Friends not involved in agriculture were most often mentioned as sources of emotional support. One woman who had experienced some painful financial problems on the farm told me, "For moral support, I have a group of friends who are separate from the farm. They may not understand all the details, but we can all relate to financial problems. I can talk to them and not worry about them judging me in any way. They are a great bunch of women!" One young woman with four years on the farm said, "I really enjoy spending time with my friends. There are two girls that I went to high school with that I am still really close to. They make me feel really good about myself and give me a lot of emotional support. They give me a compliment or just a hug, and it always helps me feel good. I know I can totally be myself with them and just relax and talk about things that have nothing to do with the farm. It is nice to have them to count on."

If the perceptions of the women inter

The church is very important. There is a part of that social interaction in the church that gives us the strength and support to go on with our daily lives, to maintain the place we are now. It is the spiritual that helps us grow, to become something more.

FARM WIFE | by SUSANNE **GEORGE** BLOOMFIELD

viewed for this study are correct, these
families are in for a rocky time in the
future. The social support networks now
in place may be vital to the ability of these
women and their families to handle the
stress that is likely to confront them in
the future. Perhaps these networks will
contribute in other ways. As one Fillmore
County woman suggested, "I feel that
the only way that the small farm is going
to make it is if we all get together to
support each other. We need to form
cooperatives and share in work and
marketing and even in machinery. We
need to help each other through what
I think is going to be a tough time."

If the women and their families are
assisted in maintaining a positive attitude
by family, the church, neighbors, and
friends, and if these farm families work
together to insure a future for the small
farm, the future may not be so bleak after
all. These fascinating women will continue
to make vital contributions to the survival
of a family-oriented way of life.

Selected**References**

Bokemeier, J. and L. Garkovich. 1987. Assessing the influence of
farm women's self-identity on task allocation and decision making. Rural Sociology 52: 13-36.

Coughenour, C. and L. Swanson. 1983. Work statuses and occupations of men and women in farm families and the structure of
farms. Rural Sociology 48: 23-43.

Dacquel, L. and D. Dahmann. 1993. Residents of farms and
rural areas: 1991 United States Department of Agriculture-
Economic Research Service.

Flora, C., J. Flora, M. Lapping, J. Spears, L. Swanson, and M.
Weinberg. 1992. Rural communities: Legacy and change.
Boulder, CO: Westview Press.

Rosenfeld, R. and L. Tigges. 1987. Independent farming:
Correlates and consequences for women and men. Rural Sociology
52: 345-364.

U. S. Bureau of the Census. 1994. County and city data book.
Washington, DC: U. S. Government Printing Office.

Heat shimmers
above the furrowed ground
as the farmer
tractor-hungry
from winter's wait
slices through
the cornstalk littered crust.
Grey gulls,
swirling like whirlwinds,
follow closely,
reaping their spring harvest.

At the row's end
he pauses.
Sunshine warms
his weathered face,
and he fills his lungs
with damp earth smell,
as rich as life
and rooted in his soul.

She watches him
from her kitchen window,
lifts the sash,
and shares with him
the fragrant breeze.

HISPANICS IN CENTRAL NEBRASKA:

1890-1996

Roger P. Davis, Professor of History

The first Hispanics in central Nebraska were, in all probability, the members of the ill-fated Villasur expedition of 1720. General Don Pedro Villasur and his party of forty-two soldiers and sixty Indian allies were sent north from Santa Fe, New Mexico, to counter French incursions along the Platte River Valley. Crossing the Platte in early August, the expedition camped at the confluence of the Loup and Platte rivers near present-day Columbus and opened negotiations with the Pawnee. The Pawnee, possibly inspired by French agents, responded with a surprise attack, which resulted in the death of the general and the retreat of the survivors back to the southwest.

From 1720 to 1900, relatively few Hispanics would make their way into central Nebraska. The territory described by Major Stephen Long in 1820 as a great "American Desert" did serve as a conduit for populations moving west along the Oregon and Mormon Trails; however, most of these travelers were native-born immigrants from the eastern United States or foreign-born immigrants from Ireland, England, and Northern Europe, and relatively few chose to settle along the Platte. At the time of the establishment of the Nebraska Territory in 1854, the census recorded only 4,494 citizens, with no formal indication of any Hispanic presence.

In 1862, the Homestead Act and the Pacific Railway Act initiated a series of developments that changed the Territory into a state by 1867, and transformed the "desert" into a productive agricultural region of over one million residents by 1900. Again, however, the Hispanic presence was slight. The railway network of the Union Pacific, the Burlington, and the Saint Joseph and Pacific both created and served the towns of Schuyler, Grand Island, Gibbon, Kearney, Plum Creek (Lexington), Cozad, and North Platte. Accompanying the development of the rail lines and new towns was the establishment of the three fundamentals of the Nebraska economy: corn and grain crops, sugar beets, and cattle. Corn production grew from 1.4 million bushels in 1860 to over 13.5 million bushels by 1900, making Nebraska the fourth largest producer in the nation. Wheat production also increased significantly over this period, from 147,000 bushels to over 3.2 million bushels.

Sugar Beet and Cattle Production

Another crop which experienced a dramatic rate of growth was sugar beets. Introduced into the United States in 1830, the first successful sugar beet factory was established in California in 1879. That success inspired local interest in central Nebraska, and, in 1890, the American Sugar Beet factory began operations in Grand Island. A year later, a second factory opened in Norfolk. In 1899, the Standard Beet

Mexicans on train to Nebraska to work the sugarbeets, 1920s

Company opened a third factory in Ames. By 1899, approximately nine thousand acres of sugar beets were being grown in central Nebraska for processing in these plants. Germans and Japanese provided most of the original labor for this crop. Some Hispanics, principally Mexicans, were also recruited to work the fields, but few reliable statistics exist for this time.

Cattle production also made its mark on the Nebraska economy. In 1870, Schuyler became Nebraska's first cattle boom town by shipping over forty thousand head of cattle to the east. By 1874, the cattle railhead moved west to Ogallala, and, by the turn of the century, over two million head of cattle were bound for the market each year. In the east, Omaha's six major meat-packing houses transformed that city into a major meat-processing center.

Initial Hispanic Settlements

From 1890 to 1910, the Nebraska economy attracted some Hispanics to the state, and they initially settled in central Nebraska. The 1890 census indicates the presence of 114 Hispanics for the entire state, and, of that number, 101 are located within five counties of central Nebraska. All Hispanics are listed in the category of "Other." Nevertheless, while their nationality is unclear, it is reasonable to suppose, on the basis of proximity and future trends, that

most, if not all, were Mexican. In the census of 1900, the designation "Mexican" formally appears as a group within the category "Foreign White Stock; by Nationality," and twenty Mexicans are reported for the state. By 1910, this total increases to 318. This increase in Hispanic population also represented a shift in that population to the eastern part of the state, as the corresponding totals for central Nebraska decreased dramatically, with no Mexicans reported for the region in 1900 or 1910.

Over the course of the twentieth century, the Hispanic population of Nebraska continued to grow, and a significant percentage of that population returned to the area of the Platte River Valley. From 1910 to the present, three distinct waves of Hispanic population growth are evident. The first wave occured from 1910 through 1930. The second wave occured from around 1950 through 1970, and the third and most dramatic wave first appeared with the 1980 census and has not yet crested.

First Wave of Hispanic Population

An external catalyst for the first wave of Hispanic growth was the Mexican Revolution of 1910. This catastrophic national upheaval kept Mexico in turmoil for a decade. Not surprisingly, many Mexicans fled the violence by heading north. From 1910 to 1920, the Hispanic population of Nebraska, almost

Union Pacific Railway work crew

exclusively Mexican, rose almost eight-fold, from 318 to 2,436. Thirty percent of these new arrivals, or 731 Hispanics, settled in central Nebraska.

The revolution abated by 1920, but, by that time, other factors helped solidify a Mexican-Nebraska link that maintained a Hispanic presence in central Nebraska. Railroad expansion, as well as corn and sugar beet production, combined to create an economy that sought and required the aid of Hispanic labor. From 1900 to 1910, over two thousand miles of new and parallel track were added to the state rail system. This expansion not only required labor but allowed for the delivery of record increases in the harvests of corn. As a result of the economic disruptions of World War I, prices for agricultural goods rose, and, from California to Nebraska, agricultural production hit record levels.

In Nebraska, as the price of corn rose from thirty-six cents to over two dollars a bushel, production increased accordingly, from 160 to 255 million bushels annually. Even before the United States entered the war, the agricultural states drew heavily upon Mexican immigration for the labor needed to plant and harvest the fields. The importance of that labor pool for agriculture was demonstrated in 1917. When the Immigration Act of that year threatened to place a literacy clause and head tax on legal guest workers,

the protests of agricultural interests succeeded in having those provisions suspended, thus insuring the continuation of Mexican immigrant labor.

In addition to the rail yards and corn-fields, the sugar beet industry proved to be a significant employer of Hispanic labor. While initially located in the heart of central Nebraska, the increased success of the sugar beet industry resulted in a shift of production to the western part of the state. In 1905, the counties of central Nebraska harvested over 9,000 acres of sugar beets, while only 250 acres were harvested in the west along the North Platte River. Over the next twenty-five years, this picture changed completely. The Great Western Sugar Company began raising sugar beets along the North Platte River to send to Colorado for processing in 1908. Two years later, the harvests of Scotts Bluff, Morrill, and Garden counties proved sufficiently bountiful for the company to relocate its Ames plant to the town of Scottsbluff.

By 1933, Nebraska sugar beet production reached over 88,000 acres, and five more processing plants were operating in Scotts Bluff and Morrill counties. Nebraska was the second largest producer in the nation, and the Great Western Sugar Company was aggressively recruiting Mexican labor to work its fields. The company contracted with labor agencies along the Texas border to recruit over 100,000 workers from 1915 through 1930. Most of these "betabeleros" were employed in Wyoming, Montana, and Colorado, but a significant number also arrived in Nebraska. For the counties of Scotts Bluff, Morrill, Garden, and Keith, the registered Mexican population rose from 405 in 1920 to 2,974 by 1930.

Hispanics in Nebraska

This first wave of Hispanic growth for Nebraska is clearly reflected in the overall census for the state. For all of Nebraska, the total count for Hispanics in 1910, defined solely as Mexicans, was 318. By 1920 that number increased to 2,436. That total nearly tripled to 6,321 by 1930.

With regard to central Nebraska, for the counties of Merrick, Hall, Buffalo, Dawson, and Lincoln, the Hispanic population increased from zero in 1910 to 417 in 1920 and 936 by 1930. Lincoln County experienced the greatest Hispanic presence as a result of its proximity to and participation in the sugar beet industry. For Lincoln County, 292 Mexicans were reported in the 1920 census and 557 in the 1930 census. The other area of Hispanic concentration for central Nebraska was in Hall County, around Grand Island. There, the rail hub, local industry, and residual population from the early sugar beet activity accounted for 63 Mexicans in 1920 and 151 by 1930. For the forty-four counties that comprise all of central Nebraska, the acknowledged Hispanic population grew from zero in 1910 to 1,274 by 1930.

By the eve of the great depression, a clear pattern of Hispanic presence in Nebraska was evident. The population appeared in a barbell shape, weighted at one end by Scotts Bluff and Morrill counties in the west and Douglas, Sarpy, and Lancaster counties in the east. Sugar beet prosperity underwrote the growth of Hispanic population in the west, and rail and meat packing accounted for the Hispanic populations in the east. Along the Platte River Valley, agricultural labor accounted for twenty to thirty percent of the Hispanics in the state. This basic pattern and proportion remain constant to the present time.

The depression years witnessed a sharp decline in both the Nebraska economy and the Hispanic population. As the Anglo communities struggled, and government relief became important for survival, opinion turned against Mexican immigrant labor. The federal government restricted the issuance of visas. Some states, like California, forced deportations of Mexicans. Across the United States, relief agencies and charities paid the railroad fare for "voluntary repatriation" of Mexicans. National estimates indicate that over fifty thousand Mexicans a year left the United States. Nebraska figures reflect the larger picture. By 1940, the Hispanic population for the state declined from over 6,000 to 1,846. The figures for central Nebraska read similarly, with a drop from 1,274 to 419.

The advent of World War II abruptly reversed the decline in the numbers of Hispanic workers in the United States. Critical labor shortages in the West and Southwest prompted the United States to negotiate with Mexico to expand and formalize the return of immigrant labor. In August 1942, Mexico and the United States negotiated the Mexican Farm Labor Supply Program (MFLSP), or "Bracero" program, to allow employers in the United States to contract for seasonal labor. Under this accord, an average of sixty-two thousand Mexican workers a year entered the United States from 1942 through 1947.

Ironically, this program had little impact on Nebraska. As the statistics indicate, the total Hispanic population for all of the state of Nebraska remained static from 1940 to 1950, increasing by only five persons, from 1,846 to 1,851. For central Nebraska, the increase of Hispanics was a bit more, 419 to 455, but the totals remained low. The reason for this was twofold. First, the greatest labor demand was from the West Coast, and, consequently, bracero labor was directed almost exclusively to Arizona, California, and the northwest. Second, as a result of Mexican complaints of overt discrimination against Mexicans in Texas, the Mexican government prohibited her workers from going to that state. Texas traditionally served as the initial transfer point for Hispanics making their way to Kansas and Nebraska.

Nebraska State Historical Society

Victoria de Ortiz and daughter came to Nebraska to avoid the Mexican Revolution turmoil, 1920s

Second Hispanic Wave

Nebraska's Hispanic population would pick up in the post-war years. The continuation of the guest worker program in a modified format, which no longer excluded Texas, coupled with the general post-war prosperity of the United States, proved to have a substantial impact and accounts in large part for the second distinct wave of Hispanic population growth in Nebraska, occurring from 1950 through 1970.

From 1947 to 1951, the national government allowed employers to recruit contract labor on an individual basis. In response to Mexican complaints that her citizens were not being fairly treated and that contracts were not being enforced, the United States Congress passed Public Law 78 in 1951. This legislation gave the Secretary of Labor authority and responsibility to monitor and regulate contract labor. The law was regularly renewed from 1953 through 1965. Over this entire period, an estimated four million Mexicans legally contracted for work in the Southwest, the West coast, and in the upper Midwest industrial regions of Michigan and Illinois. An estimated equal number of undocumented immigrants also entered the United States labor pool. Over the decades of the sixties and seventies, Mexican labor, both legal and illegal, continued to enter the United States in significant numbers. Some of these Hispanic workers found their way to Nebraska.

The mid-fifties through the late seventies proved to be prosperous years for Nebraska. Mechanization and technical advancements in agriculture were coupled with rising commodity prices and federal policies, which encouraged agricultural expansion on a foundation of cheap capital. This agricultural expansion served to attract some of the Mexican immigrant population to the state, but the overall impact of mechanization kept the numbers at moderate levels while maintaining the demographic barbell pattern for the Hispanic population.

Statewide Productivity

Across the state, as corn remained an economic mainstay, new crops and a new irrigation system laid the foundation for a healthy economy. In the east, in Saunders, Cass, Sarpy, Dodge, and Burt counties, soybean production grew from 16,000 acres in 1950 to over 1.2 million acres by 1974. In the west, in Scotts Bluff, Box Butte, and Morrill counties, dry bean production of pinto beans and Great Northerns emerged as a new major crop alongside sugar beets. In central Nebraska, pivot irrigation, represented by only 14 systems in 1965, grew to 1,100 systems by 1974, enhancing the productivity of that region. Also, in central Nebraska, new hybrids of grain sorghum, or milo, resulted in increased harvests from 5 million bushels in 1954 to over 140 million bushels by 1974.

Abundant production of corn, milo, and alfalfa, which marked Cozad as the "Alfalfa Capitol of the World," contributed to the growth of feed lots as well as livestock and poultry feed production in this region. Feed tonnage increased from 190,000 tons in 1950 to over 1.7 million tons by 1974. Across the state, the production of cattle tripled, so that by 1974, Nebraska cattle totaled over 7.4 million head. The cattle, grain, and feedlot success was the foundation of the economic centerpiece in Omaha. From the mid-fifties through 1973, the Omaha area packers were responsible for about eighty percent of commercial cattle slaughter in the state, and Omaha reigned as the nation's number one livestock market.

Much of this statewide productivity resulted from technological advances and improvements in the state infrastructure, particularly in the area of transportation. For the farm, this was the era of mechanization. By 1970, over half of sugar beet harvesting was done by machine, cutting the labor requirements by over twenty-five percent.

Irrigation, hybridization, and chemical control of weeds kept the need for labor static while production expanded. The efficiencies of production of scale also affected the feedlot business. From 1962 to 1974, the number of feedlots declined from 24,000 to 14,970, while the volume of fed cattle increased nearly threefold from 1.8 to 3.3 million.

The statistics represented the replacement of small lots, feeding under one thousand head, by larger, more efficient units. The number of feed lots that fed over that number increased from 312 to 460. Finally, Interstate 80, the new economic artery of the state from Omaha to the west, was constructed through the sixties and completed early in the seventies.

The labor requirements of this economic growth attracted a moderate number of Hispanics back into the state. Census figures indicated an increase in the Hispanic population for the state from a total of 1,851 in 1950 to 6,376 in 1960 and to 7,177 by 1970.

While the numbers are relatively low, particularly in contrast to the national figures, they represented an increase in the Nebraska Hispanic population of over 380 percent, returning this population to the pre-Depression levels. For central Nebraska, the jump is from 455 to 1,440, representing essentially the same percentage of change.

The reason why Nebraska did not attract larger numbers of Hispanic immigrants may have been due to the Mexican "miracle" of the 1970s. In 1974, significant petroleum reserves were discovered off of the Mexican coast, and, in short order, Mexico became a major oil exporter. By 1981, Mexico was the world's fourth largest exporter. For a short period, it appeared as though the Mexican economy would generate sufficient wealth to benefit even those at the lower end of

the socioeconomic scale. Ultimately, however, the dream of Mexican economic prosperity turned into a nightmare, and, in the process, provided part of the reason for the third wave of Hispanic immigration into Nebraska.

Third Wave of Hispanic Growth

The third and most recent wave of Hispanic immigrants is a result of the combination of three distinct factors. The first is the transformation of the meat-packing industry. The second is the Mexican economic crisis that ravaged that nation from the mid-seventies through the eighties, and the third is the United States Immigration Control and Reform Act (ICRA) of 1986. From 1975 to the present, these factors have combined to increase the Hispanic population of Nebraska to record levels and set a trajectory for the future.

The revolution in the meat-packing industry was led by IBP, Inc. (Iowa Beef Processors) and began in the early 1970s. Pressured in the larger cities by unionization, rising wages, and community complaints about the industrial odor and transportation noise, the meat-packing companies began to relocate to smaller rural communities where they were closer to feedlots, paid lower wages, and encountered fewer complaints from towns eager to gain the jobs and tax revenues. The decline of meat-packing in Omaha is an indication of this change. From the end of World War II through 1973, Omaha packers were responsible for eighty percent of the state cattle processing and employed over thirteen thousand workers. However, by 1996, that market share fell to thirteen percent, and the three remaining companies employed no more than thirteen hundred workers.

The new packing giants, IBP, Monfort (Con Agra), and Excel (Cargill) built new plants in smaller communities across the state. In central Nebraska, IBP opened operations in Lexington and Columbus. Monfort moved into Grand Island, and Excel began operations in Schuyler. While the initial impact of mechanization and efficiency temporarily lowered employment in the packing industry to 8,900 jobs in 1987, that trend was soon reversed. Labor statistics indicate that by 1992, the employ ment total nearly doubled to 16,000 and increased again by 1996 to over 20,200 jobs. Immigrant labor, particularly Hispanic labor, provided the corporations with the inexpensive work force they desired.

Two other events insured that a significant number of Hispanics would find their way to Nebraska to contribute to the labor pool. In 1975, the Mexican economy began a long period of decline. In late 1976, the value of the peso fell by over half, while prices for food and basics increased. By 1982, it became clear that Mexico's days of petroleum prosperity were over. World oil production began to exceed demand, and prices plummeted. No longer able to support a fixed exchange rate for the peso, the Mexican government allowed the value of the currency to be determined on the open market. The results were a disaster for the average Mexican. From 1982 through 1987, the exchange rate of the peso to the dollar grew from 25 to over 2,300. The inflation rate rose to 63 percent by 1985 and increased to over 159 percent by 1987. Over the course of the crisis, most Mexicans would lose over half of their savings and income as they watched their real wages drop by forty to fifty percent. The crisis was felt particularly hard in Mexican urban areas, which became new sources for immigration of non-rural workers. The hardships pushed many Mexicans northward, some of whom would seek salvation working in the meat-packing industry.

The Mexican crisis and increased immigration pressures prompted a response by Congress in the form of the 1986 Immigration Control and Reform Act. The act was designed to curtail illegal immigration by strengthening interdiction and providing fines and criminal penalties for employers who hired undocumented workers. However, the act also provided for an amnesty for current undocumented workers and expanded the number of immigrant visas to allow for a larger pool of legal seasonal workers. By June 1988, over one million aliens across the United States applied for amnesty, and over a half million immigrants sought legal status for seasonal work. As a result, previously uncounted, undocumented Hispanics now appeared in the census totals.

The demographic statistics for 1970 through 1996 indicate the significance of the above three elements relative to the growth of Nebraska's Hispanic population. In 1970, Nebraska Hispanics numbered 7,177. By the 1980 census, that figure had grown to 28,025, an increase of nearly 300 percent. The figure jumped to 36,969 by 1990, and the 1996 projections totaled 63,294, or an increase of over 700 percent since 1970. Specifically for central Nebraska, while maintaining the same general percentage for the region, the figures are equally dramatic. The 1970 census reported 1,440 Hispanics in the region. By 1980 that figure rose to 6,044 and by 1990 to 8,065. The 1996 count totaled 13,913 Hispanics in central Nebraska. While the real numbers changed significantly over these decades, the proportion of this region's population to that of the state remained at the level of twenty-one percent. Further projections for the turn of the twenty-first century set the Hispanic population of the state at 65,000 and the total for central Nebraska at 14,527.

Continuing increases in Nebraska's Hispanic population, which began forty years ago, represent a significant transformation in population patterns.

Future Immigration Patterns

Estimates of future internal and external Hispanic immigration patterns emphasize the growth of Hispanic populations in midwestern urban environments. Nebraska, contrary to appearances, has become a predominantly urban state. The last census to report a rural majority for the state population was the 1950 census. In that year, 53.1 percent of the population was identified as rural, and 46.9 percent were classified as urban, meaning living in incorporated cities, villages, towns, and other designated places of 2,500 or more persons. By 1960, the census figures were reversed. In that census, the rural population represented only 45.7 percent of the total, and the urban population represented 54.3 percent of the state. From 1960 to 1990, the rural population fell to 33.9 percent while the urban population grew to 66.1 percent.

The urbanization of Nebraska is not a phenomena of the east corridor of Omaha and Lincoln. While the mechanization and consolidation of farming and the cattle industrial complex has kept Nebraska a leader in agricultural production, it has also led to the growth of urban "islands" across the state. The urban pattern is consistent across the state and particularly in central Nebraska. Ten of the forty counties that comprise central Nebraska report populations that are over fifty percent urban, ranging from a low of fifty-four percent in York county to a high of eighty percent in Hall county. The urban counties account for 58.1 percent of all of the population of central Nebraska.

The rural versus urban population growth rates for key counties of the central Nebraska region over 1960 through 1996 demonstrates this change. While Buffalo county grew by only eight percent over these years, the city of Kearney experienced a ninety-two percent rate of growth. For Hall county, the rural population increased only two percent, while Grand Island expanded by sixty percent. Lincoln, Dawson, and Platte counties actually lost rural population, indicating no county growth while North Platte grew by sixty-seven percent, Lexington by eighty percent, and Columbus by sixty-seven percent. In addition, with reference to predictions of future Hispanic population growth being primarily urban, the ten most urban counties of central Nebraska account for eighty-six percent of the Hispanic population of the region.

Researchers on Hispanics in the Midwest have reported upon "The Latinization of Rural America" and "Latinos in the Heartland: The Browning of the Midwest." Studies from the Rural Migration News at the University of California at Davis and the Julian Samora Research Institute at Michigan State University emphasize the dramatic growth of the Hispanic population over the last fifteen years and predict the trend will continue. The history of the Hispanic population in Nebraska appears to confirm these observations. Census projections indicate that by 2025 over 111,000 Hispanics will live in Nebraska. If the relative percentage rate for central Nebraska holds steady, over 24,000 of these people will call central Nebraska home.

Selected References

Anderson, E.S. 1937. *The sugar beet industry of Nebraska.* Lincoln: University of Nebraska Press.

Grajeda, R. 1976. *"Chicanos: The mestizo heritage."* In *Broken hoops and plains people,* ed. P.A. Olson. Lincoln: University of Nebraska Press.

Meyer, M.C. and W.C. Sherman. 1995. *The course of Mexican history.* 5th ed. New York: Oxford Press.

Olsen, J.C. 1966. *History of Nebraska.* 2nd ed. Lincoln: University of Nebraska Press.

Samora, J. *Los majodos: The wetback story.* Notre Dame: University of Notre Dame Press.

Smith, M.M. Fall 1981. *"Beyond the borderlands: Mexican labor in the central plains, 1900-1930."* Great Plains Quarterly: 239-240.

Wheeler. W. 1975. *An almanac of Nebraska: Nationality, ethnic, and racial groups.* Omaha: Park Bromwell Press.

CONCEPTIONS OF HUMAN NATURE:

THE VALUE ORIENTATION OF STUDENTS FROM CENTRAL NEBRASKA

Richard L. Miller and Joseph J. Benz, Professors of Psychology

Human nature is a pervasive explanatory concept that has considerable influence on our attitudes and behavior. The motive for attempting to define human nature is rooted in the impact that people can have on others' lives. Substantive beliefs about people enable individuals to make well-informed decisions about how to interact with others. These beliefs can guide individuals in answering such questions as who can I trust, or is this person likely to help or hinder me?

At the core of one's conception of human nature are the values that define us as human beings. The development of values comes as a result of interactions with many significant people, including parents, teachers, clergy, peers, and others. It is a common assertion among those who live and work in central Nebraska that "folks from around here" are different from others, and that difference is often expressed in what people from central Nebraska consider to be their basic values. For example, it is commonly asserted that individuals from central Nebraska have a stronger work ethic than those from other parts of the country. Other values often mentioned as being pronounced among those who were raised in central Nebraska include independence, strength of character, helpfulness, and trustworthiness.

In order to examine the extent to which central Nebraskans' values really differ from those held by others, two value scales were administered to 133 undergraduate, in-state students enrolled in General Studies courses at the University of Nebraska at Kearney. For comparison purposes, scores were obtained from two previous studies in which 1,254 undergraduates enrolled in colleges in the North, South, and Midwest were given the same value scales.

One of the scales was the eighty-four-item Philosophies of Human Nature scale developed by L.S. Wrightsman in 1974, which measures the extent to which individuals conceive of others as trustworthy, altruistic, independent, strong willed, complex, and variable. The second scale, created by Katz and Haas in 1988, measures Protestant Ethic and Humanitarianism-Egalitarianism. In addition, the UNK students were asked to indicate their age, sex, and the size and location of the town in which they grew up.

Trustworthiness

The Trustworthiness scale measures the extent to which an individual sees others as moral, honest, and reliable. An example of an item on this scale is "If you act in good faith with people, almost all of them will reciprocate with fairness towards you." The differences in expected Trustworthiness between students from Nebraska and those from outside the state generally show that students from Nebraska were not much different from the national sample (Fig. 1). However, students from small towns in central Nebraska were less willing to see people as trustworthy than were students from larger Nebraska cities (Fig. 2), and men were more willing to believe in the trustworthiness of others than were women (Fig. 3). The attitudes expressed by small-town Nebraskans seem counterintuitive and require some explanation. Why should students from small towns see others as less trustworthy while those from cities see others as more trustworthy. Perhaps, this is a result of coming to a University campus that provides a contrast to the way of life they left. For the small town resident, Kearney is a fairly large place with some of the problems associated with a dense population. For the student from the city (Lincoln or Omaha), the town of Kearney may seem a safe haven from crime and other troubles in comparison to their home communities.

Independence

The items designed to measure Independence examined the extent to which individuals believe that they can maintain their convictions in the face of society's pressures toward conformity, or, how resistant an individual is to peer pressure. An example of an item on this

scale is "If a student does not believe in cheating, he or she will avoid it even if he or she sees many others doing it." Students from central Nebraska showed more Independence than did those in the national sample (Fig. 1). It would seem that central Nebraskans feel they can maintain their beliefs in the face of peer pressures to change them. Consistent with previous research in the areas of conformity and independence, men obtain higher independence scores than do women (Fig. 3), and older students also have more belief in their ability to resist peer pressure than do younger students (Fig. 4).

Rationality and Strength of Will

Rationality and Strength of Will were measured together. They gauge the extent to which individuals believe that other people understand the motives behind their behaviors and the extent to which they believe that people generally have control over their outcomes. Items on this scale include "Most persons have a lot of control over what happens to them in life" and "Most people have a good idea of what their strengths and weaknesses are." Students from central Nebraska have lower scores for Rationality and Strength of Will than do students in the national sample (Fig. 1). Nebraska students from small towns have higher Rationality and Strength

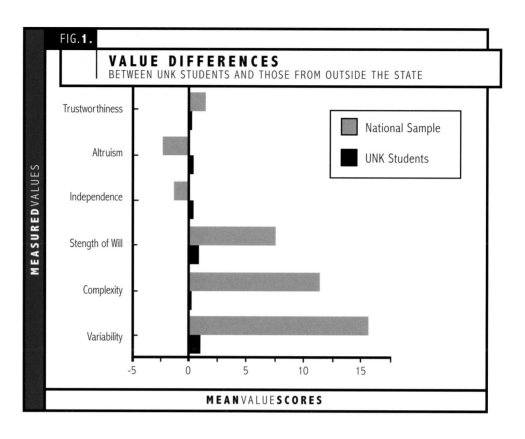

FIG.**1.**

VALUE DIFFERENCES
BETWEEN UNK STUDENTS AND THOSE FROM OUTSIDE THE STATE

MEASURED**VALUES**

- Trustworthiness
- Altruism
- Independence
- Stength of Will
- Complexity
- Variability

National Sample
UNK Students

-5   0   5   10   15

MEAN**VALUE**SCORES

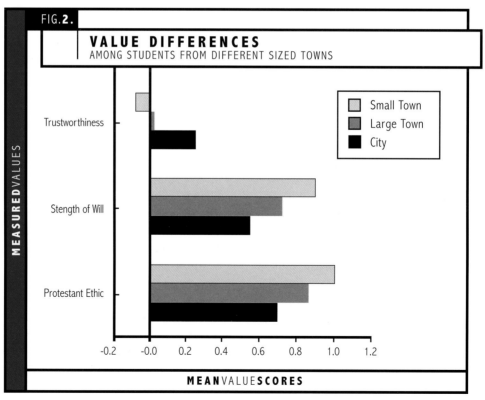

FIG.**2.**

VALUE DIFFERENCES
AMONG STUDENTS FROM DIFFERENT SIZED TOWNS

MEASURED**VALUES**

- Trustworthiness
- Stength of Will
- Protestant Ethic

Small Town
Large Town
City

-0.2   -0.0   0.2   0.4   0.6   0.8   1.0   1.2

MEAN**VALUE**SCORES

a**prairie**mosaic

of Will scores than do those from cities (Fig. 2), and men have higher scores than do women (Fig. 3). Why might Nebraskans feel that they lack control over what happens to them in life? According to some observers, it is not unusual for many college students born and raised in central Nebraska to be somewhat more self-effacing than students from other parts of the country, and this may translate into a less well-developed sense of personal control. Also, many students enrolled at the University of Nebraska at Kearney are the first in their families to come to college, and this may foster some uncertainty as to what they can achieve with a college education. With regard to Rationality, students from central Nebraska are not known for introspection, and this tendency to avoid too much self-examination may lead them to believe that most people are not clear about their self-related traits and characteristics.

Protestant Ethic

In 1904, Max Weber defined the Protestant Ethic as an individualistic value orientation that emphasizes devotion to work, individual achievement, and discipline. It encompasses the belief that people who work hard will get ahead, and that the harder one works, the farther ahead they will get. The Protestant Ethic Scale created by Mirels and Garrett in 1971 includes such statements as "I feel uneasy when there is little work for me to do" and "Money acquired easily is usually spent unwisely." Consistent with a message frequently heard in central Nebraska, students from Nebraska scored higher on the Protestant Ethic scale than did students in the national sample (Fig. 5). Furthermore, Nebraskan students from small towns had higher Protestant Ethic scores than those from the cities (Fig. 2). It is almost axiomatic in central Nebraska, and especially in the smaller towns, that the way to get ahead in this life is to work harder than the day before (Fig. 4).

Humanitarianism-Egalitarianism

Humanitarianism-Egalitarianism is a communal orientation that values adherence to the democratic ideas of equality, social justice, and concern for others' well-being.

The scale included such statements as "One should find ways to help those who are less fortunate than oneself" and "Everyone should have an equal chance and an equal say in most things." Students from Nebraska scored higher on Humanitarianism-Egalitarianism than students in the national sample (Fig. 5). This is somewhat unusual because Humanitarianism-Egalitarianism is frequently found to be at odds with Protestant Ethic. One explanation of this unusual finding may lie in the concept of social distance. For Nebraskans, the "less fortunate others" that come to mind are very likely to be well-known to the respondents, especially in the smaller towns. Thus, one would expect people to be concerned about their friends' and acquaintances' well-being, especially since they are likely to be aware of why the person is less fortunate. Like the results from the national sample, Humanitarianism-Egalitarianism is higher in women than in men (Fig. 3), and higher in older students than in younger ones (Fig. 4).

Altruism, Complexity, and Variability

The scale on Altruism was designed to measure the extent to which individuals expect others to exhibit unselfishness, sincere sympathy, and concern for others. An example of an item on this scale is "Most people would stop and help a person whose car is disabled." Complexity refers to the extent to which people are complex and hard to understand versus simple and easy to understand. An item used to measure this is "I think that you can never fully understand the feelings of other people." Variability in human nature is the extent to which people perceive that there are considerable individual differences in human nature and that human nature is subject to change and fluctuation. An example of an item used to measure this is "People are unpredictable in how they'll act from one situation to another."

Students from central Nebraska were more likely than those in the national sample to expect others to exhibit Altruism (unselfishness, sincere sympathy, and concern for others), less likely than those in the national sample to believe that people

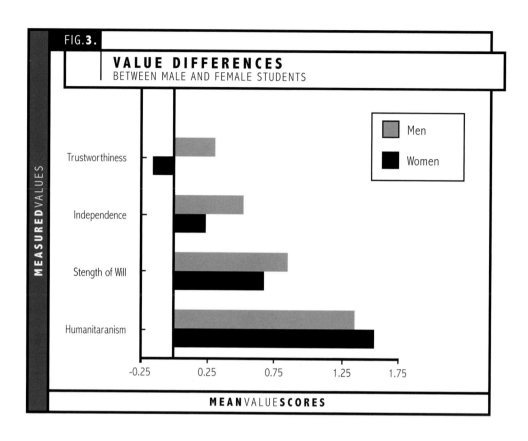

FIG. 3.

VALUE DIFFERENCES
BETWEEN MALE AND FEMALE STUDENTS

MEASURED VALUES

- Men
- Women

Trustworthiness

Independence

Stength of Will

Humanitaranism

-0.25　0.25　0.75　1.25　1.75

MEANVALUE**SCORES**

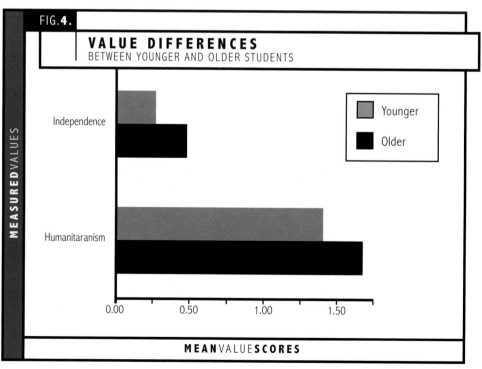

FIG. 4.

VALUE DIFFERENCES
BETWEEN YOUNGER AND OLDER STUDENTS

MEASURED VALUES

- Younger
- Older

Independence

Humanitaranism

0.00　0.50　1.00　1.50

MEANVALUE**SCORES**

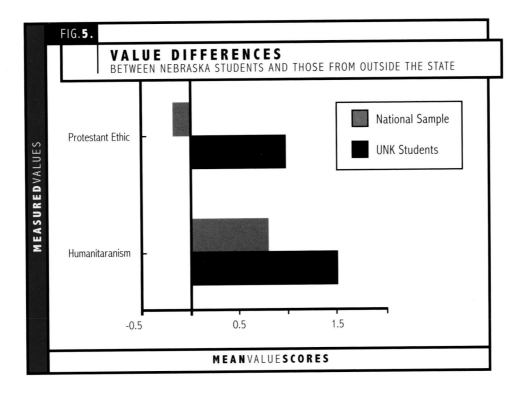

FIG. 5.

VALUE DIFFERENCES
BETWEEN NEBRASKA STUDENTS AND THOSE FROM OUTSIDE THE STATE

National Sample
UNK Students

Protestant Ethic

Humanitaranism

-0.5   0.5   1.5

MEASURED VALUES

MEAN VALUE SCORES

are complex and hard to understand, and also less likely than those in the national sample to believe that there is considerable variation in human nature (Fig. 1).

Interestingly, there were no differences among Nebraska students as a result of age, sex, or size of home town on these values. What might account for Nebraskans' belief that people are not particularly complex or variable? Part of the answer may be due to lack of cultural and ethnic diversity in Nebraska, especially in central Nebraska. Most central Nebraskans are of European descent, and many come from families that for generations have been engaged in the same occupation. Thus, for the resident of central Nebraska, the people he or she knows may, in fact, be less variable and, in some ways, seem less complex than those encountered by students at colleges and universities in other parts of the country.

Conclusions

In general, the results of this survey tend to support many popular conceptions about people from central Nebraska. Values that students from central Nebraska express, which make them different from students in other parts of the country, include: (a) higher levels of Independence, especially among men and older students; (b) higher

ratings of Altruism; (c) higher acceptance of the Protestant Ethic, especially among students from small towns; (d) greater expected levels of Trustworthiness by men; (e) higher Strength of Will among students from small towns; and (f) lower expectations of Complexity and Variability. Those results that run counter to popular conceptions about Nebraskans include (a) less expected Trustworthiness in general, especially by students from small towns; and (b) less Strength of Will.

Selected**References**

Katz, I., and R. G. Hass. 1988. Racial ambivalence and American value conflict: Correlational and priming studies of dual cognitive structures. Journal of Personality and Social Psychology 55: 893-905.

Mirels, H., and J. Garrett. 1971. The protestant ethic as a personality variable. Journal of Consulting and Clinical Psychology 36: 40-44.

Weber, M. 1904-05. The protestant ethic and the spirit of capitalism. Trans. T Parsons. New York: Scribner, 1958.

Wrightsman, L. S., 1974. Assumptions about human nature: A social-psychological analysis. Monterey, CA: Brooks/Cole.

BURR OAK:

A LEGACY OF THE ONE ROOM SCHOOL

Lynn Johnson, Professor Emeritus of Professional Teacher Education

The one-room schoolhouse in Nebraska occupies a rich page in the history of rural education in the state. Although the terms of these schools accommodated the planting and harvesting seasons in order to support the needed labor, such schools provided what the early settlers felt was a necessity for their children. During the 1930s, it was common to find one-room school houses located in almost every two sections of land that resulted in "walking distances" for all of the students. With the advent of school consolidation in the 1940s, many of the one-room schools closed, signaling the beginning of the end of this form of education.

Currently in Custer County, Nebraska, there are eleven Class I (elementary grades only) school districts, ranging from an enrollment of twenty-eight students and three teachers to a student enrollment of four with one teacher. It is interesting to review the names of the Class I districts in Custer County. Some are names of communities (Mason City, Berwyn, Oconto), some reflect geographical traits (County Line, Round Valley, Round Hill), and yet others represent more of an idyllic view (New Hope).

Last of the One-Room Schools

In 1993-1994, the Nebraska Educational Television Network filmed and produced a program titled The Last of the One-Room Schools. The major focus of this program was School District 63, Burr Oak School, in Custer County, Nebraska, and featured Sarah Jane Graham as the sole teacher along with her seven students. A visit to Burr Oak in September, 1998, found the one-room school still operating with a total of five students, including one kindergartner, two second graders, one fourth grader, and one sixth grade student, with Graham remaining as the teacher for the district.

In 1994, the ETV production noted concerns related to the declining family farm population, the ups and downs of the agricultural economy, and the constant problems connected with keeping District 63 open in light of budgetary issues. The present total budget for Burr Oak is $28,000, which includes Graham's salary. This was a modest amount in comparison to larger school districts, but for Burr Oak it stands as a major problem when considering the future of the district. In visiting with Graham, it was interesting to note that the major concerns voiced in 1994 remain today.

Graham is a graduate of the University of Nebraska, class of 1965. Her teaching experiences have included larger districts such as Minden, Nebraska, as well as Asmara, Ethiopia, where she worked in a Department of Defense dependent's school while her husband was in the military. Prior to coming to Burr Oak in 1989, Graham taught in

Miss Mary Longfellow, teacher, holding down a claim, near Broken Bow, Nebraska   Butcher Collection

another Class I district (Flatbottom) a short distance from her present school. She commutes from her home in Miller, a round trip of fifty miles. It was obvious in visiting with Graham that her dedication to teaching remains focused on the importance and success of such schools as Burr Oak.

Emphasizing a number of distinct advantages of being the sole teacher at Burr Oak School, Graham noted, "I have the real opportunity to work with the same students from kindergarten through sixth grade. Thus, I can reinforce what my students need on a more continual basis, including what their major strengths and weaknesses are. In a larger school, students change teachers every year. For me, I see a great advantage of being able to start to work on the very first day of school and not having to determine to test where my students are." Being the solitary teacher in the school has other advantages. "Here, I am paid for what I am hired to do–teach! I don't have to face constant interruptions from bells, schedules to accommodate art, music, and physical education, and lunch in the cafeteria. (At Burr Oak, the hot lunch program is a microwave and the students eat at their desks.) This means that I can be very flexible with my instructional day without interrupting others' schedules."

Graham also remarked how she can quickly establish meaningful relationships with the parents of her students, especially since she will have their children for their complete elementary educational experiences. She makes a point to take her students home on the first day of school, and has, on occasion, due to weather or illness, accompanied students to their homes. "I don't have to have a committee meeting to call off school if I am ill or if there are threatening weather conditions," Graham added. "Since I am the building administrator as well as the teacher, I have the advantage of making such decisions."

In reviewing the advantages of being a student at Burr Oak, Graham offered a number of points. First, she emphasized the importance of her students learning effectively on their own. "Here, they soon learn to rely on their own initiative and self-learning. The students realize that I cannot be with them all of the time, so they have to forge ahead on their own to complete their assignments." At the same time, Mrs. Graham emphasized that in this type of an educational environment, the students also reinforce and help each other to complete the work and to stay on task. In some schools, peer teaching is advertised as a new technique, but at Burr Oak this practice has been occurring for some time.

"To a certain extent, students here are 'protected' by this type of educational climate. Classroom rules are established and maintained on a set of values agreed upon by me

Lynn Johnson, middle, Third grade class, Knox County, Nebraska, 1943   photo courtesy of the Johnson family

Parents have always been concerned about their children's education. Here, I find it very easy to communicate with the families about problems.

and the parents on a cooperative basis," Graham continued. "This means that conflict resolutions can be accomplished with minimal interruption. I cannot send a student to the principal's office here. Also, such practices as bad language don't occur here." Finally, Graham mentioned that students from Burr Oak do well as they enter middle and senior high school. Most Burr Oak students attend Broken Bow for these years. Such evidence from these students reinforces Mrs. Graham's belief that her students receive a strong foundation for academic success.

When asked what she would perceive as the major disadvantages of being the teacher at Burr Oak, Graham was hard pressed to reply. "I suppose that I am somewhat isolated," she remarked. "If problems or issues arise, I have no principal or teaching colleague with whom to visit. There are times when I would welcome such a dialogue for reinforcement or advice." She continued that this may be more of a problem for a beginning teacher than for her, since she can rely on her experiences from the past.

"Remember that I am the building administrator, nurse, cook, playground supervisor, custodian, and secretary. Filling out the required reports does take some time and effort." On occasion, Graham may also

have to be the catcher for the ball game at recess. She does not compare herself to the pioneer school teacher, since she does not have to build a fire or carry water in from the well. And, she does not have to board with the parents since she drives from her home in Miller. Graham adds that there is a computer for her students, a small library, and a microwave; the educational service unit provides numerous services and resources for her teaching, an asset that pioneer teachers did not have for assistance.

Graham recalled some of her most memorable times at Burr Oak. Having ETV focus on the school provided some excellent support for the success of such schools as Burr Oak. In 1994, a late winter storm disrupted electrical services to the school for nearly three weeks, and the National Guard came every morning to start an electrical generator in order to keep the school open. In 1996, Burr Oak was featured in a publication, People of the Great Plains, that publicized the students and Graham by depicting the advantages of the one room school. The students greatly enjoyed this experience, especially the opportunity to visit with the author.

One experience that Graham especially recalled was the discovery of a rattlesnake underneath the front steps of the school. After disposing of the snake, Graham utilized the experience to have a science lesson on the reptiles in Custer County, and how to treat snakebites. "This was a teachable moment, so I was able to adjust my lesson plan for the day to accommodate this experience."

In recalling her most rewarding experiences as a one-room school teacher, Graham offered a number of such memories. First, she feels that she has been a part of the families of the Burr Oak district. "I have had the opportunities to attend graduations, weddings, anniversaries, and birthday parties of the various families. I am not sure that teachers in larger districts have this kind of relationship with their students' families." Graham also included the praise she has received from her students and their parents for preparing young people, not only for academic achievement but also for life itself, noting that such thanks from the school patrons is difficult to measure, yet is so

From left to right: (back) Bridget Schmid, Staci Jones, Sarah Jane Graham   photo by Lynn Johnson
(front) J.W. Schmid, Seth Lueck, Wacey Schmid

satisfying for her. "Knowing that students from Burr Oak will be able to to go on to high school realizing that they have not come from an inadequate schooling experience is very meaningful for me. In the same vein, I am confident that my students will be able to go on in life and face the challenges that all of us encounter, whether or not the students continue with formal educational pursuits after high school," Graham noted.

When asked about the future of Burr Oak, Graham related that districts such as Burr Oak face a short life expectancy. "Economic strangulation" was the term coined by this veteran teacher in discussing the present plight of the rural one-room schools in Nebraska, noting that the tax structure and rural economic conditions offer little hope for the future of these historical educational institutions. In light of this, Graham was asked what she felt the legacy of Burr Oak will be when the doors close for the last time. She offered the following thoughts: "I think that when those who attended Burr Oak recall their days here, they probably will not recall when they first learned what a verb was, or when they finally mastered multiplication. However, I feel that they will relate to their children and grandchildren other memories such as how they ran down the hill every day at recess, of having to go around the building when they yawned during school, or of putting the flag up in the morning. I think they will recall having to stand in the corner when they misbehaved, or how the small building blocks spelled out their names. They will certainly remember all of the special days and events such as Thanksgiving dinner, Grandparent's Day, the Easter Egg Hunt, and the Christmas program when the room was filled with parents, relatives, and friends. The students may recall how we waved down the Schwan's ice cream truck for special occasions. These certainly don't relate directly to academics, but they do make up the legacy and memories of a school that will soon cease to exist."

As this visit to Burr Oak came to an end, Graham was asked what her legacy to this school would be after nine years. She briefly stated, "I hope that the students will understand that I attempted to give them the tools to become successful adults and citizens no matter where they go, to be honest and to admit their mistakes, and to learn from these and to go on." Such a statement would probably be a fitting epitaph for any educator!

Selected**References**

George, S. 1993. Country school legacy. In The Platte River: An atlas of the big bend region. Jenkins A. and S.K. George. Eds. Kearney: University of Nebraska at Kearney: 75-79.

Hausherr, R. 1988. The one room school at Scrabble Hollow. New York: Macmillan.

Miller, P. 1996. People of the Great Plains. Silver Print Press: Burlington, Iowa: Silver Print Press.

Nebraska Department of Education. 1997-1998. The Nebraska education directory. Lincoln, Nebraska: Government Printing Office.

Editors note:

Burr Oak School closed its doors in the Spring of 1999. Mrs. Graham is presently teaching at Round Hill School, and has seventeen students, ranging from kindergarten to sixth grade.

It is easy for me to adjust my schedule to accommodate the students' needs. I am able to provide them with immediate feedback on their lessons.

When the doors close for the last time, I will know that I have done my best to provide my students with what they will need in life.

SARAH**JANE**GRAHAM

Burr Oak playground   photo by Lynn Johnson

Burr Oak one-room school house   photo by Lynn Johnson

EDUCATION, TECHNOLOGY AND THE FUTURE:

A 1999 SNAPSHOT

Barbara M. Audley, Dean of Continuing Education

The first recorded formal public school in Nebraska, District 12 at Holland in Lancaster County, opened in 1869. According to records in Nebraska State Historical Society archives, that first school had students from seven families. In Fall, 1998, the State Department of Education reported Nebraska's school demographics as including 401 high schools and 1,163 elementary schools in 640 districts. The Chronicle of Higher Education of August 28, 1998, listed Nebraska's higher education institutions as four public universities, three state colleges, four learning centers, twenty-one private universities and colleges, and nine community college districts with seventeen campuses. How the picture has changed in 129 years!

Education at all levels is now in a period of tremendous change. Technology is a major driving force in this transition, and what the end result will be is hard to envision, given the warp-drive speed of events today. The safest prediction is that education will be different ten years from now.

Nebraska now has over fifty percent of its population clustered in metropolitan/urban areas in the east. Educational services are and will remain easily accessible in that eight-county area around the Omaha-Lincoln metroplex in eastern Nebraska. In the other eighty-three counties of Nebraska, access to education will remain

a problem, from kindergarten through university studies.

K–12 Education

Because of recent legislation aimed at eliminating the Class I districts–rural, elementary only schools–the number of places for farm and ranch families to access education for their small children will decrease. Since schooling is a major concern for most families, will this cause young families to spurn the farm and ranch for city careers, lowering the agricultural productivity of Nebraska? Will rural areas become enclaves for the elderly who then have no one to take over the farm or ranch when they retire?

Even as districts consolidate to save administrative and instructional costs, will tax lids lower the budgets of these districts so far that a comprehensive curriculum cannot be provided? Will the smaller rural consolidated districts be forced to close because there is not enough money to provide the breadth of programs the state requires to be certified? Are we looking at most of Nebraska being without economic production because the undergirding educational infrastructure is missing? Are we eliminating the schools that allow people to move to an area for employment, so there are no employees for newly created jobs? This becomes a "Catch 22," simplistic but entirely possible.

Erection of first building at Kearney's State Normal School, 1904-1905   Butcher Collection

Post-secondary Education

Colleges and universities do not escape this population quandary either. Institutions in urban areas will have ready access to numbers of potential students. Those in more rural areas–those that normally do not draw potential students from the urban areas–will have difficulty maintaining enrollment levels and, thus, income levels. Those institutions will also have difficulty attracting qualified faculty, both because of low enrollment and low salaries. A minimum level of student enrollment is necessary to provide an appropriate spectrum of educational opportunities from a diverse, qualified faculty. In addition, a minimum level of technology must be included in any curriculum to adequately prepare graduates for success in the twenty-first century. All of this requires time, commitment, and resources.

Future Responses

Educational institutions have begun to address these concerns, and technology will be in the forefront of those answers. So-called distance education has been around for a long time. Distance education basically means the instructor is not in the same room as the students. Correspondence study, based on mailed books and materials, has been used since the mid 1800s to share knowledge. Sunrise Semester was an early attempt to use technology to teach, with faculty broad-casting classes over commercial television at early morning hours, and students responding by telephone. In Nebraska, the public television-based University of Mid-America provided televised classes with telephone callback.

With the advent of computers, some new approaches have been developed. With broad access to the Internet available even in rural areas, entire university degree programs from institutions around the world are available at the bachelor's, master's, and doctoral levels in a great many fields. The University of Phoenix and Western Governors University–of which Nebraska is a member–are prime examples. Although generally very expensive, when no other choice exists, cost does not long remain a barrier.

At the K-12 level, there are fewer academic content resources available. Traditional correspondence-based programs for high school students complement the resources of some parents who have the interest and expertise to home-school their children. The newer answer is telecommunications-based delivery, a sophisticated outgrowth of the Sunrise Semester of years ago.

In Nebraska, educational resource expansion has taken the form of satellite-based, telephone-based, and fiber optic-based delivery. As a direct result of the University of Mid-America, in 1990, the state of Nebraska leased space on a satellite and began development of a multi-purpose network called NEB*SAT, which today provides several different services. The most widely known is public television, available in most homes in Nebraska on a regularly scheduled basis. EDU-CABLE, the channel devoted to programs for K-12 classes and received by most schools in Nebraska, is another popular service.

Additionally, college courses are broadcast over satellite in one of two modes: one-way video, two-way audio (telephone return) called NEB*SAT II and two-way video, two-way audio, called NEB*SAT III. Any school with a satellite dish can downlink NEB*SAT II. Nineteen specific sites, frequently located at an institution of higher education, participate in NEB*SAT III programming. This delivery mechanism has grown astronomically in just seven years. Beginning at 52 hours a month in 1991, NEB*SAT broadcast more than 3,500 hours of programming a month in 1998. Various Nebraska institutions of higher education share the origination responsibilities for these hours of programming.

Many state-wide meetings are held on the Nebraska Video Conference Network

Lifelong learning is a requirement for a progressive society and desirable quality of life. Responding to this need necessitates using creativity, resolve, and, most probably, technology. Keeping an open mind to maximize what the future might bring will be the key to success in the new century.

BARBARA**AUDLEY**
DEAN OF CONTINUING EDUCATION

Dr. Rebecca Umland and Dr. Barbara Audley during a fiber-transmitted classroom discussion

photo by Brad Norton

or NVCN. This telephone line-based service provides compressed video and audio to twenty-five sites throughout Nebraska. NVCN, a more sophisticated version of the original videophone first proposed by AT&T many years ago, permits live two-way audio/video conversations. While mainly used for short-term meetings, on occasion the NVCN is also used for instruction when the NEB*SAT system is not available.

The newest development in using technology to deliver educational programming is the initiation of fiber optic based network consortia of K-12 districts, Educational Service Units (ESUs), and higher education institutions. These are live, two-way audio/video networks developed by contiguous schools. Known as "pods," these consortia will be interconnected to create a K-12/higher education state-wide network in the near future. Multiple reasons exist for the development of these consortia: to provide K-12 schools with curricula they need but cannot provide individually, to share faculty who have the qualifications to teach more advanced subjects, and to make connections to outside experts. Additionally, the higher education institutions and ESUs can provide professional teacher enhancement courses to the schools at their distant sites to keep rural faculty up-to-date on education trends and practices without long hours of travel to a central site.

For the higher education institutions that have a mission to serve their regions as well as their residential campuses, distance delivery using technology is a much more efficient use of faculty time and effort. Rather than driving many miles in all kinds of weather numerous times each semester, faculty can now walk across campus within minutes from their offices and return easily. This makes long-distance teaching much more attractive and efficient.

Additionally, through world-wide connections, distant experts can be connected to the various sites to enhance the content of a given class, again at a much lower cost than bringing guests to a specific location. Higher education views this capability as a major enhancement of its resources at a minimal cost. Finally, students who live far from cities or even towns, as is common in rural Nebraska, can gain access to higher education within easy driving distance–assuming their local school has joined a nework. This technology opens the doors to a much brighter future for all Nebraskans, wherever they live.

A Final Word

Education is in the process of a paradigm shift, and this is indeed an exciting time to be involved in the profession. No option is exclusive, but only one of many, each existing to serve a discrete portion of the population. Residential colleges will continue to serve the traditional college audience. Rural K-12 schools will continue to exist now that the required curricula can be accessed electronically within financial constraints. Internet-based options for college and university courses and, eventually, secondary school curricula will be expanded exponentially.

What will come next is hard to imagine, but as each challenge is identified, a new solution will be developed that might not include anything that exists today. Lifelong learning is a requirement for a progressive society and a desirable quality of life. Responding to this need necessitates using creativity, resolve, and, most probably, technology. Keeping an open mind to maximize what the future might bring will be the key to success in the new century.

LISTOFCONTRIBUTORS

Anderson, John. Associate Professor of Political Science.

Audley, Barbara. Dean of Continuing Education.

Bennett, Gordon. Associate Professor of Geography.

Benz, Joseph. Professor of Psychology.

Bicak, Charles. Professor of Biology.

Blake, Gordon. Professor Emeritus of Economics.

Bosshardt, Carol. Lecturer of English.

Bridges, Deborah. Assistant Professor of Economics.

Cisler, Valerie. Associate Professor of Music and Performing Arts.

Dart, Stan. Associate Professor of Geography.

Davis, Roger. Professor of History.

Eifler, Mark. Former Assistant Professor of History, currently Associate Professor, University of Portland.

Foradori, Anne. Assistant Professor of Music and Performing Arts.

Fort, Charles. Professor of English, Reynolds Chair.

Frasier, Tom. Former Lecturer of History, currently Doctoral Fellow at Northwestern University.

George-Bloomfield, Susanne. Professor of English.

Gilbert, James. Professor of Criminal Justice.